RETHINKING ECCLESIA

Being and Becoming Christ Communities: Towards a Borderless Church

Biblical and Theological Perspectives

RETHINKING ECCLESIA

Being and Becoming Christ Communities: Towards a Borderless Church

Biblical and Theological Perspectives

EDITORS

Daniel Rathnakara Sadananda

Solomon Paul J.

CHURCH OF SOUTH INDIA

2021

Rethinking Ecclesia – Being and Becoming Christ Communities: Towards a Borderless Church – Biblical and Theological Perspectives - Jointly Published by the Indian Society for Promoting Christian Knowledge (ISPCK), Post Box 1585, Kashmere Gate, Delhi-110006 and The Church of South India (CSI), CSI Centre, No. 5, Whites Road, Royapettah, Chennai – 600 014.

Online Order: http://ispck.org.in/book.php

ISBN: 978-93-90569-14-4

Laser typeset by

ISPCK, Post Box 1585, 1654, Madarsa Road, Kashmere Gate, Delhi-110006 • *Tel:* 23866323

e-mail: ashish@ispck.org.in • ella@ispck.org.in
website: www.ispck.org.in

Contents

Section 2
Theological Perspective

Acknowledgements

Rethinking Ecclesia publication is a result of well thought and planned series of 8 consultations in the year 2018. These consultations are indeed a historical moment in the history of CSI as we commemorated 70 years of faithful journey and Reformation 500. All the papers presented and the meaningful conversations helped the Church of South India to engage more vigorously in the process of searching new theological directions and visions as CSI steps into a new decade.

The theme "Being and becoming Christ communities – towards a borderless Church" were discussed from a) Biblical perspective, b) theological and ethical perspective, c) liturgical and missiological perspective, d) prophetic and diaconal perspective, e) empowerment and educational perspective, f) healing and reconciliation perspective, g)National and global ecumenical perspective.

The Moderator of the Church of South India, Most Rev Thomas K Oommen, who inaugurated these consultations, remarked that the theological exercise of Rethinking Ecclesia consultations has helped the Church to find new directions in the pilgrim journey of CSI. He said that these explorations should continue to challenge the church and its mission and also make way for newer forms of ministerial engagements with the people at the grassroots.

These consultations has enabled the church to make a theological audit of CSI, create a network of theological educators who are CSI and gave opportunity for the seminary and the church to bridge the existing gaps in working closely with one another for the sake of a united mission.

This book is a compilation of articles presented during the Biblical and Theological perspective consultations held at CSI Synod, Chennai. Biblical scholars and theologians of CSI came and presented their insights on the theme.

At this moment we thank the God of koinoinia who called CWM to partner with CSI from the beginning till the end of this Rethinking Ecclesia consultations helping us to encourage each other and also assuring us of God's accompaniment in our Pilgrim journey.

I also place my thanks to the Youth Department of CSI for their meticulous efforts in planning and implementation of these consultations and coordination in bringing out this publication.

Special thanks to ISPCK for publishing these books and partnering with CSI in continuance of God's mission.

Rathnakara Sadananda

Preface

It is with great joy and contentment that I present the book – **Rethinking Ecclesia: Being and Becoming Christ Communities - Towards a borderless Church**, a series of articles deliberating on the theme from Biblical and Theological perspectives.

Borders have become an undeniable reality today. Both the nation-state and the Church are governed by borders. If borders are to offer security and protection, the same borders also exclude or de-mark the other. The Church in India, since many decades now has been struggling to engage with the many identity-markers such as caste, region, denomination, tradition, gender and so on... Though the Church is called to live and profess the liberating Spirit of God which transcends borders yet, she is engaged in grappling with the many challenges imposed by the identity-markers.

These identity-markers which promote intrinsic value to the worth of an individual and betterment of the community have become a strong border/barrier among communities leading to negation of life. It is in this context that the book "Rethinking Ecclesia" tries to find meaning and sense for the existence of the CSI today and tomorrow.

The articles in this book resonate the visions, dreams, aspirations and even frustrations in re-imaging a new community centered on Christ and show the way forward towards a borderless Church. These articles are not ashamed of the grave mistakes the Church has committed in stiffening borders and building walls of animosity, but have rather lamented over them in repentance, waiting for another opportunity to set it right through theological articulations. They reflect on the present context of the Church battling even more greater hurdles as the socio-geo-political climate of the nation is going through a shift towards rightist ideological forces.

"**Rethinking Ecclesia**" is the result of a well-thought and planned series of eight consultations in the year 2018. These consultations were indeed a historical moment in the history of CSI as we commemorated 70 years of faithful journey and Reformation 500. All the papers presented, and the meaningful conversations helped the Church of South India to engage more vigorously in the process of searching for new theological directions and visions as the CSI steps into a new decade.

The theme "**Being and becoming Christ communities – towards a borderless Church**" were discussed from a) Biblical, b) Theological, c) Liturgical and Missiological, d) Prophetic Diaconal, e) Empowerment and Educational, f) Health, Healing and Harmony as well as g) National and Global Ecumenical perspectives. Around 109 papers were presented during these consultations containing voices from within and outside, voices of complement and voices of dissent, voices from the vulnerable and those in responsible positions.

The Moderator of the Church of South India, Most Rev Thomas K. Oommen, who inaugurated these consultations, remarked that the theological exercise of Rethinking Ecclesia consultations has helped the Church to find new directions in the pilgrim journey of CSI. He said that these explorations should continue to challenge the Church and its mission and also make way for newer forms of ministerial engagements with the people at the grassroots, especially in liberating the weak and the oppressed.

These consultations affirmed that the Church is the sign and the sacrament of the reign of God; that as the continuation of the incarnation and an instrument of the reign of God, the Church ventures to live out her commitment and faith as an alternative, that proclaims boldly that another world is possible, right here and now in our midst; and that the Church is the penultimate, subject to change and transformation till she is ultimately absorbed into the very reign of God. And therefore, the consultations were indeed a prophetic call to rethink *ecclesia*, not only its significance, importance and relevance, but also its being and becoming.

These consultations have enabled the Church to make a theological audit of CSI, create a network of theological educators in the CSI and provide opportunity for the theological faculties and the Church to bridge the existing gaps in working closely with one another for the sake of a united mission. Consultations also provided the much-needed space for the Church and the theological fraternity to listen to, have dialogue with one another, and work together to overcome the lacuna that exists between the seminary and the sanctuary.

This book is a compilation of articles presented during the consultations from **Biblical and Theological perspectives** held at CSI Synod, Chennai. Biblical scholars and theologians of CSI came and presented their insights on the theme. The opinions and theological assertions expressed in the articles are of the authors themselves put forth with sincere faith and hope that, they would help the people of God to clearly and relevantly articulate the self-understanding of being and becoming Ecclesia.

Heartfelt thanks to the Moderator of CSI, Rt. Rev. Thomas K. Oommen, Deputy Moderator, Rt. Rev. V. Prasada Rao, and Treasurer, Adv. C. Robert Bruce for their immense solidarity and leadership during all the consultations that took place. Special thanks to the General Secretary, Rev. Dr. Daniel Rathnakara Sadananda, who was responsible for this theological exploration and exercise, without whose guidance these consultations and this publication would not have been possible.

We thank the God of *koinoinia* who called the CWM to partner with CSI from the beginning till the end of these "Rethinking Ecclesia" consultations by helping us to encourage each other and also assuring us of God's accompaniment in our pilgrim journey towards becoming a borderless Church.

I also place my thanks to Mrs. Augustina Margaret, staff, Youth Department, CSI for her efforts in planning and implementation of these consultations and for coordinating to bring out this publication. Thanks to Mrs. Jessica Richard and Mrs. Angel Merlin for their help in proof reading and special thanks to ISPCK for publishing these books and partnering with CSI in the continuance of God's mission.

Epiphany, 2020 **Solomon Paul J.**
Chennai, India **Editor**

Concept Note

Towards a Borderless Church

At the time of independence in August 1947, the colonial masters re-drew the borders of our nation even as it wriggled in pain and tension. People began to move to safer places, many were displaced from their habitats and lives and livelihoods lost. The country paid dearly for its independence. In September 1947, our fore-fathers and mothers decided to overcome the borders of denominational faith, mission allegiance and regionalism to form the Church of South India. Inspired by the Lord's prayer for unity and oneness 'that they all may be one as we are one', our fore-fathers and mothers ventured into a radical discipleship of imitating God's oneness. To a divided India, to the divided church worldwide, the Church of South India became a parable of unity, a beacon of hope, an aroma of the Gospel.

Borders do exist. Each cell in our body has a border. However, each cell communicates and interacts with the other. Every one of us lives within certain borders and ever-widening borders, within the borders of our home, family, congregation, faith communities, village, town, state, and country. At times we share borders, we cross borders, we merge borders, we re-draw borders. We dream of borderless-ness. Thus, we live with borders, yet we yearn for borderless-ness. In our quest to understand borders and borderless-ness, we learn to understand the energy, power, potentials and the possibilities and opportunities that evolve in crossing and going beyond our borders.

A borderless Church calls us to look intently at our borders. Normally, borders are identity markers. Borders do inform us about what we are and what we are becoming. Anglican, Presbyterian, Congregationalist, and Methodist Christians in Southern India decided to redraw their ecclesial borders together to form, very consciously, a united and uniting Church of national and cultural identity. They indeed looked intently on the form of their faith, spiritual expressions, traditions, spiritual practice and how they organised themselves as congregations and churches. The varied faith expressions, spirituality, and liturgical traditions mingled together in their many-ness, yet interwoven into a colourful and powerful expression of oneness. The borders merged, were redrawn, new borders emerged.

In the first creation story, borderless-ness and harmony are evident. The varied, multiple forms and creatures created multitudes of borders that were held together in oneness and wholeness, an intrinsically connected, networked, harmonious blend is seen as good, and very good, culminating in Sabbath, the Shalom. Only the second creation story speaks of the process of self-discovery in relation to the other - in holding the other in respect and dignity, the identity of each is defined, interpreted and enhanced. The concept of identity formation, freedom with responsibility is introduced in the narrative only to affirm that when identity is misrepresented, and when the creature tries to impersonate the Creator, the connections, bonds and networks get destroyed.

The call and election narratives in the Old Testament are an invitation to understand this complex, yet beautiful interrelatedness and intrinsic value. The narratives of Abraham, Sarah and Hagar, Isaac and Rebecca, Esau, Jacob, Leah and Rachel show that they are invited to cross borders, share borders, draw new borders, and understand the mysteries beyond their borders and become a borderless community. For the writers of Genesis, their histories inform us of God's initiative that challenges human community to rediscover, reinvent and remember the borderless creation and be part of God's Shalom.

The story of Exodus is about breaking the borders that exploit and are oppressive. It is a story of empowerment for liberation; crossing the red sea - a baptism in water, is the visual symbol of overcoming borders and becoming a liberated community, a parable of liberation. The liberated community was called to represent the possibility of another world, where the world can hear its breathing and visualise its being. The commandments and the book of the covenant were given in order to make an alternative, another world possible, it was drawing new borders that would negate the borders that exploit, oppress, destroy and threaten life and proclaim the coming of justice and peace, not only within the borders of the liberated community, but beyond its borders and everywhere. Love, faithfulness, peace, justice, and righteousness are to be seen and experienced within the liberated community in order that it becomes the Gospel to the whole world.

The Deuteronomic eucharistic prayer (*anamnesis* - Deut. 26:5-10) holds together the wandering Aramean walking from the margins, crossing borders, the small and insignificant, few and negligible, strangers and aliens becoming empowered, to go through the struggles, pains, and sufferings, getting liberated from the crushing clutches of death and destruction to emerge as a people. It is a narration of resilience and resurrection, a living experience of breaking the chains of bondage and enslavement, to redraw borders that seem to extend and expand unceasingly.

The Prophetic literature which came at the time of exilic and post exilic period clearly depicts the community that was called to be an alternative, liberated community, which by losing its way and its borders emerged from its struggles of being conquered and occupied. The prophetic voice makes it clear that when the community loses its vision of liberation, corruption and injustice extinguish the power to move, connect and be open, when the community loses its dynamism and becomes static; connectivity, networks, and the power to transcend are destroyed and in the process people get marginalised and lose the creative power to overcome the borders and transcend the borders. Therefore, the prophetic call comes first as comforting, then as sowing the vision of a new heaven and new earth, but with a strong inclination to empower the community against corruption, injustice, oppression, and exploitation, so that they may discern and embrace the new that is already there and sprouting. Only in empowering the marginalised, in drawing out the inherent, innate, and immanent potentials, does the community once again regain movement, connectivity, and openness.

In the New Testament, Jesus' understanding of God as is defined in his conversation with the Samaritan woman is very instructive and profound - "God is Spirit; those who worship him must worship him in Spirit and truth" (Jn.4.24). God does not belong to one community, he is not stationary at Jerusalem or in Shechem, on the mount; God cannot be bound to certain traditions and forms of spirituality; he is boundless and borderless.

Jesus was preaching the reign of God, its imminence, and the reign of God, not the Church, was at the centre of his teaching. The reign of God is the safe space, that comforts, cares, heals and reconciles. It is a place where one receives forgiveness, grace, and loving kindness. The reign of God is where one rests powerlessness, vulnerability, frailty, weakness, insufficiency, and gets empowered. The reign of God calls the excluded, rejected, oppressed and outcastes, embraces them into an inclusive solidarity, to offer justice and peace. The reign of God is love, joy and hope, that brings integrity, wholeness, and harmony. It is the space and place where people experience the presence and accompaniment of God. The reign of God that Jesus proclaimed therefore, is not only borderless, but that which also gives assurance of eternity.

To make God's reign felt and experienced by commoners, Jesus' movement was evolved within the borders of Jewish religion. Jesus called out (*ecclesia*) twelve/seventy and created a community within the community. On this rock, I will build my Church (Matt.16.18), a rock-like, solid faith; but unlike the traditional understandings of messianic liberation, redemption was brought about by the suffering servant. Jesus standing firmly on the prophetic traditions of his faith, practiced prophetic *diakonia* as the means and instrument of liberation (Matt.16:21,24,25). Indeed, this was the culmination of a borderless, prophetic diaconal movement that moved from Nazareth to Gennesaret, to Tire Sidon, Samaria and to Jerusalem and back to Galilee. A borderless movement that empowered the margins, resisted the empire, critiqued religion and embraced the marginalised. It was a community called to be salt and light; a new life-giving and life-affirming movement, as flowing water and wind that blows wherever it pleases, a borderless new creation.

The Evangelists interpreted the crucified Christ as the one who draws all people to himself as he is lifted up. The crucified one, broken, crushed, and eliminated signifies the movement of the crucified people, and draws together those who are condemned to margins, denied of space, opportunity, rights and honour, bound because of their innocence and ignorance, excluded, made voiceless and unjustly persecuted. The crucified one in his passion and death enters the crucified communities and releases the power of life. The resurrected one who is boundless, and has overcome the limitations of time and space, inaugurates a new creation, boundless and borderless.

The early Church was indeed borderless, as it understood Jesus' command to go and make disciples of all nations (Matt.29:19), as a mandate to create borderless Christ communities. It also had a clear geographical strategy, 'you will be witnesses, in Jerusalem and in all Judea and Samaria and to the ends of the earth' (Acts 1:8). Peter also is 'converted' to the borderless Church, after the vision and real-life experience at Joppa and Caesarea (Acts 10). Paul, after his world-encircling, missional engagements writes his faith conviction; his *magna carta* "there is neither Jew nor Greek, slave nor free, male or female for you are all one in Christ" (Gal.3:28). It is very consistent with his sacramental theology which envisions a borderless Church, "Do you not know that all of us who have been baptized into Christ Jesus were baptized into his death? Therefore, we have been buried with him by baptism into death, so that, just as Christ was raised from the dead by the glory of the Father, so we too might walk in newness of life" (Rom.6:3,4). Every follower of Christ has been baptized into Christ, and therefore when he writes to Corinthians he clarifies that "The bread that we break, is it not a sharing in the body of Christ? Because there is one bread, we who are many are one body, for we all partake of the one bread" (1 Cor.10:16,17).

The ecclesiological reflections in the letter of Hebrews speaks of the visible and invisible Church. The language that 'we are surrounded by a great cloud of witnesses' (Heb.12:1), connects us with the Church of yesterday, with the Church of today and the future. The language used in the catholic epistles, of being strangers and pilgrims, to reflect the nature and being of the Church, depicts the struggles of living up to the great vision of a people of God. The theological affirmation that the Church is the Household of God (Eph.2:19) compared to the households of the time, and of the Church as God's House inform us about the profound theological affirmation: "Once you were not a people, now you are the people of God" (1Pet.2:10).

The eschatological vision of the book of Revelation depicts the New Jerusalem, the space of peace as an inclusive space, without borders. It speaks about a most valuable, yet fully transparent space, a space without a temple, as the whole space itself has the presence of God, which is light. All the nations of the earth will bring their splendor into it, it has gates that will always remain open, yet nothing impure will enter it (Rev.21:22ff). Even the heavenly space is not static; it is dynamic and transforming. The river of water of life, as clear as crystal flowing from the throne of God, and the trees of life which are for the healing and reconciliation of the nations, clearly affirm the process of being and becoming a Christ community, a borderless Church.

Today, we understand the Church as a sign and sacrament of the reign of God. She is an instrument of the reign of God and alternative that proclaims that another world is possible, that it is here and now in our midst. The Church is the penultimate, subject to change and transformation till she is absorbed into the reign of God. As a sign and sacrament of the reign of God, the Church has distinctive, discernible identity markers and borders, yet calling and exhorting people to the borderless reign of God.

As the Church of South India steps into the eighth decade of her being and becoming, may she be given grace upon grace to understand anew the gift of oneness and unity. May the 70-year celebrations be a sign of prophetic SEVA (*diakonia*), Social Empowerment - a Vision in Action upholding the sacramentality of life, where she, as a borderless Church travels beyond suspicion, fear and hostility in a multi-religious, multi-lingual, multi-cultural society. May she be empowered and emboldened to share, cross and redraw borders in order to set the energy of the margins, the crucified peoples free. May the children and the young be inspired to DARE into a process of Discernment And Radical Engagement, and be change makers and signs of transformation. May she be given grace to be a real MITHRA (friend) - Migrant Intervention Towards Holistic Responsive Action, to understand the beauty and significance of the small, frail and vulnerable, and be a movement of protest and resistance that gives DISHA, a new direction (Disability Intervention for Solidarity and Holistic Accompaniment), for those disabled, excluded, and condemned to margins. May the Church of South India be given grace to be God's instrument that brings dynamism and moves people, to connect not only with the Creator, but also with those around and all of God's creation, to open new possibilities of celebrating and living life in all its fulness. May the Church of South India be a new GEET, song (Gender Equity and Enabling Timetable), harmony that proclaims and practices equality, justice, and peace. In being and becoming a borderless Church, may the Church of South India open herself to God's eschaton, move in her radical engagement in the ever-continuous movement of unity and oneness of all and experience the fullness of Him who fills everything in every way (Eph.1:22), so that God may be all in all (1 Cor.15:28).

Rev. Dr. D. Rathnakara Sadananda

General Secretary, CSI

SECTION 1
Biblical Perspective

1

CSI's Future as the Family of God and Christ's New Creation: Rethinking being Church for this 'evil age' with Paul

For a CSI Consultation on rethinking Ecclesia

'Being and becoming Christ communities – towards a borderless Church: From the Biblical perspective'

Daniel S. Thiagarajah

Thank you for the invitation to contribute to this CSI commemoration of the 500th anniversary of the Reformation. I welcome the initiative to use this historic anniversary for our Church's reflection on what it means for us today to be and to become Christ-like communities. Our General Secretary has reflected upon where he thinks CSI needs to focus our rethinking on being and becoming Christ communities by titling this consultation 'towards a borderless Church'. I see this conference is as an opportunity for respectful, careful Bible study on our

Church's being in the face of the profound changes in Asian culture and the socio-political challenges of continuing globalisation. So following my study of the theme of being and becoming Christ communities through a study of Paul's letter to the Galatians, I will present my conclusion that CSI's rethinking of our being as church would not be enriched by becoming a borderless church. Instead, following Paul's mission to 'this evil age', I propose CSI rethink our becoming Christ communities by being 'the family of God' in the context of Christ's 'new creation' to a world subjected to militarism in the service of globalised and borderless economic growth.

I am grateful that our Synod's consultation on rethinking ecclesia begins with the Biblical perspective because I believe how we rethink what it means to be and become Christ communities is a vital methodological issue. When Martin Luther concluded the public defence of his writing and preaching in 1521 with the statement, 'My conscience is captive to the Word of God'[1], he placed his trust in Scripture firmly above the testimony of papal authority or the views of Church councils. However in today's context, Walter Brueggemann has noted that the Reformed tradition's methodological priority for scripture in our discernment of Christ's vocation for our missional obedience is 'radically deprivileged',[2] and that the church today too often reads the biblical text whilst burdened by modernist and postmodernist theological, historical, or cultural assumptions. He says 'The question is how far and in what ways can the biblical text be heard among us as an authoritative voice that is a genuine alternative that is not from the outset turned and trimmed by the pressures, demands and attractions of the dominant account of reality that is everywhere among us.'[3] My concern is that by pre-empting that CSI needs to move towards being a borderless church, it may render our listening and responding to the biblical text captive to emerging historical and cultural claims for a 'borderless world'.

In spite of the General Secretary's endeavours to present the 'border-borderless' dualism in the most benign terms in his concept paper for this consultation, the Sri Lankan experience of thirty years of civil wars has taught me that contested borders are really sites of death, violence and destruction. Attempting to establish a universal claim for a future borderless church hides the pain of our Diocese's war trauma from the scholarly community of CSI. Sadly, it also hides the experience of the GS from the Synod in helping us to understand why he has come to the radical conclusion that CSI should move towards being a borderless church. What lies hidden to me is the world he is troubled by. This is a predictable consequence when we turn a blind eye to the militarisation that underpins the rapacious economic demands for a borderless world. As Brueggemann notes, this consequence is not only born in the church, but is suffered more widely as 'the alarming diminishment of the human fabric of our common life.'[4]

A closer reading of Paul's letter to the Galatians reveals it has ever been thus. But as I will discuss later, the theological and historical consensus around this epistle since Luther's reformation, has contributed significantly to negating Paul's radical presentation of a reformed Judaism. Luther's anti-Jewish rhetoric in his commentary on Galatians diverted successive generations from Paul's original purpose by justifying their spiritual blindness to the bitter fruits embedded in Luther's demonising of Judaism.

Alongside the new perspective on Pauline studies, recent empire-critical studies of the New Testament have been transformative in helping the church read these texts with fresh eyes. Lutheran writer Brigitte Kahl vividly describes what it is like to live as vanquished people through the eyes of those defeated by Roman imperial power, and so brings fresh light to Paul's letter to the Galatians.[5] She selects two issues widely neglected in Galatian studies. 'First is the power of Rome and the representation of that power in images, most notably the images of vanquished Galatians. …Second: (she) seeks to re-imagine the historical context in which Paul and the Galatians met.'[6]

Kahl's empire-critical colleague Davina Lopez has come to similar conclusions in her own ground-breaking study of Paul, that: 'he can no longer be called an enemy of Judaism, but must be seen as an enemy of Roman imperial order. He is an enemy not of the local synagogue, but of the world wide drive toward civilization/slavery. His integration program, or alternative destiny, for the nations is relief under the umbrella of (God) the father of the promised land, not of the (Emperor as) father of the fatherland. And the terms of integration, according to Paul's Galatian formulation, are not conquest and slavery, but interconnectivity and freedom.'[7] Lopez, along with Kahl and others[8], has reasserted a political reading of the text that strips away the individualistic introspective reading of Galatians that has dominated western traditional reading since the Lutheran Reformation's dismantling of Catholic authority. Paul's letter resists the practices of the Roman imperial cult and attacks what the cult represents i.e.: 'civilisation through enslavement to empire'. Paul's declaration is a withering and decisive counter-assault on the idolatrous claims to borderless power by the Roman Empire and its Emperor.

Within the first nine verses of the first chapter of the letter to the Galatians, Paul marks out the field of battle in which life and death, peace and violence, new creation and destruction are all at stake. In empire-critical perspective, Paul wastes no time in establishing that he is 'sent neither by human commission nor from human authorities', thus stating in coded language the fact that he is not an agent of Caesar or under the power of the emperor's agents (1[1]). Kahl argues that the phrase is code to disguise Paul's opposition to the emperor, before he establishes that *his authority as an apostle is* 'through Jesus Christ and God the Father' (1[1]). The need for using coded language is evident - Paul later refers to spies in the assemblies (2[4]) who report to the authorities on any dissent to imperial law and order. Caesar was vaunted as the universal father of the Romans and conquered nations, so Paul's claim to be authorised by another divine Father would be seen as treasonous - and therefore punishable by crucifixion. We can imagine that this reality was understood all too well by the Galatians; such coded language minimises the risk to Paul and his congregations of courting trouble with the imperial authorities.

This is the reality of the everyday threat of violence that pervades life in the midst of war. During our country's civil war, remembering the Tamil dead, especially any who were associated with the LTTE, often held dangerous and violent political consequences. For a JDCSI pastor to conduct a Tamil person's funeral, especially anyone connected with the LTTE, meant being caught between the competing and deadly political forces. Yet this was the circumstance I faced when a JDCSI theological student asked me as his Principal at our Theological Seminary to conduct a Christian funeral for his LTTE-brother who was killed during the fighting. It is not difficult for me to understand why Paul would choose his words carefully and use words and images that would be understood by his audience, but at the same time hid their deeper meaning from the imperial powers. I believe I was able to conduct the funeral for my student's soldier-brother through the same grace and peace Paul affirms comes from God our Father and the Lord Jesus Christ. Whatever comfort the funeral service gave to the gathered mourners was also Christ's gift, which 'set us free from the present evil age' (1^{3-4}). Paul understood that being the church was a gift of God's grace and that any service we may offer in a hostile and evil age is made possible by the freedom from sin and death Christ has given to us.

In our fragmented and corporatised world, perhaps the concept of 'family' as a unifying and reconciling agency has become less popular. Perhaps our church need to reclaim the larger concept of 'the family of God'. For when Paul declares his authority is through 'God the Father', he not only asserts his coded resistance to Caesar's claim to divine fatherhood of Rome's conquered nations, but he boldly asserts that all those conquered nations amongst whom he ministers are united in solidarity as 'the members of God's family who are with me' (1^{2}). Their family status is affirmed three times in four verses ($1^{2,\ 3,\ 4}$) as gifted by 'God our Father', authoritatively describing both sender(s) and receivers of the letter as being part of this family. Against recalcitrant Galatians and false teachers are 'all God's family' who are in solidarity with Paul. For the troubled Galatian communities' members it is vital that they recognise one another again as belonging to one family: 'Paul, the brothers/sisters, and the Galatians alike, comprising both Jews and Gentiles/nations.'[9] This is Paul's powerful reading, that across all their differences of race and nation, the community of Jesus' followers are together in solidarity as one human family out of Abraham's and the Messiah's offspring ($3:^{16\ \&\ 29}$).

Paul's counter claim to Roman imperial ideology represents Judaism as a 'light to the nations' (Isaiah $49^{:6}$) through solidarity among the defeated nations, who are led by God's servant to turn away from life under Caesar's violent domination toward the invisible, liberative one God of Israel.[10] So our church receive our solidarity with victims of injustice as Christ's gift 'to set us free from the present evil age' (1[4]). This wonderful gift is not the result of our personal mission to set 'others' free. It is God's gift of new creation that embraces us all, and it comes with a calling and an ethical imperative – a call to be freed in solidarity with all those suffering from this increasingly borderless world dominated by the economic imperative for growth and progress.

The church as the 'family of God' are thus those who know what it means to yearn for liberation 'from this evil age'. While the concept paper focuses quite narrowly on a biblical survey to promote the possibility of a future borderless church, Paul's first four verses of his letter to the Galatians locate the fundamental intention of God's grace and peace as liberating the family of God from the idolatry of the world. How blessed is CSI to be united in grace and peace as the family of 'God the Father and the Lord Jesus Christ' (1[3]) under the promise of God's liberative project. That is, we receive this unity as Christ's gift 'to set us free from the present evil age' (1[4]).

Yet our Diocese experiences the Sri Lankan post-war environment as a source of ongoing suffering and injustice. Soon after my consecration as Bishop, a group who supported another candidate created a schism with CSI and attempted to establish their own church. In the violence that ensued, people on both sides were demonised, enmity flourished, mirroring our nation's war and leading to our own despair. This schism then poisoned our relationship with several international partners, including their withdrawing of funding. Almost a year ago, I brought to the Synod meeting our pain at the schism that occurred in Jaffna Diocese. The Synod resolved to take appropriate steps with one of our international partners supporting pastors who claim to have left the CSI. It pains me to report to this gathering of the CSI family that nothing appears to have been done to implement the Synod's resolution.

I understand we are called by Christ to give ourselves in love to those who have harmed our Diocese if we are to counteract the logic of a borderless world that pursues its own self-aggrandisement, law, victory and righteousness. But if we are to be part of an initiative engaging a national ecumenical partner, we stand in need of the solidarity of our CSI family so that we may be strengthened in our attempt to withdraw our perception of the schismatics as 'the unrighteous … and undeserving *other*.'[11] Can the freedom that Christ has won for us from this present evil age provide solidarity in the CSI family of God to strengthen one another to serve those we have seen as 'other', as Paul admonished? May we yet trust in Christ's promise of a new exodus and a new creation so that in solidarity with our Synod, our Diocese may give ourselves in love to those who have harmed us? So I pray that the grace and peace with which Paul blesses God's family may renew the sense of relationship that exists at the heart of being part of God's family, including the CSI family, the family of international ecumenical partners, and the family of churches in Sri Lanka. CSI may then live as Christ communities when our Synod strengthens its solidarity with all our Dioceses when they give voice to their suffering and injustice.

The reality of civil war gives urgency to our Diocese's understanding of what it means to be captive to the death, destruction and violence of 'this evil age'. So we cannot read Paul's proclamation that 'God the Father, (who) raised him (Jesus Christ) from the dead' (1^1) without a deep and profound awareness that Jesus died the most violent and public death imaginable. We understand full well that crucifixion was a tool of empire. 'It was imposed on the rebellious territories ..., the inferior *others* of the underside of empire, as a brutal restatement of Roman law and its re-inscription on the body of subject and slave.'[12] In Roman perspective, as a Jew and member of a conquered nation, Jesus is '*other*', and no different from all the others who were crucified by the state. The imperial 'gospel' is that the creation of universal peace and new life for barbarian nations entails the murderous violence of conquest and continual repression of the conquered.

But now, in Paul's gospel, God becomes father - not by imposing death like the Roman gods of war, nor by imposing death under the will of the fatherhood of Caesar - but by undoing the imperial power's politics in its use of violence and death. The Roman world could never imagine that a *crucified* man, an enemy of the empire, and a member of a conquered nation could be raised to life. Paul's affirmation that Jesus has been 'raised from the dead' (1[1]) is a public mockery of Roman law enforcement; 'it clashes with the most sacred images of cosmic order'[13]. Paul's gospel is profoundly counter-cultural in proclaiming to the despised Galatians that God's messiah, a despised 'Other' from the ranks of conquered Jews, has been raised from the dead (1[1]). In four verses, Paul has pronounced his assault on Roman cosmology which will unfold in Galatians. 'God's appearance on the side of the *other* destroys the dominant image of God, of law, of the world, and worst of all, it destroys the image of the enemy. ... For Paul ... it is the beginning of a new creation – or of an exodus out of the old world order "from this present age".'[14]

It is my experience that Christ's gift of new creation simply cannot be planned for in the same way we might plan to become a borderless church. For our church is in danger of being self-limiting if we adopt the language of 'borderless' that serves the interests of corporations and governments. The rethinking that may be required of us is whether we are open to receive God's grace and its acts of radical newness. For example, I give thanks and praise that God came to me from outside my past experience of God's presence in the church through the approach of a Singhalese pastor. This man sought me out with his request to join the Jaffna Diocese, which until that moment had been a historic Tamil national Church since 1948. Later, I was called to stand in solidarity with another Singhalese pastor who was assaulted and his church attacked by Buddhist fundamentalists. In a post-war context, our mission is to be in solidarity with people from different ethnic backgrounds and to serve others different from ourselves in their religious beliefs. Our Diocese has been enlivened by God's newness forming our being as an exodus community of Singhalese and Tamil, burdened in different ways by suffering and injustice yet trusting in the good news of Christ's liberating purpose to free us from this evil age. To this end, our being as church shares Paul's prayer of praise for the freedom conferred upon us, 'according to the will of our God and Father, to whom be the glory for ever and ever. Amen (1^{4-5}).'

Paul's gospel of a 'new creation' also challenged the prevailing worldview of Roman religion, law and order that the cosmos consisted of opposing (or binary) forces that were irreconcilable. This conclusion brings forward my fundamental disquiet about absolutising one half of the binary 'border-borderless' in order to frame CSI's future ecclesiology as a borderless church. 'The "slavery" involved in these binary opposites is both spiritual and physical, since it results from a systemic politics of conquest and is based precisely on the bonds between Roman religion, Roman law, and the Roman construction of Self and Other.'[15] That is, when one side of a dualism is absolutised, it demonises the other side and sets us on the path to idolatry. Paul's letter to the Galatians is an urgent, full-fronted assault on interpreting creation as consisting of binary (or opposing) forces. Embedded in Paul's new creation was a gospel of love that collapsed the 'Self' and 'Other' into a new humanity that under-cut and transformed the imperial need for violence and war.

For a war-weary church and a war-weary nation, Paul's trust in Christ's new creation is joyful good news. However that this 'new' binary seems to have brought dualistic thinking back into our theological reflection at the time we are observing the 500th anniversary of the Reformation may encourage us to take this opportunity to look more closely at how such ancient dualisms persist.

Kahl argues that Luther's doctrine of justification by faith and grace justified an anti-Judaism that entrenched an ancient dualism of "Us versus Them". This doctrine became 'a powerful ideological weapon in subsequent warfares conducted by the Christian occident (west) against its "Others".[16] Kahl argues that Luther absorbed or inherited his binary (that is, dualistic) view of the world from the Hellenistic and Roman dualisms, where the *Self* was always defined as 'good' against the barbarian *Other*. Through this binary or dualism, the Romans' belief in their righteous *Self* was sustained by their need to have a perpetual enemy. Thus Luther's theology carried within it the same conviction of the Roman Empire - that peace could only be won through war and violent conquest by the power of Empire.

Luther founded the liberating power of his theology of the cross over and against what he called the 'theology of glory', as evidenced in the prevailing theological and ecclesiastical culture of his day. 'Gerhard Forde tells us that for Luther the theology of glory and the theology of the cross are "two ways of being a theologian." These two theologies are diametrically opposed: "the two theologies are always locked in mortal combat."'[17] For Luther, these two theologies are mutually exclusive. The success of Luther's assault on the political structure of the Roman Catholic Church was in large part due to the power of his theological reform that shifted authority from the church hierarchy to the individual's direct relationship with God. But for Paul, to believe that the universe is structured according to a dualistic worldview as evidenced in Hellenic and Roman thought is to succumb to the 'treacherous and illusory attraction of the "idols", the other gods'[18] he described as being 'enslaved to the elemental spirits of the world' (4^3).

Now what strikes me about Forde's image of Luther's conflict between the theology of the cross and the theology of glory, is its violence. Luther's theology of the cross appears to hide within its reforming zeal both a spirit of hatred of its opposition and a self-justifying rhetoric of redemptive violence. The US theologian Walter Wink coined the term 'redemptive violence' to describe the belief that violence saves, that war brings peace, that might makes right.[19] Each of these tendencies may be discerned in Luther's attacks on the Roman Catholic Church and what he believed was its theology of glory. As our diocese seeks to make headway in a post-war environment, what troubles me is that in the CSI inheritance, the Reformation's spirituality of hatred lies hidden in the theology of glory. The spirituality of self-justifying hatred of the 'other' contains the seeds of 'holy' violence and war.

This bitter fruit seems present in the theology of the American Board of Commissioners for Foreign Missions (ABCFM), which sent missionaries to southern India and Ceylon. The policy of the ABCFM throughout the 19th century was for their missionaries to avoid politics in foreign lands, and to withdraw from the political struggle over slavery at home. By the early nineteenth century, the seed that was planted by Luther's reform had become embedded as the spirituality of individualism 'into the very fabric of European life and shaped the modern world.'[20] The theologies of the Presbyterian and Congregational missionaries of the ABCFM were formed by an individualistic piety that often blinded them to the reality that by accommodating the modernist binary that set politics ('bad') and religion ('good') in opposition, their churches in Ceylon and India were unwittingly and uncritically accommodated to the economic and political status quo of the British colonial government. Abolishing the political context from their theological worldview produced the bitter fruit of national politics detached from the liberating impulse of Christ's gift of freedom from the evils of the day.

But Paul insists there is a cosmic dimension to the conflict Christ has joined for the sake of our freedom from the evils of our age. In 1[8], an angel from heaven is mentioned as a potential messenger with a contradicting gospel. Paul responds to this threat to the gospel of Christ from a 'different gospel' (v.6) or 'another gospel' (v.7) with a double curse on the false messengers in verses eight and nine. Kahl hears in Paul's double curse the powerful curse formula of Deuteronomy 27-30 and 13 against those who succumbed to idolatry.[21] This is not a curse on Judaism as has been traditionally read, for the Jewish Torah is the foundation and source for Paul's own curses.

Paul places a curse on those enmeshed in idolatry. And 'as we have seen, in Paul's time the most overbearing and all-encompassing form of idolatry was the Roman imperial religion with its claim to integrate and dominate all other religion.'[22] The other gospel referred to no fewer than four times in 1:6-9 (v.6, 7, 8, 9) is more likely to be the gospel of imperial salvation, peace through the violence of war and conquest, and imperial salvation and patronage through military and economic might. Paul's curses therefore must apply to the violence of enslavement and coercion, exile and death that in biblical faith is the consequence of idolatry. Paul is pointing to the deadly destructiveness inherent in Roman imperial law and order itself, and the Empire's ambition to be the dominant power of its borderless world.

The powerlessness of the Church is God's gift to open our hearts and minds to receive Christ's saving work. This is the point to which I believe Paul is inviting us, to trust one another as members of God's family to be in solidarity through our deep listening to one another's pain. There is much I sense in the life of our CSI family that causes pain: conflict in our Dioceses and wider society, the status of Dalits, atrocities against vulnerable minorities, the prevention of child sexual abuse. None of these are outside our experience in Sri Lanka, and to the extent that we are able to share our pain, we will enter the cruciform space made open for us in the death and resurrection of our Lord. This is where our being as Christ communities will find its integrity and mission.

I believe we can truly be Christ's church and proclaim 'good news' to our world when the humanity of warring parties is 'restored from the likeness of Caesar's image into the image of God.'[23] So I do not find that describing the church I yearn for as 'a borderless church' adds anything of substance to what I believe the church today needs to become more truly church. I have suggested Paul's Galatian's letter warns strongly about how Christ communities modelled on becoming a borderless church will render us vulnerable to being captive to the idolatry of a borderless world, our 'evil age'.

I trust that in our conversation as CSI we may reflect prayerfully on what St. Paul is teaching us about the need to transform the world's dualisms through the unifying grace of Christ's new creation. We may be encouraged in our vocation as church by the exciting biblical scholarship that continues to enliven Pauline studies. For fundamentally it is Paul's great good news in our scriptures that recalls us to our worship and mission through Christ's promise of our solidarity in God's family, living in obedience as Christ's new creation. This is good news for CSI as we seek to be and become Christ's church for a world increasingly subjected to the elemental spirits of this evil age: militarism in the service of globalised and borderless economic growth.

Endnotes

[1] https://blog.cph.org/around-the-house/did-luther-really-say-here-i-stand/ (accessed 17/10/2017)

[2] W. Brueggemann, *Ichabod Toward Home: the journey of God's glory*, Wipf & Stock, Eugene, Oregon, 2002, p.86.

[3] Brueggemann, *Ichabod Toward Home*. p.87.

[4] Brueggemann, *Ichabod Toward Home*. p.86.

[5] B. Kahl, *Galatians Reimagined: reading with the eyes of the vanquished*. Fortress Press, Minneapolis, 2014.

[6] Kahl, pp. 3-4

[7] D. Lopez, *Apostle to the Conquered: reimagining Paul's mission*. Fortress Press. Minneapolis. 2014. p. 167.

[8] See also: J. Crossan and J. Reed, *In Search of Paul: how Jesus' apostle opposed Rome's Empire with God's kingdom*. HarperOne. New York, 2005. N. Elliott, *Liberating Paul: the justice of God and the politics of the apostle*. Sheffield Academic Press. Sheffield England. 1995.

[9] Kahl, *Galatians Reimagined*. p.248.

[10] Lopez, *Apostle to the Conquered*, pp.167-168.

[11] Kahl, p.262.

[12] Kahl, *Galatians Reimagined*, p.259.

[13] Kahl, *Galatians Reimagined*, p.260.

[14] Kahl, *Galatians Reimagined*, p.260.

[15] Kahl. P.20.

[16] Kahl, p.11

[17] G. Forde, *On Being a Theologian of The Cross.* Grand Rapids: Eerdmans, 1997, p.10, and p.4, quoted in op.cit., Palmer, *Africa Journal of Evangelical Theology*, pp. 131-132.

[18] Kahl, *Galatians Reimagined*, p.253.

[19] See W. Wink, *Engaging the Powers: discernment and resistance in a world of domination.* Fortress Press. Minneapolis. 1992.

[20] B. Keane, 'The Birth of Modernity' (cited https://www.crikey.com.au/2016/12/09/birth-of-modernity-and-capitalism-in-the-reformation/, 16/04/2017)

[21] Kahl, p.253.

[22] Kahl, p.254.

[23] Kahl, p.262.

2

Isaiah 2: Boundaries and Boundary Crossers – Walking up to Zion together with People

Royce M. Victor

Introduction

In recent years, the concept of boundaries has been at the center of research agendas in anthropology, sociology, history and political science. These studies show that the word "boundary" can be a misleading term. On the one hand, it conveys the idea of keeping a person separate from others. On the other hand, boundaries are connecting links since they provide healthy rules for navigating relationships. Boundary is meant to protect a person from danger and to improve his or her relationships and self-esteem. It actually brings everyone together than farther apart.

Boundaries are also identity markers since they give distinctiveness to those who are inside the boundary. Boundaries allow you to make yourself a priority. However, it cannot be a rigid marker. In this era of migration, displacements and refugees, no one can be isolated by oneself. More specifically, in today's world, nobody can live without connecting with others. Therefore, one's identity is associated with the context in which he or she is living and thus it always becomes relative and hybrid. From this background of movements and interconnectedness of human race, I would like to read Isaiah chapter 2.

Church and Her Boundaries in the Old Testament

The Greek word *ekklesia* is translated as "church" in the New Testament. This word is formed from *ek*, meaning "out of" or "away from," and *kaleo* meaning "to call." So, **it literally means "the called-out assembly**." The one who is calling is none other than God. Therefore, *ekklesia* can be translated as "**assembly**" and/or "**congregation.**"

Ekklesia **is used several times throughout the LXX to translate the Hebrew word** *qāhāl* (or *kahal*). *qāhāl* is translated into English as **multitude, company, congregation**, and **assembly.**[1] Notice that **two of the four definitions of *qāhāl* are identical to those of *ekklesia*.**

God promised Patriarch Jacob that He would make his twelve sons into a harmonious worshipping "community of nations" (Gen. 28:3) that would be known by his new name, "Israel." Significantly, the Hebrew word used here for "community" is *qāhāl*, which the Greek translation of the Old Testament often renders as *ekklēsia*, "church."

Qāhāl and Mission:

Although there is no direct command for mission found in the Old Testament, there are stories which provide hints and observations as well as some explicit statements that uncover the mission of God's people. These incidental expressions witness the mission strategy in a different form, and they are not as straightforward as one could wish.

The metanarrative of the Old Testament unfolds only progressively God's universal plan for the whole world. It helps to realize that God had a global plan, a proposal for the people of God to fulfill, but it has not always been plainly perceived. As Christopher Wright states, "the mission of God is to bless all nations on earth. . .. Israel in the Old Testament was not chosen over against the rest of the nations, but for the sake of the rest of the nations."[2]

David J. Bosch points out: "If there is a missionary in the Old Testament, it is God Himself who will, as God's eschatological deed *par excellence*, bring the nations to Jerusalem to worship him there together with his covenant."[3] If this is so, then one can deduce that God will not do it by Godself, but God's working method is to utilize humans to accomplish God's objective (Gen. 12:1-3; Ex. 19:4-6). It is obvious that God wanted God's Chosen One Israel to be a blessing to the nations. John A. McIntosh defines God's mission as doing everything possible to communicate or *to bring* salvation to the world.[4] Thus, God's universal purpose is actually the "basis for the missionary message of the Old Testament."[5] In sum, God has a mission, and the people of God is expected to participate wholeheartedly in that mission.

This was the common understanding of God's people about her mission in the pre-exilic period. The boundary of God's people was open and the call/invitation was extended to all. That is how people like Melchizedek, Balaam, Ruth and Jethro could enter into the Israelite fold and acquire prominent positions there. God was concerned about the wellbeing of all nations, and the message of the Hebrew Scripture transcended Israel's borders and boundaries. God did not provide warnings to people without a purpose; God always wanted to see all the creations living in peace/shalom (see Gen. 6:3). Isaiah chapter 2 comes from this period of time.

One cannot find much change in this hospitable attitude even during difficult times of exilic and post-exilic period. God's plan for humanity is clearly expressed in several of the exilic and post-exilic texts. For example, the statement found in Isaiah says: "'Turn to me and be saved, all you ends of the earth; for I am God, and there is no other'" (Isa. 45:22). In other words, Israel believed that she was bestowed upon a responsibility to perform a mission to the nations, the outside world (even to the distant islands [Isa. 66:19]). There was a clear vision about the mission of the People of God. The mission had an outward focus (centrifugal). The mission of Israel was directed toward others who did not belong to the community/congregation of Israel. The Prophets were not only speaking to their own people, but they also prophesied about many nations as well; God will judge all (e.g., Jer. 46–51; Ezek. 25–32; Obadiah; Jonah 3).

Isaiah 2: Joy of Pilgrimage

Although the United Nations is not, and does not claim to be, a Christian organization, outside its building in New York there is a wall bearing the inscription, "They will beat their swords into plowshares and their spears into pruning hooks. Nation will not take up sword against nation, nor will they learn war anymore." (Isa 2: 4). The phrase "swords into plowshares" has been adopted by countless organizations campaigning for peace and is also frequently associated with the UN's mission and international law more broadly. Also this verse of Isaiah corresponds closely to the prohibition on the use of force in Article 2(4) of the UN Charter (UNC): "All Members shall refrain in their international relations from the threat or use of force against the territorial integrity or political independence of any state, or in any other manner inconsistent with the Purposes of the United Nations."

According to form analysis, Isaiah chapter 2 can be classified as "Prophetic announcement of Joy and Judgement" and can be divided into two sections: The first five verses talk about the future of the House of God and rest of the chapter speaks of the pronouncement of judgement on the House of Jacob.[6] The Lord is the source of justice and peace and this is the fundamental theme of this chapter; and it is the connecting link between these two major sections of the episode. These verses of the chapter are written clearly with future orientation.

The chapter starts with an introduction of the prophet, which is a repetition of 1: 1. Also vv. 2-4 are nearly identical to Micah 4:1-3

> In days to come the mountain of the LORD'S HOUSE shall be established as the highest of the mountains, and shall be raised up above the hills. Peoples shall stream to it,[2] and many nations shall come and say: "Come, let us go up to the mountain of the LORD, to the house of the God of Jacob; that he may teach us his ways and that we may walk in his paths." For out of Zion shall go forth instruction, and the word of the LORD FROM JERUSALEM.[3] He shall judge between many peoples, and shall arbitrate between strong nations far away; they shall beat their swords into plowshares, and their spears into pruning hooks; nation shall not lift up sword against nation, neither shall they learn war anymore;

These verses of Micah speak of the nations' voluntarily submission to the Lord, seeking Torah and the refashioning of their weapons into agricultural implements. Nations' submission and their voluntary pilgrimage to the Lord were a prominent topic of theological discussion during exilic and post-exilic era, when themes like international peace and justice became more relevant to the life of the people. Therefore, many scholars consider these verses as later addition to the older text.[7]

Four major events take place in the first four verses: [1] The mountain of the Lord's house will be elevated and exalted (v.2); [2] There will be a pilgrimage of all peoples to the Mountain/ Zion. It is a purposeful journey to the holy place; [3] Singing a song of call to pilgrimage that expresses their reason for coming to Zion; and [4] Attraction of Zion is stated: Torah and the Word of the Lord go forth from Zion.

These verses talk about a pilgrimage of a large number of people from all over the world to the Lord's place, Zion, which is the centre of God's rule. The pilgrims travel to Zion seeking God's peace and justice. It is not an individual movement but a collective enterprise of pilgrimage. It is a challenge to the self-centeredness and mere individualism that is prevailed in the world of today. It is also a challenge to the self-created walls of the church/people of God. The prophet envisions a voluntary people's movement towards the House of the Lord. These verses demand everyone to work together in harmony to bring God's rule in this world. This is ultimate aim of the pilgrimage.

Invitation to Pilgrimage of Justice and Peace:

The Lord is pictured as teacher in v. 3, which traditionally was held by the priests in ancient Israel. Moreover, God is not depicted as king in these verses. Through these verses, God teaches the nations the importance of bringing justice and peace to the society. It is an open invitation to pilgrimage of justice and peace. Also, this verse shows the transformation that takes place among the audience/nations by learning from the Lord. After learning from the teachings of the Lord, the nations destroy their weapons of war and transform them to agricultural implements. It is not God who destroys the weapons of war but the people themselves change their attitude and convert them to devices that can be useful for the wellbeing of all creations. In these verses, we see the reversal order of human nature, which is often moves from peacefulness to destruction. Whereas here the movement is from peacelessness to peace.

The nations trust the Lord's ability to settle the issues and bring peace and justice to the world. This belief attracts them to go near to the Lord. It should also be noted that the nations come to Zion to learn from the Lord the ways of justice. In other words, the pilgrimage is meant to learn from the Lord the value of justice and peace and then to carry those values to the rest of the world. The pilgrims are commissioned to function as channels of God's peace and justice in the world. This commissioning is similar to the purpose of calling of Abraham and his descendance mentioned in Gen. 12:1-3. In other words, the calling and commissioning of Israel and other nations are understood as one and same.

These verses speak of a two-way movement of pilgrims. First, people travel from all over the world to Zion to learn from the Lord the meaning of justice and peace; and then move out to the world to become channels of justice and peace in the world. The pilgrimage is possible only when there is no restriction in Zion to entry or exit. God envisions a borderless Zion where there is no control over pilgrims to move back and forth. Here, what is role of those who are already dwelling in Zion, the congregation of God's people? God visualizes the people of God be a facilitator of this movement rather than being an obstacle to the pilgrimage. As facilitators, the role of the people of God becomes significant to the process of bringing peace and justice to the world.

God not only teaches instructions but also God pronounces judgements. The rest of the chapter (vv. 5 – 22) speaks of God's judgement on those who stand as a hindrance to bring peace and justice. No partiality can be seen in God's judgement. Everyone, including God's people will be treated equally with others. God shows no difference between God's people and "Others" or "no people". There is no "we" and "other" or centre and periphery for God. These verses are God's invitation to go to God's place to learn justice and peace and to establish them in the world. Also, it is a warning to those who depend more on their achievements, self-dependent attitudes and distorted worldviews (v. 8), which will be obstructions to the welfare of the society. There is no space for individualism or self-centeredness in the process of bringing peace and justice. The journey to the Lord's place for learning God's peace and justice will be a collective movement; a journey of the people of God with all creations. It is a pilgrimage of people rather than a lonely journey. In this travel there is no difference between the inhabitants of Zion and the people from rest of the world. Everyone is expected to move forward with others – journeying together in a pilgrimage, holding hand in hand – and work together to bring God's reign of peace and justice to the world.

Conclusion

Isaiah chapter 2 talks about radical transformation from nationalism, conflict and dispute to unity, justice, peace and harmony. Both, People of God and rest of creations, are commissioned to be channels of God's blessing to the world. The chapter envisions a collective pilgrimage of People of God and "others." An unrestricted movement of people back and forth to Zion is envisioned. Human participation in bringing peace and justice to the world is highlighted throughout the chapter. Conflicts and tensions continue even in the new age – the age of pilgrimage. But there will be a peaceful settlement, which transcends individual or national interest. It talks about compromise and accepting each other. There is a contrast existing between the ideal Zion presented in 2: 2-4 and the status of its people that must overcome their present state of being to achieve this ideal in the rest of the chapter. This is frequently portrayed through metaphorical use of the imagery of height and depth. On the one hand, the ideal Zion is pictured as the highest and (2:2); on the other hand, the people are portrayed as symbol of height to emphasize their self-pride and failure to rely upon the Lord (2: 12-16). That is, the people are in their lowest state of being and that state demands a pilgrimage to the Lord's place to establish peace and justice in the world.

The pilgrims portrayed in Isaiah chapter 2 are on the move responding positively to the call of the Lord. They transcend their social, cultural, political and religious boundaries to attain a higher goal, which is to learn the value of justice and peace from the Lord. They have become boundary crossers and their task is to transform the world according to the will of the Lord and to fulfil the commission that has been bestowed upon them by their creator. Their identity has changed from their initial one to a hybrid one. Most importantly, these verses of Isaiah clearly convey the message that the boundaries of Zion are open and welcoming. The borderless and hospitable Zion challenges today's Church, which still works hard to build new walls of borders and margins every day.

Endnotes

[1] Francis Brown, S.R. Driver and Charles A. Briggs, *Hebrew and English Lexicon of the Old Testament* (Oxford: Clarendon Press, 1952), 874 – 75.

[2] Christopher J. H. Wright, *Knowing the Holy Spirit Through the Old Testament* (Downers Grove, Ill.: InterVarsity, 2006), pp. 99, 100.

[3] David J. Bosch, *Transforming Mission: Paradigm Shifts in Theology and Mission* (Maryknoll, N.Y.: Orbis, 1991), p. 1719.

[4] John A. McIntosh, "Missio Dei," in *Evangelical Dictionary of World Mission,* A. Scott Moreau, ed. (Grand Rapids, Mich.: Baker, 2000), pp. 631, 632. *Italics* is mine.

[5] Johannes Blauw, *The Missionary Nature of the Church: A Survey of the Biblical Theology of Mission* (Grand Rapids: Eerdmans, 1974), p. 17.

[6] See Marvin A. Sweeney, *Isaiah 1-39 With an Introduction to Prophetic Literature, Forms of the Old Testament Literature Vol. 16* (Michigan and Cambridge: B. Eerdmans, 1996), pp, 87-106.

[7] See the discussion in Brevard S. Childs, *Isaiah, Old Testament Library* (Louisville and London: Westminster John Knox Press, 2001), 28-31.

3

Borders, Boundaries and the Bible

John Samuel

Our churches in India are poised at a significant juncture while facing some hostile situations, we are also showing signs of maturity and strength in several ways. The very fact that we are so plural and yet hold on to one faith is a mark of generosity and openness. The transitions happening from one end of the church to the other are mind-boggling. The theological thinking being articulated now is unprecedented. Mutual respect and acceptance among different churches are growing day by day. Efforts to transcend barriers and move beyond liturgical and organisational differences are increasing day by day while we are able to hold firm to different faith positions. We have grown to the point of beginning to discuss the "borderless church".

This essay is an attempt to reflect on the theme, "borders and borderlessness". We all have borders and boundaries in our life. We also continue to make newer forms of boundaries. In one sense borders sometimes become necessary. From a different angle, borders are a hindrance to our future. Our theology, our history, our sexuality, our economy, our spirituality can simultaneously build some boundaries and remove some borders. We easily move over some boundaries whereas we get stuck when some other borders are concerned. Church of South India emerged as a borderless church. In the process, it also became a border for some churches. In spite of the tremendous opening up, there are areas where we are unable to open up any more.

When we come to the mission of the church, we are concerned about maintaining the secular nature of our society. We are involved in active dialogue with other faiths. We have an open mind to relate with people of other sexual orientations. We are struggling for a casteless society and to break all the dividing walls in our society. We want to engage with ecological commitments. We are moving towards gender and class equality. We stand up for the cause of girl children and otherwise abled. These are the real expressions of our borderlessness as a church. We have come a long way.

Borders are Inevitable

Hebrew Bible introduces Israel as a nation. God promised a land for the descendants of Abraham. The land was defined with clear borders:

> On that day the Lord made a covenant with Abram, saying, "To your descendants, I give this land, from the river of Egypt to the great river, the river Euphrates, the land of the Kenites, the Kenizzites, the Kadmonites, the Hittites, the Perizzites, the Rephaim, the Amorites, the Canaanites, the Girgashites, and the Jebusites." (Genesis 15:18:21)

It is further mentioned elaborately in Numbers 34:2-12 where the Lord spoke to Moses, saying: Command the Israelites, and say to them: When you enter the land of Canaan (this is the land that shall fall to you for an inheritance, the land of Canaan, defined by its boundaries). Isaiah too shares the surprise of how Israel became a nation: "Who has heard of such a thing? Who has seen such things? Shall a land be born in one day? (Isaiah 66:8)

If Israel is a nation, it must have a boundary which separates Israel from the other nations. Any boundary, of course, is an imaginary line between one nation and other nation(s), separating the imaginary rights of one from the imaginary rights of the other. Any nation has three claims: 1. There exists a nation with an explicit and peculiar character.2. The interests and values of this nation take priority over all other interests and values.3. The nation must be as independent as possible.

An ancient concept of Israel as a nation can be traced back to biblical times. The story of the Jews narrated in the Bible seems to confirm the antiquity of nations. The biblical Jews were the Chosen people of their God, sharing common descent from Abraham, distinct from other peoples, with a manifest destiny plotted out in history. As part of their Covenant with God, they had conquered a territorially bound kingdom, their Promised Land. Their covenant was a collective pact between the Jews and their God and was to a degree egalitarian, as under Jewish Law all Jewish men were equal. When they failed to maintain their covenant, God providentially intervened and deprived them of their sovereignty over the Promised Land, and they had to wait for a Messiah to restore that kingdom. This is the classic story of a nation.

Space, Borders, and Boundaries

In the Hebrew Bible, Space is not only the place where something happens, but it includes the whole web of life. Space is divided by boundaries. Boundaries divide not only space but also divide all those that belong to that space.

Separation and exclusion are not the only functions of boundaries. They can also put people together in order to constitute a group. Boundaries very often have social functions in setting limits for constructing an identity and constituting a group. Therefore, boundaries do have an important impact on the constitution of society – in reality as well as in fiction. Thus, special attention must be paid to boundaries as to how they are constructed, how they include or exclude, how they stabilize identities, and who is able or allowed to cross the border and who is not.

Boundaries quite often have a paradoxical function: In arranging structures, they seem to "tidy up" the world. By doing so, boundaries frequently present a clear and often very simplistic view of the real or fictional world. They place subjects in this or that space, allow or forbid, enable or reject. But a closer look quite often shows that these boundaries are much more fluid than they appear to be at first: selectivity, fluidity, dynamism, permeability are all intrinsic to the construction of boundaries

Bible from the beginning engages in the description of the land and its boundaries. The description does not follow the travel route, but instead starts at the Temple, then goes to the palace and the city of Jerusalem, and ends with the country. This account places the Temple at the beginning and goes out in the description of the topography from this center to the periphery. Space is marked in circles, the center is the holy of the holies. It is surrounded by the temple. Temple is surrounded by Jerusalem. Jerusalem is the center of the nation. Israel is in the center of the world.

If space representations testify to the value system and culture model in which they are anchored, then this organisational principle shows a world view that describes not only Jerusalem but places the temple in the center of the representation (Temple → castle → city → country) and, originating from it, the world. It is equally revealing that all four subspaces described are closed spaces that were created (circular walls) or are naturally present. While there are clear demarcations within the space, there is also intra-border relationship. All are related as one whole.

There are other boundaries also. For example, The Hebrew Bible has legislation on food and drinks. Why was it that creation being one, some things are regarded as unclean for food and are not allowed even to touch" First, they explain the theological foundation that there is only one God and then goes on to speak of the laws in detail. Therefore our law-giver, Moses, equipped by God gained insight into all things, surveyed each particular object and consequently, he fenced the pure and clean from the impure so that Jews should mingle in no way with any of other nations, and remain pure in body and in spirit. The food and purity laws do not serve to ensure health, but rather are only there to establish a boundary with the people of the nations, and thus a stable identity is established. However, the boundary-setting food and purity laws have another function, in that they serve, not only to separate but to define the boundaries of belonging also.

Borders and Privacy

Generally, every human being constructs borders in their individual and collective life. The boundaries created may be sociological, psychological, religious, political and gender-based. It is globally agreed, in a charter on refugees, that any refugee camp should not reduce the personal space for a person below the level of at least 4.5 to 5 square meters. However, in reality, in many refugee homes, many more people could be found occupying such a space. These issues are complex and they reveal the character of our society. They are one of the many basic problems concerning boundaries.

While notions of "personal space" are culturally constructed and differ throughout the world, it seems to be a universal human requirement that some sense of personal space is necessary for all people. Invasion of that space or a transgression of such boundaries causes tensions, often violence, and even the spread of disease. When someone is homeless, he/she has been denied the personal space which gives them an identity and security.

Churches and social institutions working with children need to establish clear behavioural boundaries in the relationship between adults and children. Professors must either have windows in their office doors, or those doors must be kept open when they are alone with a student. Healthy borderlines are very important for the ethical conduct of our affairs in business, politics, the church, and the academy. All the families or households need boundaries if the home is to be a place of security and comfort for all.

"Strangers are people without a place" (Walter Bruegemann). In ancient Israel, they are often people whose "boundary stones" have been moved. To be placeless is to live in the tenuous vulnerability of life without the bounded security of home and shelter. Boundaries that demarcate in and out, mine and yours, ours and theirs, my body in distinction from other bodies, private and public, are necessary if life is to be secure. "Strangers" are people who have been stripped of such boundaries.

A boundary is "that which defines and gives identity to all kinds of systems." Such boundaries can be concerned with "names and stories, traditions and values." Boundaries are constitutive to identity and "unless we can draw a line – a boundary – and say that something lies outside its domain, then we can speak about nothing that lies inside with deep meaning."

Boundaries are lines that afford definition, identity, and protection – for persons, families, institutions, and nations. A boundary gives us something to which we can point and ascribe a name. Without a boundary, we have nothing to which we can invite or welcome anyone else. Without boundaries, there can be no sense of place as home, as a site of hospitality, security and intimacy with local knowledge; Without boundaries, there is no locality, and therefore no sense of membership in a particular community, family, or neighbourhood. Without boundaries identity is impossible.

Boundaries and Ghetto Mentalities

In the context of one nation to the other nations, borders become sacrosanct at the cost of the relationships between peoples beyond the borders. The demonization of the others, the ideological differences and cultural dissimilarities are used to separate the peoples on both sides of the border. Those who are outside our borders, outside the bounds of our civilization are thought to be unsafe, and as those who will become detrimental to our geopolitical, economic and cultural interests. If so, how can we meaningfully speak of boundaries and borders as necessary and good dimensions of human life together?

All boundaries require certain categories to describe who or how "we" are and "they" who are not "like us" or we who are not like them. And the whole idea of others is constituted by the imposition or acceptance of someone's understanding of boundaries. Boundaries are created on ideas like the colonial and the colonised, fair and dark, powerful and powerless, rich and poor. And the recent trend is to recognize the constructed character of all such boundaries and therefore their inherent deconstructability.

We cannot get along without demarcating boundaries. However, all "boundary fixing", cannot go unscrutinized. And the questions that will be raised emerge from the perspective of the "peripherated" - those who are pushed to the outside. If we still need some sort of demarcated boundaries, then how will they be drawn? What are the criteria by which people draw up boundaries, even if these boundaries are never finally fixed? This is a theological question.

The Concept of *Eruv* Vs *Gibul*

The book of Leviticus presents a pattern of borders between the communities based on ritual purity and others. Sabbath is a sign of the eternal covenant between Israel and God. As long as there are days and nights, there will be a covenant between God and Israel. Sabbath is a time of great rejoicing and resting. Sabbath is a time of becoming united with God, the creator. Sabbath is separated from the other days of the week. When the first three days are paired with the second three days of the week, Israel paired with the Sabbath who had no pair. Sabbath and Israel are inseparable. Having said this, while Israel and Sabbath are inseparable, Sabbath divides Israel from the rest of humanity.

a. Eruv

The concept of an *eruv* goes back to the principle of Sabbath rest. Under Jewish Law on Sabbath, it is forbidden to carry anything - from a "private" domain into a "public" one or vice versa, or more than 6 feet within a public domain. An enclosed area is considered a private domain, whereas an open area is considered public for the purposes of these laws. Practically, it is forbidden to carry something, such as a *tallit* bag or a prayer book from one's home along the street and to a synagogue or to push a baby carriage from home to a synagogue or to another home, on Sabbath.

It became obvious even in ancient times, that on Sabbath, as on other days, there are certain things people wish to carry. The answer is a technical enclosure which surrounds both private and hitherto public domains and thus creates a large private domain in which carrying is permitted on Sabbath. Colloquially this is known as an *eruv*. The *eruv* is usually large enough to include entire neighbourhoods with homes, apartments, and synagogues, making it possible to carry on Sabbath, since one is never leaving one's domain.

It is technical because theoretically, the *eruv* should be a wall. However, a wall can be a wall even if it has many doorways creating large open spaces. This means that a wall does not have to be solid. As such, the entire "wall" is actually a series of "doorways." Added to that there may be existing natural boundaries and fences.

An *eruv* does not give one a license to carry everything. It does not allow the carrying of objects whose use is forbidden on the Sabbath. For example, it is forbidden to carry an umbrella since opening or closing it is forbidden. Therefore, an umbrella cannot be carried anywhere on Sabbath regardless of whether it is within the *eruv* or not. Pens cannot be carried within the *eruv*, since pens cannot be carried on Sabbath at all. Finally, items that will only be used after Sabbath also cannot be carried on Sabbath, even within the *eruv*. The purpose of the *eruv* is to allow certain basic necessities to be carried, such as a *tallit* or a prayer book, house keys, clothing which is removed on warm days, and reading glasses. And it allows the pushing of a baby carriage along with food and diapers. While there are an increasing number of *eruvs* being established throughout the world in traditional Jewish communities, support for the practice is not universal.

b. Gebul

Gebul is a concept that is the opposite of *eruv*. It is an unviolable boundary. It came to be used in the context of inheritance of land: "Do not move the ancient boundary which your fathers have set" (Proverbs 22:28). "Do not move the ancient boundary" (Proverbs 23:10). What are the Scriptural ancient landmarks (boundaries)? Who set them? Can we remove them? From the definitions of the word "landmark," we can see that the word means to set a marker by a rope, a pile of stones, or an erect pillar to set the boundaries that are to mark off a territory or an inheritance. It served as a visible reminder or notice that one was entering into a land or place that had been set apart by a covenant ceremony. To trespass across the marker or to remove it was considered an offense to the owner of the land and God.

According to Deuteronomy 19:14, the Torah Forbids the moving of the Boundary and there are several Old Testament texts that also stress this: " Do not remove your neighbour's boundary, which those in the past have set, in your inheritance, which you inherit in the land that YHWH is giving you to possess" (Deuteronomy 27:17).

Landmarks were so revered that even the Romans placed a death penalty upon their removal. "Cursed is he who moves his neighbour's boundary"; "They remove landmarks; they rob and feed on flocks; they drive away the donkey of the fatherless, and take the widow's ox as a pledge; they turn the needy out of the way; the poor of the earth have hidden together (Job 24:1-3); "The chiefs of Judah shall be like those who remove a border-on them I shall pour out my wrath like water" (Hosea 5:10). Maybe Jesus was citing these two verses in John 8:56: "Your father Abraham was glad that he should see my day, and he saw it and did rejoice." The Jews of Jesus' day were guilty of moving the landmarks, because of the hypocrisy of their leaders while they were actually devouring the homes of widows and orphans (Matt.23: 14; Mark 12:40; Luke 20:47).

Their guilt was, they had started by removing the Torah's landmarks or boundaries which also YHWH has set through his servant Moses. Remember that sin starts when we remove or replace a commandment of the Torah, and begin to substitute the teachings of men and their interpretations of the Torah. Isaiah 10:12-13: For he has said, 'By the power of my hand I have done it, and by my wisdom, for I have been clever. And I remove the boundaries of the people and have robbed their treasures..." The Torah is not a heavy burden for Israel to bear. Only when the ancient landmarks have been moved it becomes a yoke too heavy for anyone to bear. "Do not add to the word which I command you and do not take away from it, so as to guard the commands of YHWH your Elohim which I am commanding you" (Deuteronomy. 4:2). All the words I am commanding you, guard to do it-Do not add to it nor take away from it" (Deuteronomy 12:32). "Do not add to his words, lest He reproves you, and you be found a liar" (Proverbs 30:6). We are not to add to them, increase them, change them, replace them, or impose more upon people as Torah any more than what has been given to us in the perfect law of YHWH (Psalms 19:7- 11).

Opening Up the Borders for Others:

> 6 The wolf shall live with the lamb,
> the leopard shall lie down with the kid,
> the calf and the lion and the fatling together,
> and a little child shall lead them.

7 The cow and the bear shall graze,
their young shall lie down together;
and the lion shall eat straw like the ox.
8 The nursing child shall play over the hole of the asp,
and the weaned child shall put its hand on the adder's den.
9 They will not hurt or destroy
on all my holy mountain;
for the earth will be full of the knowledge of the Lord
as the waters cover the sea. (Isaiah 11:6-9)

This is a classical passage that speaks about a borderless community (church). The wolf and lamb cannot be safe without boundaries. The calf and lion cannot coexist where there are no borders. The cow and the bear must remain as far as possible from the other. A small child and an asp cannot remain together. However, the prophet proclaims that all boundaries will become obsolete. Borders will be meaningless any more. No hurt, no destruction as the final times of harmony are arriving. Isaiah 19:24 says:

> 23 On that day there will be a highway from Egypt to Assyria, and the Assyrian will come into Egypt, and the Egyptian into Assyria and the Egyptians will worship with the Assyrians. On that day Israel will be the third with Egypt and Assyria, a blessing in the midst of the earth, whom the Lord of hosts has blessed, saying, "Blessed be Egypt my people, and Assyria the work of my hands, and Israel my heritage."

This is another prophetic text which speaks about the future of the world, where there will be border-crossing. Borders and boundaries will become forgotten from the minds of the people. There will be a highway instead of barbed wires and heavily guarded gates. They will all live with a borderless religion. Perhaps they point towards the messianic era. Egypt, Assyria, and Israel, nations who waged wars and inflicted violence over the others become spiritual and united people. Politics and religions become borderless.

Conclusion

The Bible invites us to experience the joy of one God and one humanity. Israel has the privilege of being God's servant for the sake of humanity. Israel must maintain its holiness if it should serve the purpose of God. Israel must be secure with its boundaries to practice Torah. Israel will be separated from the rest of the world as God has chosen Israel. Israel becomes a different nation by virtue of its rituals and laws. While Israel discovers mechanisms to overcome the boundaries, it also becomes committed to the boundaries imposed on her. Israel, as it maintains the borders, cannot remove the borders of ancient times. Israel cannot add or remove from the Torah, as it would violate the territory beyond its power. While Israel will be bound by the borders by virtue of the covenant, it is also called to transcend or overcome the boundaries. Thus, will the messianic era be ushered in. Borders and boundaries are both securities and dangers. The aesthetic dialectics between being bound to and to cross over the boundaries will be the beauty of God's children. How will the church identify and respond to these border issues within and without in our local, national and global context?

4

Genealogies: Widening Borderlessness

A Reflection on Genesis 10:1-5

Chilkuri Vasantha Rao

The formation and existence of the Church of South India is in itself an example of an initiative towards a borderless church that has and is still doing away with denominational borders and marching forward into doing away with more existing borders. William Carey, a reformer, an illustrious missionary and the father of Modern Missions who derived inspiration to widen the borders of his ministry, time and again quoted Isaiah 54:2 stating, "enlarge the site of your tent and let the curtains of your habitations be stretched out; do not hold back; lengthen your paths and strengthen your stakes."

More often then not we hear that it is better to build bridges than to build walls. The Indian ecclesia has, however, succumbed to the temptation of confining itself to the borders by creating boundaries along the lines of social identities, economic statuses, gender biases, and the like. In our attempt to rethink ecclesia towards a borderless church, we take a look at how in the Old Testament sages struggled with the idea of a borderless community and from them derive inspiration and vision for the new borderless ecclesia.

Our text for studying this would be Genesis 10 in general, particularly verses 1-5; 32, which is normally titled as "Nations descended from Noah". These are the descendants of Noah's sons, Shem, Ham, and Japheth. Children were born to them after the flood. The descendants of Japheth: Gomer, Magog, Madai, Javan, Tubal, Meshech and Tiras; The descendants of Gomer: Ashkenaz, Riphath, and Togarmah; and the descendants of Javan: Elishah, Tarshish, Kittim, and Rodes. From these, the coastland peoples spread. These are the descendants of Japheth, living in their lands and nations, with their own language, and with their families. Verse 32 speaks of the families of Noah's sons, according to their genealogies, in their nations; and from these, the nations spread abroad on the earth after the flood.

Genealogies

Once I was visiting a museum at Delphi in Greece. As students of the Old Testament, we were aware of the famous prophecies of Delphi in the study of the ancient world. In the museum at Delphi, there was a big round stone which was called the navel of the earth. That meant that at one time when the Greek civilization flourished, Delphi was considered to be the navel of the world or center of the world. And once in Rome, there was another stone that was also called the navel of the earth. So at a time when the Roman Empire was in power, Rome was considered to be the navel of the earth. And today, many who visit Jerusalem and preachers who preach about Jerusalem consider Jerusalem as the navel of the earth or the center of the world. Now, this is the trend and the thinking pattern that civilizations want their own places to be considered the center of the world and construct their worldview from that point and then as the world evolves, with a particular point as center, we end up referring to other locations as Near East, Far East, Middle East and so on. Everything is measured from the center as you try to measure the distance of the peoples, of the nations or anyone.

Genealogies are often skipped without being read, because we think, "well what do we get in genealogies!" When I was a pastor in one of the congregations, there was a family living beside the church. Every time I went to the church, I had to pass their house. Every time they saw me, they used to hail me saying, "Pastor, Praise the Lord". They used to invite me into their house saying, "Pastor pray for us". I used to read the Bible, give a short meditation and pray. And the next time I passed by their house this would be repeated. This sort of intervention in my pastoral work increased in frequency. Next time they called me I told them to bring their Bibles and asked them to read the texts that had the genealogies. Because they were probably reading it for the first time it was like a tongue twister and they were so annoyed to read those lines. After this, they stopped calling me into their house when I happened to pass by. So genealogies don't seem to interest people because we just don't tend to read them, and if we read them then we don't apply thought to understand it.

Sometimes we read the genealogies without understanding them because we have to complete the Bible reading. The general notion is that there are no spiritual values inherent in genealogies. They are seldom incorporated into the scriptures reading in Sunday worship. If at all we get some meaning, sometimes, we end up thinking that in those days men used to give birth - because

Abraham begets Isaac, Isaac begets Jacob and so on. So, these are the thoughts that come to mind when we think about the genealogies but genealogies have their own significance.

While genealogies are supposed to be dry and meaningless, they have a clear-cut form and format. Every form of writing has a purpose. If there was a purpose to employ such a form of writing as genealogies, then the names and the nations mentioned in these genealogies like Gomer, Magog, Madai, and so on are not just mere names. In these genealogies borders, people, people's cultures and languages are taken into cognizance. In these genealogies, we have names of individuals, groups of peoples, and nations. Genealogies acknowledge that the world is divided on the basis of nationality, language, cultures and geography.

So now one could easily get mixed up being unable to discern which is a proper name for a person and which is a proper name for a place as sometimes the name of a person may be identical with the name of a place. So this play on words/names exists in the genealogies. So genealogies present personalities and whose descendants they are. They detail a nation and its important places, its people with their respective religious, cultural and political systems. So in reality, if a reader wishes to understand the names in Genesis 10, one must read other books of the Bible where most of these names appear in the prophecies of Ezekiel like Gomer, Margok, Mardai, Tubal. All these names are mentioned at one time or other with reference to a place for example when a curse on Tyre is mentioned.

So we understand that these writings or sources come from a period of the Babylonian Exile when those exiled were deported and they were trying to make meaning of their lives in a new location. Hitherto, Jerusalem was everything for them, Jerusalem was their identity, Jerusalem was their culture, Jerusalem was their

God, Jerusalem was their theology, Jerusalem was everything to them. But then once they went into exile, their thinking pattern changed and they began to ask, "what are we, where are we, why do we not sing the Lord's song, near the rivers of Babylon". So this change in thinking comes from a change in the geographical location which was so dear to them and has now disappeared, raising questions like, "what meaning do we derive from being in a foreign land? What is this foreign land? where did it come from, why are we here? Does being here make us aliens? Does being here mean we are no more a people of the Land?"

The phrase, "people of the land," in the Old Testament refers to the Jewish people, the Israelites. But when Abraham's wife died, he goes to the "people of the land" to buy a little place. So the "people of the land" in this case are primarily Canaanites but then Israelites appropriated the term to themselves once they moved there. But now forced to move to Babylon how do they understand their identity being in a foreign land, being in Babylon?

So the names in the book of Ezekiel and the genealogies are similar and they coincide. So the writer, whoever it was, now knows his geography very well because he had to place the nation in a particular geographical location. The author does it in an excellent manner. He/she begins to unify continents in a very simple way in 5 verses in Genesis 10. But when one takes note of the geographical location and political framework of a nation, where they are and how they are, he/she begins from the location of their exiled geography. It also follows the direction of the Hebrew alphabet from right to left.

So the author begins slowly by quoting the continents in this manner and he/she connects one nation or the other nation from right to left. He begins in Mesopotamia, and mentions Asia Minor next, then he goes into Europe and comes down to Egypt and then later into the Arabian Peninsula. These are not just names but show a world that is divided by several reasons. The author is slowly trying to knit them by removing these borders to make the whole world one inhabited world.

The author also has a very good knowledge of historic timing. Some nations moved - these were people who were moving all the time. Abraham started somewhere in Mesopotamia, and he identifies himself and his ancestors as a people from Syria and then sojourning into Canaan, going to Egypt and coming back. So they all are people on the move. They are all migrants, as we are all migrants at one time or the other. Just because we happen to stay longer in one place does it mean we belong there? This migrant nature is there in all of us. So even in these five verses, the redactor recognized even nations who were at one time in one place had at some point moved to another place. This movement of nations means, boundaries are moving. So at one stage, the author shows us fixed boundaries and by moving up in the timeframe he also shows that one nation has already moved from the north. A nation in Mesopotamia has moved to Asia Minor. He spots therein fixing of the boundaries, taking note of the boundaries and then also moving of boundaries.

So, the author takes history into consideration. As Old Testament scholars or students of the Hebrew Bible, we do not normally entertain questions that fall within Genesis chapters 1-11 because once these questions are raised at some point one realizes that no answer is sufficient. Chapters 1-11 are considered pre-history, and there is no set geography or people or time factor pertaining to this section. Genesis chapters 1-11 give us the genesis of every phenomenon that is in existence. Chapter 10 falls into this category, telling us about the nations of the world.

If one accepts chapters 1-11 are pre-history, then this author or the redactor is also trying to outline the aetiological saga of how these nations came to be. Genesis chapters 1-11 are full of aetiological sagas that explain the origins of existence. But then, the genealogies that begin in chapter 10 are also moving into chapter 11. That means the author or redactor is trying to form a bridge between pre-history in order to connect it to history, then the reader understands both these pre-historical elements and the historical elements are now taken into consideration. In this instance, the author does away with the borders of pre-history and history.

The redactor also demonstrates with this exercise, the removal of boundaries from their sources also. If one talks about Genesis 10, then we immediately jump into the question the sources the redactor is using. Is it J or D or E or P? The redactor seems to be borrowing from both J and P sources and making a redaction and then presenting it to the world as what he thinks about these boundaries, how these boundaries came to be and how these boundaries are moving and what we do with these boundaries later.

So this chapter 10 is a commemoration of both the Yahwistic source and the Priestly writing. Chapter 10 incorporates elements from both the sources without losing the thought pattern. I submit that the main motive of the redactor in these 5 verses and through the chapter, is unifying the border between two histories, the pre-history, and the history. He is unifying the borders of two sources - J and the P, and the two specific theological ideologies inherent in these sources as J and P had different theological perspectives. But the redactor brings his own theological perspective of dealing with these fixed boundaries, moving boundaries and moving borders. Ultimately what he wants to achieve is making it into a borderless world by unifying the bigger borders.

Now coming to the cultural borders, or the linguistic borders, when the redactor is working on the sources, and when we are reading these names as Japheth, Gomer and so on he also mentions the coastland peoples. As chapters 1-11 are pre-history, it cannot really help answer questions on the factual exact name of names, its locations, and its languages. But the Hittite, the Assyrian, the Babylonian, the Egyptian and the Canaanite inscriptions, give us cross-references to these nations. They talk about their own language in verse 5 and say that from these coastlands the people spread. These are the descendants of Japheth and their lands. Note the way the author identifies people in their land, with their own language, linguistically by their families, the social identity and their nations, and cultural identities. People are identified by their political, cultural, linguistic and social systems. These are further clarified by other Assyrian, Hittite, Egyptian and Canaanite inscriptions for us. Thus the redactor also goes on to unify political borders.

The redactors mention different political entities in the genealogies because different lands are mentioned. He moves from one continent to another continent. He takes Mesopotamia, and then takes into consideration the places there and tries to connect them from where they came, then moves on to Asia Minor, moves on to Europe, moves on to Egypt and move on to the Arabian Peninsula. They are even identified by their families. So the political boundaries are taken into cognizance: Different cultures, different languages, and different families.

When we look at what the author does, we identify that this piece has come from the Priestly source, the Priestly source writer follows exactly writings in Genesis 1, as chapters 1:1 - 2:4a in the Masoretic text, is very liturgical in presentation and form. In Gen 1, we see liturgical formats: "it was evening and morning and again it was evening and morning and again it was evening and morning" – such examples of writing that are set out in such a wonderfully rhythmic way, belongs more to the liturgical format of writing. "Then it was day 1, then it was day 2, then day 3, then day 4, then day 5, then the 6th day"; then again he goes on to say "God saw it was good, it was good, it was good" repeatedly and ultimately to say, "God saw it was very good". This pattern is also visible in chapter 10.

In v. 5, the author comes up with the knitting together of the coastland people. These are the descendants of Yahweh in their lands, with their own language, by their families, in their nations. Four elements: the social, the linguistic, the political, and cultural are reflected. Now in Genesis 10: 20 he jumps from verse 5 to verse 20, to say that these are the descendants of Ham by their families, by their language, by their lands, and by their nations. Again we see that these boundaries of political, cultural, social realms are here recognized. Again in a rhythmic way, it is presented in a liturgical form in verse 31, and the same pattern is repeated after the few verses where he comes back to the same rhythm. "These are the descendants of Shem, by their families, languages, lands and their nations". This is a beautiful expression. He describes the nation and then says these are the boundaries and we are going to overcome these boundaries. Just as in the Genesis 1 account every day is culminating into the last verse saying, "… and God saw that it was very good", appears in verse 32, here too the author sums up everything at one point to say, "these are the families of Noah's sons according to their genealogies, in their nations, from their nations spread abroad after the flood." This is the total scenario that we are given to understand that Ham, Shem and Japeth are the descendants spread all over the world.

Now, if P is writing at the time of Babylonian exile, then he has knowledge about the J document already as other creation stories already existed. And for me, Genesis 10 is a very very important piece, because the compiler P, in exile, has this Yahwestic document. In chapter 2 of J document, it talks about the Garden of Eden, and that in the Garden of Eden, a spring comes up, and divides itself into four rivers that now flow to all corners of the world. Now, this is a beautiful ecological borderless expression that comes from the ecological sphere to us: a river comes up, there is a source of the river, and it divides itself, and it spreads to all over the world. This same pattern is now adapted into ch. 10 where all nations are of one source, dividing itself, into several streams and spheres, and then it covers the whole earth. Here also, the political system is to be taken note of how the already divided nations slowly get connected to one source i.e. Noah after the flood. This is to convey that although the world is divide by nations, by lands, families, languages, yet we are one human family. So the nationalities are done away with, the lingual barriers are done away with, the social barriers are done away with. The author is telling us: "Whoever you are, name yourself, whatever you are, name yourself, whatever nation you belong to, name yourself, whatever continent you belong to, name yourself, whatever language you belong to, claim it, but I want to tell you that all of us are only one common humanity stemming from that one person, Noah."

So this is a borderless community that the redactor is trying to bring about and tell us, we are but one human community stemming from one root that is Noah. So we are not many families but we are one big family in God (Gen 10: 5, 20, 31, 32). So, it is in a way a political documentation, a geographical documentation, linguistic documentation or it may even be an ethnographic documentation, but in whatever name you call it, the redactor wants us to affirm and say, "we are one human community, transcending these political, national, continental, linguistic, and social boundaries, thereby we are one. We are one single big human community and human family. All these boundaries are thereby overcome, and these boundaries are done away with."

So, the message of the redactor reverberates and is akin to what Paul writes, if anyone is in Christ, there is no Jew or Gentile, no female or male, no master or slave (Gal 3:28). So also, there is no longer family, language, culture, political system that divides us, but we all belong to one common human community having the same roots in one personality in the person of Noah.

We are a new human community that is one without borders of social, linguistic, cultural or political systems. The boundaries are there but the boundaries are also changing. The Genesis 10 author seems to declare that even those nations that are yet to come into being are also taken into cognizance and knit with this line to trace back to one person, Noah.

We had Czechoslovakia and now we don't have Czechoslovakia. It has become two countries Czech Republic and Slovakia. You know what was one has now become two countries. So the Genesis 10 author would say that even the future nations that would be born, whatever political, lingual boundaries they profess, they still belong to the one common human root thereby they are one family. This is what the redactor or the genealogies which we otherwise do not delve in to tell us. This has a big message for the struggle that the Church of South India encounters. We are struggling with many boundaries like the redactors who have already struggled with this long ago. They had a solution, they had a vision and a perspective on how to make the divided world into one human family. May we will find such solutions, visions and perspectives too.

5

The Communion of Saints as Ecclesia and Christ Communities

D. Sam Christopher

'Unity in diversity' is the uniqueness of India with its multiplicity of castes, classes, cultures, faiths, and languages. In the history of Christianity, in addition to the diversities of the Indian nation, there existed various mission agencies with its unique traditions and practices. The formation of the Church of South India is significant in that it forged unity by broadening the borders in spite of their doctrinal differences and practices.

While we envision a borderless church, it must be acknowledged *prima facie* that divisions or borders in Christianity from the times of early church have been inevitable. It is evidenced in Paul's address to the Corinthian church, when he says, "What I mean is that each one of you says, 'I belong to Paul,' or 'I belong to Apollos,' or 'I belong to Cephas,' or 'I belong to Christ.'"[1] Paul appeals to the nascent church to be united in the name of the crucified Christ instead of fostering factions.

In the history of Christianity, racism, political intimidation, theological and linguistic differences and social factors have caused divisions and created borders. However, from the beginning of the Protestant Mission in India, the Indian Church has shown courage to forge unity by breaking down borders. The protestant mission in India was launched by the joint effort of the pietism group and its antagonist group. In the 18th century, two German theological students of Halle University who were pietists were sent by the Danish King, who belonged to the Danish Church that did not accept pietism.[2]

In due course, the union of Church of South India and later, the union of Church of North India glorified the name of Christ by attaining unity amidst the diverse missions in India. At present, the attempt of Church of South India in envisioning a borderless church which may possibly lead us further towards breaking borders and achieving the prayer of Jesus, "that they may all be one."[3]

The Communion of Saints

"The Communion of Saints," is a creedal statement that possibly emerged from the Pauline concept of "saint" and its usage in his epistles. It may be reflective of apostle Paul's thinking along the lines of the borderless church. At a time when the Jewish Christians thought the Church belonged only to them, Paul re-drew the borders of Christianity by including Gentile Christians and addressing them by the term, αγίος (*hagios*). In recent times, this term has a wider spectrum of meanings that tends to divide people by virtue of their conduct and character, rather than unite people into an inclusive community. But in Pauline epistles, this term addresses every Christian as a saint and leads them towards an understanding of universalism rather than particularism.

Connotation of the Term Αγίος

Αγίος (*hagios*) means set apart to or by God; consecrated; holy; morally pure; and, upright.[4] It is a term that perhaps in its linguistic sense divides people by one's character; but in the Bible, it is used to identify people as a result of their election by God and qualifies them as the people of God. Especially in the New Testament, it has the connotation of the Christ Community. This idea of God's people might have evolved from the ideology expressed in Lev 11:44 -45: "… you shall, therefore, be holy, for I am holy."[5] Generally, in the Old Testament, Israel as the Chosen people are known as holy[6] as well God's saints.[7] In the New Testament, the believer of Christ is acknowledged as a saint, by virtue of one's own position "in Christ."

Although we may be tempted to understand the word *hagios* as something that divides or separates people as holy and unholy, in biblical understanding, it does not divide but differentiates people. As light and darkness are differentiated from one another, and when the light comes, darkness disappears, so also in a Christian understanding, *hagios* denotes the difference between people in terms of their identification with Christ. In Christ, one lives a new life or stays in one's old in life. As Paul states in 2 Cor. 5:17, one's character and life are changed in Christ.

W. Barclay points out that the term *hagios* refers to differentiation from ordinary things.[8] W. Pannenberg considers it not of separation from the world but of sanctification in the midst of the world.[9] Above all, according to Cranfield, *hagios* signifies the character of the Church in Christ as pardoned sinners by the Grace of God in Jesus Christ; *hagios* then is a free gift possessing no righteousness of its own.[10]

It is implicit in Peter's deliberations with God, as it is seen in the Peter - Cornelius episode concerning clean and unclean food where it is said, "What God has made clean, you must not call profane,"[11] and subsequently ends with the baptism of the Gentiles in Ceaseria in accepting all people into the Christ Community.

In the New Testament, the term 'saints' is applied to Christians in the churches of Corinth, Ephesus, Rome, and other places who upheld their unity and relationship with Christ as well with one another. It is used inclusively and everyone is addressed as a 'saint' without any question of one's own moral integrity. As testified to in Gal 3:28, there is no disparity shown in addressing people who are in Christ as saints - poor or rich, male or female, elder or younger, slave or master, Jew or Gentile. In general, it must be noted that the term, 'saints' was applied to Christians because they are a called and sanctified communities.[12]

Ecclesia: A Called and Consecrated Community

While sainthood has commonly been understood as referring to the holiness of a person, it is used to refer to both a person who is living on earth as well as a person who is dead and lives among the heavenly community.[13] The latter are known as saints with haloes. But, in Pauline writings, he uses the term, 'saint' to indicate a hold person living on earth.

Paul uses the term 'saint' in the salutations in his epistles to address the congregation members of local churches: "To all God's beloved in Rome, who are called to be saints…" (Rom 1:7); "Greet … all the saints who are with them" (Rom16:15); "To the church of God which is at Corinth, to those sanctified in Christ Jesus, called to be saints together with all those who in every place call on the name of our Lord Jesus Christ…" (1 Cor 1:2); "…To the church of God which at Corinth, with all the saints who are in the whole of Achaia" (2 Cor 1:1); "...To the saints who are also faithful in Christ Jesus" (Eph 1:1); "...your love toward all the saints" (Eph 1:15); "...To all the saints in Christ Jesus who are at Philippi..." (Phil 1:1); "Greet every saint in Christ Jesus. The brethren who are with me greet you. All the saints greet you, especially those of the emperor's household" (Phil 4:21); "To the saints and faithful brethren in Christ at Colossae..." (Col 1:2).

Apart from these salutations, Paul uses the term saint in other instances also with the same inclination: Rom 8:27; 16:2; 1 Cor 6:1; 14:33; Eph 1:18; 3:8; and, 1 Thess 3:13. Moreover, he refers to the Christians at Judea suffering persecution and tribulation using this term, saint: Acts 26:10, "... I not only shut up many of the saints in prison..." So, it is obvious that Paul uses the word saints to denote the Christians of every Church as the ones who are called and set apart for God as God's own people without any question about one's moral integrity.

Besides, in a few other non-Pauline New Testament passages also the usage of this term 'saint' refers to the Christians. For instance, in Ananias' statement regarding the atrocity of Saul against the Christians that states "... how much evil he has done to thy saints at Jerusalem" (Acts 9:13). Further it is also used with the same reference to Christians in Acts 9:32 & 41; Heb 13:24; Jude 3; Rev 5:8; 13:7, 10; 19:8 & 20:9.

Hagioi, in plural form, represents the people of God in Paul's writings and indicates that the Church is called collectively to be a consecrated community. Paul might have perhaps borrowed the ideology of saints from the Hebrew word, קָהָל (*kahal*) which means congregation, assembly; especially the congregation of the people of Israel.[14] In the Old Testament, it denotes Israel as God's people who are the holy assembly of the Lord (Num 16:3). In the New Testament, Greek word ἐκκλησία (*ekklesia*) also means the same; and, κυριακόν (*kuriakon*), the derivative of the term Church, means "belonging to the Lord."[15] However, it should be noted that in the New Testament, the plural usage, *hagioi* not only represents the covenant people but also includes the Gentiles and addresses all of them as saints: "So then you are no longer strangers and sojourners, but you are fellow citizens with the saints and members of the household of God…" (Eph.2:19)

Another possibility to understand the term 'saints' is as Paul uses it in his writings to contrast it in the *Sitz im leben* of Christians' identity crisis at that time.[16] Amidst the identity crisis, it enables every Christian to construct true catholicity and ecumenicity. It befits Paul's metaphor of the Church as the body of Christ, which O. Cullmann points out is the risen body of Jesus. This is in line with that we may vision as the borderless church which ought to be the reality of the visible Church. It reiterates the call and commission of every Christian to be channels and partakers in building up the community.

Ecclesia: A Commissioned Community

It may perhaps be said that each one is commissioned: "…to equip the saints for the work of ministry for the building up the body of Christ…" (Eph.4:11-12). In other words, from Paul, we learn that the church is called to care for each other as a custom-built community. In Rom 12:13 he says, "Contribute to the needs of the saints …" Along with the commission, Paul proceeds to help people who are in need which is understood from his words as expressed in Rom.15:25-26, 31: "At present, however, I am going to Jerusalem with the aid for the saints. For Macedonia and Achaia have been pleased to make some contribution for the poor among the saints at Jerusalem… my service for Jerusalem may be acceptable to the saints."

Further, he uplifts the help of the churches to one another as another dimension of a commissioned community in several references in 1 and 2 Corinthians: "Now concerning the contribution for the saints..." (1 Cor.16:1)"; "...they have devoted themselves to the service of the saints" (1 Cor.16:15); "For, as I can testify, they voluntarily gave according to their means, and even beyond their means, begging us earnestly for the privilege of sharing in this ministry to the saints" (2 Cor.8:3); "Now it is superfluous for me to write to you about the offering for the saints"(2 Cor. 9:1).

In all these references, it is obvious that the early Christian communities as the body of Christ took care of each other during difficulties like drought and poverty. So, the ecclesia can be understood as a vibrant community which is commissioned to take care of one another in building up community life within its own and beyond its border. It also indicates the early church in its praxis as a moving community aware of the other and accomplishing the needs of the other in their struggles (cf. 2 Cor 8:1-5; 9:1; Rom. 15:26-28).

Ecclesia: A Micro to Macro Moving Community

Pauline salutations and other references to saints indicate a specific local community at a micro-level. Although he addresses them with the name of their local church or place, he encourages them to help the other micro-communities at a macro-level. It breaks the boundary/border of particularism and leads towards universalism. It breaks the local boundary/border of exclusivism and leads towards the mission of inclusivism.

Generally, Pauline ecclesiology of inclusivism is said to be captured in Gal.3:28, the *Magna Carta*, "There is neither Jew nor Greek, there is neither slave nor free, there is neither male nor female; for you are all one in Christ Jesus." This inclusiveness seems to be not only among human beings but also along with Christ. This vision of inclusiveness portrays Christ as the head of the borderless church.

Although the usage of the term 'saints' indicates both the local Christians as well the Christians of other churches, it is very clear that Paul insists on wider union of borderless church in its mission. On the whole, in Paul's terminology within the New Testament image of Church as the body of Christ, 'saints' lead everyone towards communion with one another from micro to macro-level by having oneness of mind and deeds in their living, as is confessed in the Apostle's Creed that we believe in 'the holy Catholic Church' and 'the communion of saints.'

Ecclesia: The Communion of Saints

According to Pannenberg, the communion of saints would mean the communion of Christians.[17] From the New Testament understanding of ecclesia, the body of Christ, is one under the head of Christ (Eph 5:23).[18] Early Church father, Bishop Cyprian of Carthage says, "No one can have God as his father who does not have the church as his mother."[19] It implies the idea that Christians unite themselves in a borderless, single family of God.

Prophet Malachi also says, "Have we not all one father? Has not one God created us?" (Mal 2:10a). So, basically, it is clear that no individualism or parochialism stands in the fellowship of saints. The phrase, communion of saints leads us towards the understanding of a church not only at the micro-level but also at the macro-level of One Church or Catholic Church, which we are currently discussing as a "borderless church."

A. McGrath says that the phrase, communion of saints can also be pronounced as "a fellowship of forgiven sinners, who are in the process of becoming holy."[20] It may be viable to think that the concept "fellowship of forgiven sinners" along with the ideology "communion of saints," opens up the praxis of the borderless church like the charming harmony of music.

While we move towards the understanding of the communion of saints, there may arise another issue: Can we include the saints with haloes who are in heavenly places or only the living Christians? Early father Nicetas says:

> Patriarchs, prophets, apostles, martyrs, all the just who have been, are, or shall be, are one Church, because sanctified by one faith and life, marked by one Spirit, they constitute one body... the communion of saints is defined as the fellowship that all Christians have with one another, those in this world, and those who will yet be, those who have passed into the world beyond ... [21]

I. Puthiadam and X. Irudayaraj also hold the view that it is "our communion with the saints, who are already in heaven."[22] Their opinions may perhaps be a holistic understanding of an invisible Church. But, as it has been noted earlier, the usage of *hagios* referring to a living person is clearly and practically demonstrated in Paul's writing and it denotes the fellowship of caring and sharing as well portrays the Eucharistic life of the Church.

Ecclesia: Eucharistic Life

The statement of the creed, "the Holy Catholic Church" indicates the unity of Christians rather than the division among them. The Church is "catholic" means general or universal.[23] The mission of the Church is not to detach one from another but to unite all. The body of Christ, the ecclesia leads everyone to have fellowship in the sharing of the elements of Eucharist, the body and blood of Jesus Christ. The Latin phrase, *communion sanctorum* means either communion of saints or communion in holy things.[24] Participation in the Eucharistic celebration leads the believers of Christ to be aware of and give up their sinful life. Also, the communion of saints in Eucharistic celebration implies the concept of κοινωνία (*Koinonia*), which means fellowship; a close mutual relationship; sharing in; or partnership.[25] Both communion with Christ and one another in Eucharist fulfil the essence of the church and lead towards the rule of God as well the borderless church.

Pannenberg says, "The definition of the church as communion with Christ also has its location in the context of the hope of the kingdom of God."[26] In this, one should not confine it to the Kingdom of God as the kingdom only for Christians, but open it up to embrace the whole humankind.

Conclusion

In biblical understanding, the term 'saint' is used inclusively to the ones who are in Christ irrespective of their diverse status in the society. On the basis of such a New Testament understanding when we speak of "the communion of saints" in India, it leads those who are in Christ towards unity without any divisions based on our identity of caste, creed, class, dialect, and culture.

To accomplish our Lord's prayer, "that they may all be one" let us move as Christ communities towards such an understanding of the communion of saints and in living this out attain the envisioned borderless church.

Endnotes

[1] 1 Cor.1:12.

[2] C. B. Firth, *An Introduction to India Church History* (trans. A.D. Manuel; Madras: C.L.S., 1962), 201-202. (Tamil)

[3] Jn.17:21.

[4] "Dictionary" in *The Greek New Testament* (ed. Barbara Aland, et al.; Stuttgart: United Bible Societies, 2001), 2.

[5] Cf. Lev.19:2.

[6] Deut.7:6.

[7] Ps. 31:23.

[8] William Barclay, *The Apostles Creed for Everyman* (New York: Harper &Row, 1967), 256.

[9] Wolfhart Pannenberg, *The Apostles' Creed* (London: SCM Press, 1972), 146.

[10] C.E.B. Cranfield, *The Apostles' Creed* (London: Continuum, 2004), 61.

[11] Acts 10:1ff.

[12] 1 Cor.1:2.

[13] A.S. Hornby, *Oxford Advanced Learner's Dictionary of Current English* (Oxford: University Press, 1974), 765.

[14] H.W.F. Gesenius, *Hebrew-Chaldee Lexicon to the Old Testament* (Grand Rapids: Baker Book House, 1979), 726.

[15] "Dictionary" in *The Greek New Testament*, 55 & 105.

[16] J. A. Adewuya, "The People of God in a Pluralistic Society: Holiness in 2 Corinthians," *Holiness and Ecclesiology in the New Testament* (ed. K. E. Brower & A. Johnson; Grand Rapids: Wm B. Eerdmans, 2007), 203.

[17] Pannenberg, *The Apostles' Creed* 149.

[18] Eph. 5:23.

[19] A. McGrath, *Affirming your Faith: Exploring the Apostle's Creed* (Great Britain: Inter Varsity Press, 1991), 111.

[20] A. McGrath, *Affirming your Faith*, 120.

[21] Barclay, *The Apostles Creed for Everyman*, 295.

[22] I. Puthiadam and X. Irudayaraj, *The Christian Faith Creed in the Indian Context* (Bangalore: ATC Publishers, 2008), 240.

[23] Barclay, *The Apostles Creed for Everyman*, 257.

[24] Puthiadam and X. Irudayaraj, *The Christian Faith*, 239.

[25] "Dictionary" in *The Greek New Testament*, 101.

[26] Pannenberg, *The Apostles' Creed*, 155.

Bibliography

Adewuya, J. A. "The People of God in a Pluralistic Society: Holiness in 2 Corinthians." 203 in *Holiness and Ecclesiology in the New Testament.* Edited by K. E. Brower & A. Johnson. Grand Rapids: Wm B. Eerdmans, 2007.

Barclay, William. *The Apostles Creed for Everyman.* New York: Harper & Row, 1967.

Cranfield, C.E.B., *The Apostles' Creed.* London: Continuum, 2004.

Firth, C. B. *An Introduction to India Church History.* Madras: C.L.S., 1962.

Gesenius, H.W.F. *Hebrew-Chaldee Lexicon to the Old Testament.* Grand Rapids: Baker Book House, 1979.

Mc Grath, A. *Affirming your Faith: Exploring the Apostle's Creed.* Great Britain: Inter Varsity Press, 1991.

Pannenberg. Wolfhart. *The Apostles' Creed.* London: SCM Press, 1972.

Puthiadam I., and X. Irudayaraj. *The Christian Faith Creed in the Indian Context* Bangalore: ATC Publishers, 2008.

6

A Johannine Perspective of Jesus' Public Ministry

A Call for Christ Communities towards a Borderless Church

I. Franklin

According to the Fourth Gospel, Jesus' public ministry starts and ends at Cana. His first public ministry travel took him from Cana to Jerusalem, into Judea, Samaria, and back to Cana. The circle of his first missionary journey was completed with his second miracle or sign.[1] Jesus performed his first two miracles namely, the wedding at Cana (Jn 2: 1-11) and the healing of an official's son (Jn 4: 46-54) during his first public ministry travel. These two miracles are generally distinguished from the other signs because they were both performed in Cana of Galilee. This article focuses only on these two signs of Jesus' first public ministry tour.

The two Cana stories form an obvious frame around the narrative that extends from John 2:1-4:54. In John 4:54 the evangelist looks back to John 2:1-12, thus closing the episodes that run from Cana to Cana. Gerald L. Borchert explains the geographical bounding of the Cana Cycle which moves the reader's attention from Cana (Jn 2:1-11) and Capernaum (Jn 2:12) through Jerusalem (Jn 2:13-24) to an unclear Jewish/Judean context (Jn 3:1-36), then to Samaria (Jn 4:1-42) and back to Cana in Galilee (Jn 4:43-54).[2]

Cana becomes the center for both the first and second miracles.[3] Cana of Galilee is a vital place in Jesus' fist public ministry cycle. There is not much information about this village because every time the evangelist refers to it, he explains it simply as being ἐν κανὰ τη!ς γαλιλαίας – "In Cana of Galilee" (Jn 2:1, 11; 4:46; 21:2). It is a distinctly Johannine village appearing nowhere else in the New Testament besides John 2:1, 4:46 and 21:2. The exact location of Cana in Galilee is still disputed with at least four locations vying to be recognized as the Cana of John's gospel: Ain Kanah, Kanah, Kefr Kenna, and Khirbet Kana.[4]

Both Cana signs are alike in that those who witness them are able to see the revelation of Jesus' identity in and through the miracle. The first Cana miracle reveals Jesus' glory; the second reveals his ability to give life. John 2:11 grips the interpretive key. Jesus' disciples saw him turn water into wine at Cana, but it was not the miracle in and of itself that led to their faith. Rather, they saw Jesus' glory in the sign, and it was in Jesus, not the miracle, that they believed. Similarly, the royal official moves beyond a preliminary faith in the miraculous power of Jesus' word (Jn 4:50) to complete faith (Jn 4:53).

First Cana Miracle

John's first miracle account (Jn 2: 1-11) describes a wedding celebrated in a small village called Cana. The evangelist mentions six characters namely: the mother of Jesus,[5] Jesus, his disciples, the servants at the wedding banquet, the chief steward and the bridegroom. But except Jesus, none of them are named. This pericope is placed immediately following the calling of the first five disciples[6] and is contextually vital because the results of the miracle center on the disciples' faith. This sign serves a dual function of closing the evangelist's introduction of Jesus while detailing the inauguration of the Cana cycle of his public ministry.

Women Participation and Leadership in Jesus' First Miracle

Mary is called the ἡ μήτηρ τοῦ ἰησοῦ - "the mother of Jesus" - three times in this miracle (Jn 2:1, 2, 5). The imperfect ἦν (Jn 2:1) confirms that Mary is there at the wedding party even before Jesus' arrival. She appears only twice in the Fourth Gospel: at the wedding at Cana (2:1-12), and at the foot of the cross (19:25-27). The phrase 'οἶνον οὐκ ἔχουσιν, "They have no wine," is the starting point of the sign. It shows Mary's courage and leadership quality in a critical situation. οἶνου has no article which could mean that the wine was absolutely finished in the wedding party. ἔχουσιν (present, active) indicates the action which is presently happening at the moment and this meant loss of face for the host family. According to Andrew Lincoln:

> To run out of wine was not simply a social embarrassment but entailed a serious loss of family honour.[7] It suggested a lack of cooperative friends and had dire implications for the web of reciprocal obligations in which a person was involved.[8]

The bridegroom was facing great embarrassment and loss of face because the wine had given out and guests were still present.[9] When the wine ran out, the host family became desperate, including Jesus' mother who suggested that Jesus do something about it (Jn 2: 3).[10] There was a need to urgently appeal to someone to resolve the lack of wine since it is related to the honor of the bridegroom in society. The chief steward was not aware of this important issue, so the mother of Jesus took leadership and initiative to solve the problem so that it did not mar the joyful occasion.

Jesus' reply, "Woman, what concern is that to you and to me? My hour has not yet come," can be understood in two ways. It can mean either a critical refusal of an affiliation between people and a profound hostility or the beginning of a difference of opinion. Jesus uses this term γφναι often when referring to women in the Gospel of John (Jn 4:21; 8:10; 19:26; 20:15). It is understood to be a term of respect and affection yet it is undoubtedly an unusual way to address one's mother.[11] It may be that when Jesus addresses his mother this way he is denying her maternal claims on him and distancing himself from her by placing her on par with the other women he so addresses.[12] Morris explains this as "indicating that there is a new relationship between them as he enters public ministry."[13]

The mother of Jesus continuously does her duty to resolve the crisis. Her words to the servants: "Do whatever he tells you," (Jn 1: 5) responds to the invitation of Jesu where she enters onto the plane of openness to God's project. Mary places everything in the hands of the Son and arrives at the point where he lives and sees things. It is not difficult to compare the expression used by Mary with that which the Israelite community expressed at Sinai while wandering in the desert: "Everything that the Lord has spoken we will do" (Ex 19, 8; 24, 3,7). The parallel between Mary and Moses is eloquent. Just as Moses on Mount Sinai was the mediator between God and the people, introducing them to the Covenant with God, so too Mary at Cana introduces the servants, after she herself had submitted to the will of God. Just as on Sinai the gift of the Law followed the act of faith, so too at Cana, with Mary's faith passed on to the servants, there follows the gift of the new wine, which is the 'joyful tidings' brought by Jesus.

Contextually Mary might have played the role of chief steward or bridegroom in the wedding but theologically the image of Mary can be seen as representing the Church. Jesus addresses Mary as "woman" and the evangelist never mentions her by her proper name. With the title of Woman, from this moment Mary will not only be the Mother of Jesus but the Woman-Mother, who will carry out a specific role in the messianic mission of her Son: to represent the people of the Covenant with an attitude of openness and of availability to the Word of God. She is the Mother-Zion (Ps 87: 5, cf. Isa 2: 2-5; Mic 4: 1-3; Zech 8: 20-23), the new Jerusalem which assembles her children for the construction of the new people of God (cf. Isa 18:20; 66:8), the new Israel in its eschatological setting.[14]

It is very clear that Mary's request is accepted by Jesus, thus he blesses the wedding with the abundance of best wine. She played the main role in his first miracle. This shows how Jesus uses women in his mission right from the beginning. In fact, it may not be entirely wrong to assume that the servants involved in this miracle might have been women since their gender is not specifically mentioned by the evangelist. Thus, his first sign invites the church to grant leadership to women.

Leadership is different from participation. Jesus' first sign invites us to rethink women's leadership in churches. For the past seven decades, the Church of South India has taken many efforts towards the empowerment of women. Ordination of women, women's education, women's participation in pastorate committees, diocesan and synod executive committees have been encouraged. We also have affirmative action to increase women's participation in church administration. Such affirmative action breaks the heretofore guarded borders that curtailed women's participation in church administration, governance and decision-making. When we create reservation for women in key positions of power and decision-making like Office Bearers, Secretary, Treasurer or Chairperson at the pastorate, diocesan and synod level, we cross the border from mere participation afforded by empowerment and move towards a new borderless space for women's leadership in the Church.

Accepting and Adopting Other Cultures

In his first sign, Jesus adopts at least two cultures from Gentiles. First is about the significance of the number 'Six' in this sign. There is no doubt that the Bridegroom was a Jew since he had arranged everything according to Jews rites (Cf Jn 2:6). The water jars were not simply vessels for holding water but vessels used for the Jewish purification rituals. The customs mentioned here undoubtedly refer to the washing practice described in Mark 3:1-4.[15] These rituals were grounded in Levitical Law and stone jars were often used because impurities cannot pass through it unlike earthen vessels that must be broken if made unclean (Lev 29:11-38).[16] The water jars used for Jewish purification rites represent the old order of Judaism. Through his first sign, Jesus indicates that he will replace the old order with a new one.[17] The fact that there are only "six" jars (Jn 2:6) further signals the failure and incompleteness of the old order. For Jews, 'seven' is a complete number. The saving of good wine shows that Jesus is the fulfilment of Judaism (Jn 2:10).[18] Jesus provides wine in superabundance. By placing the incomplete number of jars, Jesus breaks the border that his abundance of wine is not only for Jews but also for the Gentiles who were unfamiliar with the Judaic customs.

The second cultural adaptation is about the usage of water and wine. There have been attempts to reconstruct an original pre-Johannine miracle story, and a Dionysus background is sometimes suggested. Scholars from varying fields have noted the similarities between this Cana miracle story and the myth of the Dionysus cult. In the Dionysus legend, once a year the temple springs would produce wine instead of water and this would fill large jars in the temple. The notion of wine coming from water predates the Johannine tradition. Bultmann suggests that the Cana pericope was originally a pagan legend that was applied to Jesus.[19] Greeks who may not have grasped the messianic significance of the sign would have understood that the miraculous gift of wine revealed the presence of deity.

Throughout the Mediterranean world, wine was associated with the god Dionysus, who was said to have been the first to cultivate the vine and ferment its fruit. At Andros, in the festival called 'the gift of God', a spring would flow with wine; and at Elis, three empty jars were placed in a sealed room and the following morning were always found full of wine. The legends of Dionysus tell us little about how the story of the first Cana miracle originated, but they do help us understand how the story could communicate the significance of Jesus to Greeks as well as Jews. The widespread associations between a miraculous gift of wine and the presence of a deity would have helped many to understand that the sign revealed the presence of God in the person of Jesus.

The many Jewish elements in the Gospel account would not necessarily have screened out connotations from the wider Greco-Roman environment. Dionysus was said to have been born in Palestine, at Scythopolis southeast of Cana. Before the Maccabean revolt, the Syrians introduced the worship of Dionysus into Jerusalem for a time (2 Macc 6.7). This did not continue, but Dionysus was venerated at Tyre, just north of Galilee. Some Greek and Latin authors even thought that Dionysus and the God of Israel were the same.

The miracle at Cana testifies to the messianic and divine aspects of Jesus' identity by evoking associations from a broad cultural and religious spectrum.[20] Strengthening this claim, Bultmann contends that the date traditionally ascribed to the wedding at Cana is January 6th, the same date as the Dionysus Feast.[21] In using sources from the Hellenist cultural environment the Johannine author breaks the border and opens a creative way to communicate the good news to all groups of people, especially non-Jewish people.

Second Cana Miracle

In John 4: 46-54 a royal official son lay ill in Capernaum, so he went to Jesus when he heard Jesus had returned from Judea and, notwithstanding the dignity incumbent to his royal position, begged Jesus to come and heal his son, who was on the verge of dying.

There is no attempt by the evangelist to describe the miracle itself. The supernatural character of the miracle which in turn reflects back on Jesus' supernatural character, is shown by the immediacy of the cure as soon as Jesus spoke. Only God can act that quickly and across a considerable distance in space and time.[22] Faith is one of the main themes in this sign. The verb πιςτεφω, "I believe", is used three times in this second Cana sign (Cf. Jn 4:48, 50, 53) and is clearly a primary motif in John.

The royal official came to Jesus because he "heard that Jesus had come from Judea to Galilee." The act of hearing is very important in this context. Because he heard about Jesus' deed, the royal official took the decision to meet Jesus. Thus, hearing about Jesus and his deeds was what led the official to put his faith in Jesus.[23] Instead of helping the distressed human's need, Jesus, somewhat unexpectedly, replied, "Unless you see signs and wonders, you will not believe" (Jn 4:48). The declaration is addressed beyond the royal official to 'you' in the plural.[24] Judge comments that the βαςιλικὸσ, the royal official, thus steps out from among a new group of people who respond to Jesus, the Galileans - a group of mixed background.[25]

Status of the Royal Official

βαςιλικὸσ is in itself simply an adjective meaning "royal" and could be applied to any member of a royal family, or of the royal household.[26] In John 4, the word almost certainly denotes an official in the service of the king, that is, of Herod Antipas, Tetrarch of Galilee, who, though not technically a king, was often given the title.[27] Some scholars speculate that the royal official could be identified with Chuza, the manager of Herod's household mentioned in Luke 8:3.[28] Considering the plural form of Galileans, Van Belle opines the Royal official was the representative of the Galileans.[29] Keener also calls the Royal official a Galilean aristocrat.[30]

Scholars debate whether the βαςιλικὸσ was a Gentile or a Jew. However, with regard to ethnicity, it pays to recognize that either option is possible. Some scholars[31] assume that the Johannine βαςιλικὸ σmust have been a Jew. A βαςιλικὸσ could be either Jewish or a foreigner employed in Herod Antipas' bureaucracy. The word βαςιλικὸσ often denotes military forces for Roman or Herodian rulers.[32] Some scholars[33] presume that the Johannine βαςιλικὸσ must have been a Gentile. Mead concludes that the βαςιλικὸσ of John 4:46-53 is a Gentile officer, perhaps in the service of Herod Antipas, but quite probably, in the service of Rome.[34]

What is more important to note is that βαςιλικὸσ was a socially and economically wealthy person. Jesus performed his first Cana miracle for the welfare of a poor family in Cana at the wedding and his second miracle for the welfare of a rich family. Jesus reveals his glory in the midst of a poor family in the first miracle and in the midst of a rich family in the second miracle. Thus, while his first miracle invites us to rethink the socially and economically deprived people in our ministry, his second miracle invites us to rethink the socially and economically wealthy people as well.

For the past seven decades, the Church of South India has kept very much in view the poor, exploited and needy. But what about the rich, wealthy and so-called upper caste/class people? Christ is for all. There is neither Jew nor Gentile, neither slave nor free, neither rich nor poor, neither so-called upper caste nor so-called low caste, nor is there male and female, for we are all one in Christ Jesus. Thus, we need to break some of our borders to broaden who we focus our ministries on so that we can create a borderless church.

Endnotes

[1] Mark W. G. Stibbe, *John* (Sheffield: JSOT Press, 1993) 70.

[2] Gerald L. Borchert, *John1-11,* New American Commentary (Nashville: Broadman & Holman, 1996) 151.

[3] Gerald L. Borchert, *John1-11,* 151; Keener notes that every reference to Cana in this Gospel explicitly adds its connection with Galilee (Jn. 2:1, 11; 4:46; 21:2). This could be to distinguish it from some other 'Cana' elsewhere, but because its mention in John 2:11 comes so quickly after John 2:1, when the reader would not need a reminder, it may be intended to draw attention to its representative Galilean character. Craig S. Keener, *The Gospel of John: A Commentary* (2 vols.; Peabody, Mass.: Hendrickson, 2003) 1.630.

[4] J. Carl Laney, *Baker's Concise Bible Atlas : A Geographical Survey of Bible History* (Grand Rapids, Michigan: Baker Book House, 1988) 91-94.

[5] The evangelist mentions 'the Mother of Jesus' character even before Jesus' name, thus signaling her importance.

[6] Andrew, Peter, Phillip, Nathaniel and an unnamed disciple from John1: 37.

[7] Honour serves as a kind of social rating representing a person's social standing within the community, along with the rights and responsibilities that go with it. All members of a family share in its accumulated honour and are concerned with preserving and defending that honour. A person's honour is primarily a consequence of one's birth. It is the male head of the family, however, who represents the family's honour in the public realm and who is responsible for publicly defending it, and if possible enhancing it. Bruce J. Malina. *The New Testament World: Insights from Cultural Anthropology* (Louisville: Westminster John Knox 1993) 96-97.

[8] Andrew T. Lincoln, *The Gospel According to Saint John.* (Black's New Testament Commentary; London: Hendrickson Publishers, 2005) 27.

[9] Colin Kruse, *The Gospel According to John,* (Tyndale New Testament Commentaries; Michigan: William B. Eerdmans 2003) 91.

[10] Steven S. *Kim*, "*The Significance of Jesus' First Sign–Miracle in John*" *Bibliotheca Sacra 206* (2010) *167.* The context reveals that Mary expected Jesus to do some kind of miracle, although he had not yet performed any miracles (cf. 2:11).This is also proof that she had already observed many evidences of his supernatural and messianic identity: his supernatural conception and the announcement by the angel Gabriel, the events preceding his birth such as Zechariah's song, the events surrounding his birth such as the angels' announcement, Jesus' presentation in the temple, and Simeon's exultation (Luke 1-2). In short, she had good reasons to believe in Jesus' messianic identity.

[11] Rudolf Bultmann, *The Gospel of John: A Commentary* (trans. G. R. Beasley-Murray; Philadelphia: Westminster, 1971) 116; Leon. Morris, *The Gospel According to John,* Revised Edition (The New International Commentary on The New Testament; Grand Rapids, Mich.: William B. Eerdamans Publishing House,1995) 158; and Schnackenberg, *The Gospel According to St John*, 328.

[12] Ben Witherington III, *Women in the Ministry of Jesus: A Study of Jesus' Attitudes to Women and Their Roles as Reflected in His Earthly Life* (SNTSMS 51; Cambridge: Cambridge University Press, 1984) 84-85.

[13] Morris, *The Gospel According to John*, Revised Edition (The New International Commentary on The New Testament; Grand Rapids, Mich.: William B. Eerdamans Publishing House,1995) 158.

[14] Giorgio Zevini, *The Gospel According to John.* (NBSR 13; Roma: LAS, 2009) 195.

[15] Morris, *The Gospel According to John*, 160.

[16] Baltensweiler, H., H.G. Link and J. Schattenmann. "Pure, Clean." *The New International Dictionary of New Testament Theology.* (Gen Ed. Colin Brown. Vol. 3. Grand Rapids: Zondervan Publishing House, 1967) 100-108.

[17] Cornelis Bennema, *Excavating John's Gospel*, (Eugene: Wipf & Stock Publishers, 2008) 39.

[18] Mark W. G. Stibbe, *John* (Sheffield: JSOT Press, 1993) 43.

[19] R. Bultmann, *The Gospel of John,* 118-19.

[20] Koester, *Symbolism in the Fourth Gospel* (Minneapolis: Fortress Press, 2003) 85.

[21] Bultmann, *The Gospel of John,*119. Others have refuted this connection saying the similarities are not enough evidence. For instance, Morris argues that if anything, this similarity is used by the evangelist to show the superiority of Christ; Morris, *The Gospel According to John,* 154. He continues by pointing out that the evangelist totally disregards the actual transformation of the elements, which is in stark contrast to the pagan metamorphosis. Raymond E. Brown, *The Gospel According to John* (2 vols. AB 29, 29A. Garden City, N.Y.: Doubleday, 1966-1970) 1.100-101. This author's point is more that the final form of the Fourth Gospel calls us to think about different kinds of sources which eventually circulated to multiple groups of people within the community to portray Jesus' Salvific mission. However, the resemblances exhibited between these stories cannot be ignored.

[22] *Witherington, John's Wisdom* (Louisville: Westminster John Knox Press, 1995)128-129.

[23] This is an important concept in the Fourth Gospel, as Craig Koester has established in his article. Craig R. Koester, "Hearing, Seeing, and Believing in the Gospel of John," *Bib* 70.3 (1989): 327-48.

[24] Andres T. Lincoln, *The Gospel According to Saint John,*(BNTC: 2005)186

[25] Peter J. Judge, "The Royal Official: Not so officious" in *Character Studies in the Fourth Gospel: Narrative Approaches to Seventy Figures in John* (ed. Steven A.Hunt, D. Francois Tolmie and Reuben Zimmermann Tübingen: Mohr Siebeck, 2013) 309.

[26] John F. McHugh, *A Critical and Exegetical Commentary on John 1-4* (ICC; London: T&T Clark, 2009) 316; The term βαςιλικός is used also in Acts 12.20f., where it describes the territory and robes of Herod Agrippa; but he was a real king. A. H. Mead, "The βαςιλικός in John 4:46-53," *JSNT* 7.23 (1985):69.

[27] cf.Carson, *The Gospel According to John,*238; Brown, *The Gospel According to John,*1.190; Schnackenburg, *The Gospel According to St. John,1*.465; McHugh,

A Critical and Exegetical Commentary on John 1-4, 316 ; Köstenberger, *John,* 169; Stibbe, *John,* 72; Strictly speaking Herod was not a king at all, but a tetrarch. Ile was, however, of the royal house, and exercised kingly rule, so on occasion he could be called King (cf. Mark 6:14). Morris, *The Gospel According to John,* 256.

[28]Köstenberger, *John,* 172; Morris, *The Gospel According to John,* 256. Richard Bauckham also believes it nothing more than a "possibility" that this royal official is Chuza, ἐπιηπόποσ manager of Herod Antipas in Luke 8:3. Richard Bauckham, *Gospel Women: Studies of the Named Women in the Gospels Commentary* (Grand Rapids, Michigan: William B. Eerdmans Publishing Company, 2002),138

[29] *see* the plural form οὐ μὴ πιστεύσητε in John4:48 and οἱ γαλιλαῖοι in John 4:45.

[30] Keener, *The Gospel of John,*1. 630

[31] J.A.T. Robinson, *On Redating the New Testament* (London: SCM Press, 1976), 265; Brown, *The Gospel According to John,*1.192. Carson, *The Gospel According to John,*234. Morris, *The Gospel According to John,*255 John P. Meier, *A Marginal Jew: Rethinking the Historical Jesus. Volume 2: Mentor, Message, and Miracles* (ABRL; New York: Doubleday, 1994), 2. 722.

[32] Michael F. Bird, *Jesus and the Origins of the Gentile Mission* (Library of New Testament Studies, 331; New York: T & T Clark, 2007)118.

[33] Mead, "The βαζιλικός in John 4.46-53," 71; Barrett, *The Gospel According to St. John,*245; *Witherington, John's Wisdom,*128; Moloney, *The Gospel of John,*153; Bultmann, *The Gospel of John,* 206; Sandra M. Schneiders, *The Revelatory Text: Interpreting the New Testament as Sacred Scripture* (Collegeville, *Minnesota*: Michael Glazier Books, 1999), 187. Schnelle, *Antidocetic Christology in the Gospel of John,* (Louisville: Fortress Press, 1992) 86.

[34] Mead, "The βαζιλικός in John 4:46-53," 70.

Bibliography

Bennema, Cornelis, *Excavating John's Gospel.* Eugene: Wipf & Stock Publishers, 2008.

Bird, Michael F. *Jesus and the Origins of the Gentile Mission.* New York : T & T Clark, 2007.

Borchert, Gerald L. *John1-11,* New American Commentary. Nashville: Broadman & Holman, 1996.

Brown, Raymond E. *The Gospel According to John.* N.Y.: Doubleday, 1966-1970.

Bultmann, Rudolf . *The Gospel of John: A Commentary.* Philadelphia: Westminster, 1971.

Keener, S. *The Gospel of John: A Commentary.* Peabody, Mass.: Hendrickson, 2003.

Koester, Craig R. "Hearing, Seeing, and Believing in the Gospel of John," *Bib* 70.3. 1989.

Koester, Craig R. *Symbolism in the Fourth Gospel.* Minneapolis: Fortress Press, 2003.

Kruse, Colin. *The Gospel According to John.* Michigan: William B. Eerdmans, 2003.

Laney, J. Carl, *Baker's Concise Bible Atlas : A Geographical Survey of Bible History.* Grand Rapids, Michigan: Baker Book House, 1988.

Lincoln, Andrew T. *The Gospel According to Saint John.* Black's New Testament Commentary; London: Hendrickson Publishers, 2005.

Mark W. G. Stibbe, *John.* Sheffield: JSOT Press, 1993.

McHugh, John F. *A Critical and Exegetical Commentary on John 1-4.* London: T&T Clark, 2009.

Meier, John P. *A Marginal Jew: Rethinking the Historical Jesus. Volume 2: Mentor, Message, and Miracles.* New York: Doubleday, 1994.

Morris, Leon. *The Gospel According to John.* Michigan.: William B. Eerdamans Publishing House,1995.

Robinson, J.A.T. *On Redating the New Testament.* London: SCM Press, 1976.

Schneiders, Sandra M. *The Revelatory Text: Interpreting the New Testament as Sacred Scripture.* Minnesota: Michael Glazier Books, 1999.

Schnelle, Udo. *Antidocetic Christology in the Gospel of John.* Louisville: Fortress Press, 1992.

Witherington III, Ben. *Women in the Ministry of Jesus: A Study of Jesus' Attitudes to Women and Their Roles as Reflected in His Earthly Life.* Cambridge: Cambridge University Press, 1984.

Witherington III, Ben. *John's Wisdom.* Louisville: Westminster John Knox Press, 1995.

7

Mutual Submission in the Ephesian Church

A Biblical Paradigm for Envisioning a Borderless Church

Jayachitra L

Setting the Ephesian Church in the Backdrop of Roman Imperial Context

As far as the origin and progress of Christianity is concerned, Ephesus under Roman captivity played a significant role so much so that scholars like Von Harnack call it, the third capital of Christianity.[1] Emperor worship and Roman–imposed rules in Ephesus tremendously influenced the life of Christians to the extent that Roman imperial social and moral codes were incorporated into Christian ethics. The Roman government tried to bring about external political and economic unity; however, it was difficult to achieve social integration of all the cosmopolitan people living under Roman imperialism.[2]

It is quite evident that the emperor worship in Rome and the imperial social codes tremendously influenced the writing of the letter to the Ephesians as well. The Jews in Ephesus had been forced to absorb and affirm the socio-political hierarchical system that the Roman government had designed for civil society in general. Against their religious and moral codes of living, the Jews had to constantly negotiate with the demands of Roman administration in order to foster a peaceful living.

As far as the Jewish Christians were concerned, there were clear indications of heresies creeping into the Ephesian church (Eph 4:17–32; 5:10–20) due to the overarching impact of Roman religions, the imperial cult and their social codes of living.[3]

The epistle to the Ephesians reflects overtones of imperial ideology as it struggles to keep the pressures from the colonial environment in check. As far as the author is concerned, God's empire is in the heavenly realms with all the spiritual blessings (Eph 1:3), which in fact becomes the starting point for narrating a whole theology against the colonial backdrop. The superior power of God is manifested in raising Jesus from the dead and placing him at His right hand in the heavenly realms (1:20). The members of the Ephesian ecclesial community were already seated with Christ in the heavenly realms (2:6). Interestingly Pheme Perkins comments that the exalted Christ in Eph 2:11–22, if read against the ideology of the Roman emperor cult, resembles the emperor who was exalted through the speeches in favour of him.[4]

The empire of God's spiritual/heavenly realm was incarnated into the household of God (Eph 2:19), where no one remains foreigner or alien but everyone is a fellow citizen with God's people. Interestingly the terms like 'citizen' or 'foreigner' or 'stranger' are all relevant in a political context of an empire.

A study on the ethnic, religious and linguistic groups in the multicultural Rome in first century CE supports the view that Jewish and Christian communities were treated as 'foreign' to Roman culture and social life.[5] But, in the epistle to the Ephesians, the empire is replaced by the household, while retaining other political terms. A household in a Roman society plays a significant role in that the social order is established beginning from the smallest unit of the society i.e. family. The concept of the household of God comprising all the members of Ephesian church links to the author's intention of making God's empire very much relevant for the church in a colonial environment.

The household of God is comprised of all those who were treated as aliens and foreigners, who had become fellow citizens with God's people (Eph 2: 19). This household was built on the foundation of the Apostles and prophets, with Christ as the chief cornerstone. So it is Christ who holds together the whole building of the household of God, making it a holy temple in which God dwells by his Spirit (Eph 2:20–22).

All the members who were saved by the Gospel of Christ have been sealed with the mark of the Holy Spirit (Eph 1: 13). Jennifer G. Bird comments that once they are marked with the Holy Spirit of promise, they are claimed by God and

> ...are given the assurance that this counter–emperor will be true to the promise of redeeming them and offering them the inheritance of the empire of G(o)d. Instead of the emperor's gospel of salvation, we have the counter-gospel of a different deity, whose salvation is far greater than that offered by the Roman Empire.[6]

Here, the sealing of the Holy Spirit becomes a subversive anti-colonial tact. For the seal of a king constantly reminds the subjects about him "as both the maintainer of justice and order and the source of authority; it also indirectly referred to the power of his kingdom, which sustained him in his role."[7] Now, this loyalty of a believing person/a church is changed from the Roman emperor to the God almighty through the gospel of Jesus Christ and by the sealing of the Holy Spirit. In the face of an empire that rules through military and economic control, what is the shape of a community that serves a ruler who brings reconciliation and peace by sacrificial death rather than military might? …How does a Christian community live its life in the Empire?[8]

In Ephesians, Christ's death plays a major role in the development of the theology of this epistle. Christ's love is measured by his sacrificial death for the redemption of the church. And this is evident from the two verbs, 'loved' and 'gave up' (Eph 5:25), which are repeated from 5:2, "Christ loved us and gave himself up for us, a fragrant offering and sacrifice to God." Eph 1:20 says, God raised Christ from the dead and seated him at his right hand in the heavenly places and Eph 2:5–6 says the death and resurrection of Christ has promised the same privilege for the believers to be raised up and seated with Christ in the heavenly places. Eph 2:13 assures that the blood of Christ has brought the believers closer to God.

The effect of Christ's death on the church is reiterated in Eph 5:25–27 by three sub-clauses. In the first two clauses, Christ is the subject acting upon the church: "in order to make her holy by cleansing her with the washing of water by the word so as to present the church to himself in splendor, without a spot or wrinkle or anything of the kind…" (Eph 5:26a and 27a); and the third clause says: "so that she (the church) may be holy and without blemish" (Eph 5:27c). Church is the subject showing the result of Christ's action. The sacrificial act of Christ in making the church holy and without blemish indicates an alternative model to the Roman imperial hierarchical model of those times that did not have any such sacrificial approach to its subjects.

"Submit to One Another in the Fear of the Lord" (Eph 5:21): Towards Mutual Submission

As Ephesus and the surrounding places in western Asia Minor were strongholds of the Roman Empire in the second half of the first century CE and the churches were predominantly comprised of Gentile Christians, it may be presumed that the ethical living of Christians was heavily influenced by Roman imperial ideology. Roman laws, especially family laws, were applicable to all Roman citizens anywhere in the Empire including among the Greek-speaking Jewish and Gentile Christians.[9] This raises questions regarding how the Christian Church maintained its identity amidst growing influences of the socio-political environment.

The pericope Eph 5:21–33 begins with an exhortation to the members of the Ephesian church to submit to one another in the fear of Christ (5:21). The Greek word, *hupotasso,* to submit, is "a hierarchical term which stresses the relation to superiors,"[10] for instance, the submission of soldiers in an army to those of superior rank. This word which belonged to the sphere of worldly order of state and politics is used in Ephesians with a similar understanding of bringing order in the household.[11] This word connotes "to submit to the orders or directives of someone—'to obey, to submit to, obedience, submission' " or more forcefully, "to bring something under the firm control of someone- 'to subject to, to bring under control.' "[12] Josephus uses *hupotasso* in the active voice to mean "place under", "subordinate", and in the middle voice to imply "order oneself under" a leader.[13] Helton affirms the notion of domination as he concedes that this verb presupposes a hierarchical structure in which some people are in authority over others.[14] These references show that the verb *hupotasso* carries an overtone of authority and subjection or submission to it.[15]

While the author uses *hupotasso* to denote the submission of wives, the verb, *hupakouo,* to obey, is used for children (Eph 6:1) and slaves (Eph 6:5). Generally however, the word *hupakouo* (to obey) was also used in the Hellenistic Jewish and Greco–Roman contexts to refer to the submission of wives to their husbands. Therefore some scholars are of the opinion that *hupotasso* is uniquely used by the Christian author/ the community to place wives on an equal basis with husbands.[16] Harold Hoehner raises three objections to such distinctions between the two verbs, *hupotasso* (to submit) and *hupakouo* (to obey). Firstly, he shows the historical use of *hupotasso* to denote a subordinate role of one person to another. Secondly, *hupotasso* is used for the slaves in the household codes in other writings of the New Testament (Titus 2:9; 1 Pet 2:18). In 1 Pet 3:5–6, when Peter deals with wives in households, he uses *hupotasso* and *hupatouo* interchangeably. Thirdly and finally, Hoehner thinks that one who is subject to another is not qualitatively inferior.[17] Yet, *hupotasso* is a term strictly used for order, presuming a hierarchical social structure and reserving the first place for the man.[18]

Categorically, *hupotassomenoi* in this introductory verse (Eph 5:21) in the pericope is understood in two ways, either as a participle dependent on the previous finite verb 'be filled' as in verse 18 or as a participle in a paraenentic pericope with an imperative function (without dependence on any finite verb).[19] Andrew T. Lincoln suggests that this verse can be best understood as "transitional, completing the series of participles which are dependent on the verb 'be filled,' from verse 18, while itself providing the verbal form on which the first injunction in the following household code is dependent."[20] The filling of the believers with the Holy Spirit is linked with mutual submission of believers. It may indicate an obliging behaviour to one another. Drawing cue from Eph 4:2, Rudolf Schnackenburg suggests that the subordination or submission in verse 21 denotes "an embracing expression for the behaviour of the Christians in community," or in other words, a "specificum of the early Christian Haustafel."[21] The call to mutual submission indicates readiness to renounce one's own will for the sake of others and to give precedence to others.[22] Hence the notion of subordination in this verse cannot be treated as an external legal demand, but an ethical exhortation to characterise their Christian living.

Following a variant reading, Wayne Walden suggests that *allelon* accompanied by the prepositions *eis, en, meta,* and *pros* could be translated "among yourselves/themselves" (cf. John 6:43, 52). This rendering is technically reflexive instead of reciprocal. According to him, the pronoun *allelon* basically denotes random or distributive activity among a group.[23] He translates verse 21 as "Out of reverence for Christ, be in subordination among yourselves. Therefore, in his opinion, this verse teaches "Obey whom you are supposed to," a general principle illustrated with the following examples: wives (5:22–24), children (6:1), servants (6:5).[24] In a countering article to Walden, Stanley N. Helton comments that the reciprocal pronoun *allelon* (one another) in all the occurrences in Ephesians (4: 2, 25, 32 and 5:21) indicates reciprocity or mutuality. Helton analyses the semantics, syntax, literary structure, and the rhetoric intention of the passage to negate Walden's attempt to remove reciprocity/mutuality from the passage. For him, the level of reciprocity does not depend on the pronoun, but on the semantic limits of the verb and the prepositions.[25] Helton thus acknowledges the hierarchical thrust of the verb, *hupotasso*.

In other parts of the New Testament, submission is required only from women (1 Cor 14:34; Col 3:18; 1 Tim 2:11; Titus 2:5), children (1 Tim 3:4), and slaves (Titus 2:9; 1 Pet 2:18). Elsewhere it is required of believers to the state as well (Rom 13:1, 5; Titus 3:1), from the church to her leaders (1 Pet5:5; 1 Cor 16:16), the believer to God (Heb 12:9; Jas 4:7), Jesus' relationship to his earthly parents (Luke 2:51), demons to the disciples of the limited commission (Luke 10:17, 20) and even Christ's ultimate submission to the Father (1 Cor 15:28).[26] Helton bases his argument for mutual submission neither on the phrase, reciprocal pronoun of "one another" nor on the verb, "to submit", "but in the *actual content* of Paul's argument developed under each paired relationship… Paul *subverts* the notion of submission."[27]

The motivating force for mutual submission is drawn from the fear of Christ. The Hebrew Scriptures attests to the fear of the Lord as "the appropriate attitude of a creature to the Creator, producing obedience to his will."[28] The concept of "fear of the Lord" (interchangeably with fear of Christ and fear of God) has strong allusions to the Jewish concept of God as found in the Hebrew Scriptures.[29] The fear of the Lord is the fitting reaction to the awesome works of God. The same concept recurs in the laws (Lev 19:14, 32; Deut 13:11, 17:13) and in the general piety of Israelites (Ps 103: 11, 13, 17; Prov 1:7, 23:17).[30]

The household code in Col 3:22 has reference to "fearing the Lord" as a motivation for slaves, however, here the emphasis is laid on all. In cases of human relations, fear involves observance of the appropriate authority structures.[31] "Fear can denote the obedience demanded by the superior authority of masters or husbands as lords".[32] "In Paul's writings "fear of the Lord" or "fear of Christ" is virtually interchangeable with "fear of God." 2 Cor 5:11 sounds an eschatological note, "knowing the fear of the

Lord, we persuade people," while 2 Cor 7:1 exhorts that holiness should be made perfect in the fear of God (cf: also Phil 2:12)."[33] The concept of fear in Phil 2:12 is based on Paul's admonition to consider others better than oneself out of humility. Against this backdrop, mutual submission is directly related to their attitude of fear of Christ.

A Biblical Paradigm of Mutual Submission towards a borderless church

Is "mutual submission" calling for a radical change in the perception of church? John Paul II highlights "a conspirational egalitarian *Kerygma*" by which "the gospel does not disown lay cultures but engages them in their historical particularity and presses for their recreation. The strategy for social reform is to enter into every day relationships and to effect "transformation from within" by inserting radically new theological leaven that subverts the inner core of *hierarchical* (emphasis mine) codes."[34] Envisioning a borderless church purely lies on the church's call to bring about social reform by entering into everyday human relationships of hierarchical order and by transforming them into responsible mutuality out of commitment to God.

As far as the Church of South India is concerned, the challenges to envisioning a borderless church predominantly evolve from the socio-cultural impact on the church. Can a borderless church propose a church that is freed from the clutches of patriarchy, caste discrimination, and class disparities? Is thinking of a non-hierarchical church a utopian concept or a realistic one that will result in tangible changes in the everyday life of the church? Why has the Church of South India fallen prey to the slavish entanglements of patriarchy, caste hegemony, and class domination?

In any discourse on hierarchy and hegemony, 'self' and 'other' are dealt with. In order to establish their "first principles" (their grounding claims about reality) in the forms of argumentation (reasoning), Western philosophers like Plato, Aristotle and Descartes defined a principle by reference to what it is not. "It must have an 'other' to establish the borders of its own existence. This 'other' serves as the conceptual point of difference that makes not only the birth of the principle but also its continued existence."[35]

For Western philosophy, the first principle needs to be self-evident without any origin, and therefore, for instance, having defined the parameters of the male first principle by means of the 'other', they deny the feminine 'other's very existence.[36] Thus the feminine 'other' ceases to exist. This may apply equally well with all the binaries or dualistic concepts like "high caste"- "low caste", rich-poor, adult-child, and west-East or the rest that we have allowed to intertwine with the human psyche. Irigaray further suggests, "this dynamic repression not only structures our thoughts; it is also linked to pervasive social practices that follow similar patterns of exclusion and silence."[37]

Mutual submission that we have derived from the letter to the Ephesians is a clarion call to move away willfully from the oppressive dichotomies created by dominant western philosophy. Do we strictly need to envision a worldview that is conditioned by the binaries of western philosophy? If we alternatively explore Indian philosophies for instance, we may come across the models of the uniqueness of every single human being and their potential to merge with the Ultimate reality of God. Mutual submission provides clear pointers to envision a borderless church that might remove the hierarchical ordering of human relations by replacing them with functional models of human interactions on the basis of respect, dignity, and equality. The call to mutual submission indicates readiness to renounce one's own will for the sake of others and to give precedence to others.[38] Hence the notion of mutual submission proposed for the Ephesian church cannot be treated as an external legal demand, but an ethical exhortation to characterise their Christian living. An ethical perspective of mutual submission by all spirit-filled Christians in the household of God/ church aims at nullifying hierarchical relationships, thus ensuring a borderless church.

Endnotes

[1] Von Harnack quoted by Ernst Best, *Essays in Ephesians* (Edinburgh: T & T Clark, 1997), 14.

[2] Andrew T. Lincoln, *Ephesians*, (World Bible Commentary; Michigan Gand Rapids: Zondervan Academic, 2014), lxxxiv.

[3] C. I. David Joy, *Revelation: A Post–colonial View Point* (Delhi: ISPCK, 2001), 7–10.

[4] Pheme Perkins, *Ephesians* (Abington New Testament Commentaries; Nashville: Abington Press, 1997), 51.

Bird, *Ephesians*, 267.

[5] Noy. D cited by Beryl Rawson, "'The Roman family' in Recent Research: State of the Question" *Biblical Interpretation,* vol. 11, no.2 (2003): 131.

[6] Bird, *Ephesians,* 269.

[7] Irene J. Winter cited by Bird, *Ephesians,* 269.

[8] Brian J. Walsh and Sylvia C. Keesmaat, *Colossians Remixed. Subverting the Empire* (Downers Grove, Illinois: InterVarsity Press, 2004), 61.

[9] Carolyn Osiek, "The Family in Early Christianity: 'Family Values' Revisited," *The Catholic Bible Quarterly,* 58/1 (January, 1996): 10.

[10] Delling, "ὑποτάσσω," in *The Theological Dictionary of New Testament, vol. VIII*, edited by Gerhard Friedrich (Grand Rapids: WMB Eerdmans Publishing Co., 1972), 41.

[11] Delling, ὑποτάσσω, 45., Peter T.O' Brien, *The Letter to the Ephesians (Leicester, Apollos, 1999), 399.*

[12] Johannes P. Louw and Eugene A. Nida, eds., *Greek–English Lexicon of the New Testament Based on Semantic Domains,* 2d ed. (New York: United Bible Society, 1989), 92.

[13] (Jewish War 2:566, 578; 5:309)

[14] Stanley N. Helton, "Ephesians 5:21: A Longer Translation Note," *Restoration Quarterly, vol. 48, no.1 (*2005): 37.

[15] O'brien, Ephesians, 399.

[16] Hoehner, *Ephesians*, 734.

[17] Hoehner, *Ephesians,* 734–5.

[18] Rudolf Schnackenburg, *The Epistle to the Ephesians. A Commentary,* translated by Helen Heron (Edinburgh: T & T Clark, 1991), 246.

[19] Sampley, *And the Two Shall Become One Flesh*, 114.

[20] Lincoln, *Ephesians*, CD–Rom.

[21] Schnackenburg, *Ephesians,* 245.

[22] Lincoln, *Ephesians*, CD–Rom. See also Delling, *hupotasso,* 45.

[23] Wayne warden, "Ephesians 5:21 – A translation Note," *Restoration Quarterly* vol. 45, no. 4 (2003): 254.

[24] Walden, *Ephesians 5:21*, 254.; and idem, "Translating Ephesians 5:21," in *Restoration Quarterly* vol. 47, no.3 (2005): 179–82.

[25] Stanley N. Helton, "Ephesians 5:21: A Longer Translation Note," *Restoration quarterly,* vol. 48, no.1 (2005): 34.

[26] Schnackenburg, *Ephesians*, 244, n. 6., Lincoln, *Ephesians*, CD–Rom., Helton, *Ephesians 5:21: A Longer Translation Note*, 37.

[27] Helton, *Ephesians 5:21: A Longer Translation Note*, 37– 38.

[28] Balz, *fovbo"*, in *Theological Dictionary of New Testament, vol IX,* ed. Gerhard Friedrich (Grand rapids: WMB Eerdmans Publishing Co., 1974), 217–8.

[29] Sampley, *Two Shall Become One Flesh,* 119.

[30] O'Brien, *Ephesians*, 404.

[31] Fear of citizens toward the State (cf. Rom 13:3,4,7), children to parents (*Barnabas* 19.5, *Didache* 4.9), slaves to masters (Eph. 6:5; 1 Pet 2:18; Did 4.11), or, as here, wives to husbands (cf. also 1 Pet 3:2).

[32] Balz, fovbo", 7–8.

[33] Lincoln, *Ephesians,* CD–Rom.

[34] John Paul II, *On the Dignity and Vocation of Women* (United States Catholic Conference: Washington, D.C., 1988), 9.

[35] S. Jones, "Bounded Openness: Postmodernism, Feminism, and the Church Today", in *Interpretation* 55.1 (January, 2001): 53.

[36] Luce Irigaray, *This Sex Which is not One*, (trans. Catherine Porter; New York: Cornell University, 1985), cited by Jones, *Bounded Openness*: 53.

[37] Irigaray, *This Sex Which is not One,* cited by Jones, *Bounded Openness*: 53.

[38] Lincoln, *Ephesians*, CD–Rom. See also Delling, *hupotasso,* 45.

Bibliography

Best, Ernst. *Essays in Ephesians.* Edinburgh: T & T Clark, 1997.

Delling, "ὑποτάσσω," in vol. VIII of *The Theological Dictionary of New Testament.* Edited by Gerhard Friedrich. Grand Rapids: WMB Eerdmans Publishing Co., 1972.

Helton, Stanley N. "Ephesians 5:21: A Longer Translation Note," *Restoration Quarterly,* vol. 48, no.1 (2005).

Hoehner, Harold W. *Ephesians*. Grand Rapids, Michigan: Baker Books, 2002.

John Paul II, *On the Dignity and Vocation of Women.* United States Catholic Conference: Washington, D.C., 1988.

Joy, C. I. David. *Revelation: A Post–colonial View Point.* Delhi: ISPCK, 2001

Lincoln, Andrew T. *Ephesians.* World Bible Commentary; Michigan Gand Rapids: Zondervan Academic, 2014.

O' Brien, Peter T. *The Letter to the Ephesians.* Leicester: Apollos, 1999.

Osiek, Carolyn. "The Family in Early Christianity: 'Family Values' Revisited," *The Catholic Bible Quarterly,* 58/1, January, 1996.

P. Louw, Johannes, Eugene A. Nida, eds. *Greek–English Lexicon of the New Testament Based on Semantic Domains.* New York: United Bible Society, 1989.

Perkins, Pheme. *Ephesians.* Abington New Testament Commentaries; Nashville: Abington Press, 1997.

Rawson, Beryl. "'The Roman family' in Recent Research: State of the Question" *Biblical Interpretation,* Vol. 11:2, 2003 .

S. Jones, "Bounded Openness: Postmodernism, Feminism, and the Church Today" in *Interpretation* 55.1 (January, 2001).

Sampley, J. Paul. *And the Two Shall Become One Flesh*. Cambridge: Cambridge University Press, 2009.

Schnackenburg, Rudolf. *The Epistle to the Ephesians. A Commentary.* Translated by Helen Heron. Edinburgh: T & T Clark, 1991.

Walsh, Brian J, Sylvia C. Keesmaat. *Colossians Remixed. Subverting the Empire.* Downers Grove, Illinois: InterVarsity Press, 2004.

Warden, Wayne. "Ephesians 5:21 – A translation Note," *Restoration Quarterly* vol. 45, no. 4 (2003): 254.

8

Borderless Church as an Epitome of Unity:

Revisiting the Judges Account of Settlement and Genesis 12:1-10

Laila Vijayan

There is a constant struggle to understand the term borderless church. I struggle to place myself in this process of envisioning and materializing 'borderless church' amidst biblical understandings wrought with tensions of binaries, pluralities, and diversities in its understanding of the term. I also struggle to place my own understanding in the context of churches that practice different traditions and policies which claim their own border and borderlessness.

With this confession of my personal struggle with the concept of "borderless church", I would like to place a number of questions for our combined reflection: Can there be a borderless church? Can there be a borderless church that will be just and inclusive society; a church that transcends all barriers which make exclusive claims of tradition, authority, space and so on?

This paper attempts to analyze the Judges account of the settlement of the people of Israel in the land of Canaan to see trajectories of entry, possession and the later development of Israel as a strong nation in Ancient West Asia. Could this be a borderless model which can help us understand the values, traditions, and faith convictions that could make the mission of the church a living experience for all people today? Can we aim for a Universal or Global or Local church which can help us experience pluralities without discrimination and oppression?

Church and Perception

The Hebrew term *qahal* (assembly, congregation or gathering) is equated with the Greek term *ecclesia* (church) and these two terms refer to the gathering of the covenant community or specially called out people; generally termed as people of God in the Old Testament (people of Israel) and the people of God in the New Testament (Christians). These two groups had their own socio-religious and political world views that were interwoven with a strong faith element. Ancestor Abram stands as the founder of this called out community and Jesus as the incarnation of God becomes the source and instrument for the new community.

Biblical records make the readers affirm that it is not historiography but the life and faith record of the people that reflect the historical elements and traditions. Often biblical passages are understood from the particularistic approach rather than the universalistic approach. In the particularistic approach, there is specificity on particular people, faith, and actions and it seems that God is compartmentalized for them alone. The particularistic approach makes the norms or the faith affirmations serve as the borders that create divisions and tensions. But in the universalistic approach, there is no border and the call account of Abram is a great pillar for this borderless approach – One man Abram is called to be a blessing to all other nations.

Journey of Abraham: Borderless Experience (Genesis 12: 1-10)

The history of Israel as recorded in the Hebrw Bible basically begins from the life of Abram. Abram was called to move forward from his own land (Gen 12:1-3), became a migrant and continued to worship Yahweh all through his journey. Abram worshipped Yahweh in all the worship centers which he crossed and he made altars and invoked the presence of Yahweh (Gen 12:6,7,8) in each instance. He went down to Egypt to reside there (Gen 12:10). The story of Abram is the journey of a migrant along with his household who after a few generations, becomes a nation that entered into the land of Canaan. The migration of an individual after many experiences of migration ended up in the making of a nation. This new nation is bordered with their culture, tradition, religious beliefs and ideologies. They are a covenant-based people with commandment-oriented life who enter into the Promised Land and build up their own community among many nations. To live "with them" (their neighbouring nations) was a great challenge, but they experienced the inclusivist approach of the people of Ancient West Asia. In contrast to the migration story of Abram the Conquest model displaces the exclusivist approach of the people of Israel. In the religious secularist context, these two approaches are intertwined and both approaches are needed.

Garbini[1] identifies the period of migration of Abraham to the time of Nabonidus. During the time of the Babylonian king, Nabonidus, who was a fervent adherent of the cult of the moon god Sin (Nabonidus did not support Marduk) and the sanctuaries to this god are visible in Ur and Haran. The journey of Terah from Ur and settling in Haran makes a relative connection with the worshipping places of Ur and Haran. Abram is called to move towards Canaan which became the Promised Land for the people of Israel and is ascribed as the land flowing with milk and honey, holy land and so on. Abram's migration that began from Haran and is also connected to the places of Laban and Paddan-Aram.

Abraham or the ancestors were depicted as the peace loving people who tried to avoid friction with the neighbours[2]. Abraham was in search of the God who called him and so Genesis records Abraham's approach to worship and sacrifice[3]. A person who expects to receive a blessing should never displease the power/ Supreme power of that land. This was the belief practiced from generation to generation.

Ancestors used different divine names which makes it clear that the situational experiences made them attribute different names to God. The divine experience and God's encounter cannot be placed within the borders of language, rhetoric, or rituals. Borders bring safety and security but the same word border can be a bondage, chain which curtails the life of an individual, society and the nation. Border and borderless are contrasting and conflicting words with bipolar experience and nature. In the ancestral narratives, these two ideologies are intertwined. The religious identity of God is later restricted to Yahweh but before they reach that conviction, they identified God in response to their life experiences.

Bright calls their experiences as a cult religion and later ancestral religious practices merged into the Yahweh worship stream of Israel. Abraham, Isaac and Jacob stand at the beginning of the Israelite history and faith. These three ancestors identified Yahweh as El Shaddai (God almighty) which is also recorded in

Exod. 6:2. The divine name Yahweh is not revealed to ancestors but as El Shaddai. When the ancestors crossed Shechem, Bethel, and Beersheba, they observed the religious practices in these places on their journey to Palestine[4]. Other divine names used for God are, El olam (Eternal God), El roi (God of seeing), El zeba'ot (God of Hosts), Fear of Isaac, Mighty one of Jacob and so on. God's identity has been bordered by people at times and then it crosses the borders of religious, social, cultural structures and pluralistic cultures. But the borderless identity carried the divine name Yahweh and proclaimed God as 'I AM WHO I AM' (Exod. 3:14,15). Literally, this name is a four-letter word of the Hebrew consonants YHWH, and its origin is attributed to the Hebrew word *hayah*, which means, 'to be' and therefore the divine name Yahweh means the 'one who causes to be'. This phrase breaks the borders of religion, culture, tradition and it is more a cosmic term that covers all spheres and the cosmos. Abraham's call to be a blessing to the nations is visible in the revelation of the divine name to Moses.

Three major factors are involved in the journey of migrant ancestors visible also in the rest of the Israelite history. They are adaptation, adjustment, and consolidation. The borders are diluted so that they are able to reach the expectation of the divine call without compromising the essence of their social, cultural and religious values on nation-building.

Entry and Settlement at Canaan

Israel as the people of Yahweh under the leadership of Moses was anticipating the entry into the land of Canaan. But that leadership role or ministry and mission was carried out by the successor Joshua. The settlement of the people of Israel in the land of Canaan is recorded in the book of Joshua and Judges chapter one. Judges account is strung as a series self-contained episodes with peaceful interludes and alternate crisis events.[5] The Joshua account clearly exposes the traditional tribal identities in the form of individual units as well as the geographical divisions. (Individual name, collective name and also the place name, example: Judah). Names of ancestors mentioned are similar to the names of the gods of other nations.[6] For example, Gad was a well known Mesopotamian god and was even worshipped on Mount Hermon. Asher was a variant pronunciation of the god Ashur, a god Laban had known.[7]

The account of Judges however also presents a different view about the history of settlement often called Peaceful entry or co-existence[8] theory. From this view, I attempt to use the phrase *bahem*[9] (in/with/among them) and how this concept created space for the migrant people under Joshua to dwell, to break the barriers and made the universalism of the people of Israel visible. Israel as God's special chosen ones, covenant oriented community, who proclaimed their faith in the God of Israel, Yahweh (Lord) alone, receive all honor and glory. Possession of the land and the settlement shows the covenant unity with Yahweh as an ongoing process rather than culminating with one or two events. That means faith journey is an ongoing process. It continues to revisit, envisions and takes courage to face the challenges to move forward. Every historical event signifies the life-giving process and experience of the covenant community as an experimenting community. Leaders of the people of Israel developed strategic plans to overcome the challenges of the world and it is often attributed to the mighty act of Yahweh.

Peaceful Entry and Co-Existence : *Bahem* Perspective

Albrecht Alt proposed that the people of Israel entered the central highlands with the strategy of semi-nomadic infiltration[10]. Central highlands were thinly populated area and therefore there was no resistance from the people of the land. This settlement was developed when the semi-nomads with their flocks came from the east of Jordan river to hills off the west of the river. Later they began to build villages and became sedentary[11]. Archaeological evidence was not able to support the conquest possibility suggested in the Jericho and Ai narratives. So Alt's suggestion was supported by Martin Noth. The possibility of thinly populated areas supports the view of easy coexistence seen in Judg 1:16, 21. There is a reference about the Jebusites during the time of the monarchy. King David took the land of the Jebusites and made it the "city of David".

Borders continue to exist, but the adaptability and adjustment of borderless attitude and nature is the need of the hour which the church is anticipating for. Church must be a place where people find peace, shelter, security, unity or togetherness to experience the fullness of life which Jesus Christ has channelized in this world.

Challenge for Action

Life experience of the migrant Abram and the Judges account outlines a long period of history, which is a journey from semi-nomadic life to the settlement with new leadership who were called Judges. Life experiences and faith elements took different forms and became more systematized by the time of the monarchy. Judges period is often understood as successful in terms of each Judge, but in totality, it is a failure account of the nation. There was no stability of leadership and sustainability of the nation because of the break in leadership with different people arising at different points in time through different challenges that necessitated their leadership.

Here I tried to look into a formative period of Israel where a *bahem* perspective of "living in, with and among," has a scope for the borderless church. Calling Abram to come out of a border and to travel towards a new situation which is invisible and as he journeyed in anticipation he turned into Abraham. The places where he built altars were not the bordered worshipping centers of Yahweh, in these open places Abraham experienced the borderless nature of Yahweh and was accommodative with different names peculiar to those situations.

Borders can blind persons, systems, institutions and churches to perceive the presence and the power of God and thus forget to challenge injustice, corruption, discrimination and oppression. Yahweh is the God of justice and righteousness who demands the church to carry the inclusivist approach, where one can embrace togetherness with pluralist ideas and practices, without losing individual perceptions.

The challenge of *bahem* to the present church is to act as an agent for peace which transcends all barriers. Borderless Church can witness to the *bahem* perspective, which means without compromising the real essence of the witnessing community church can continue to hear, act, and accommodate the pains and sufferings of any community. An empathetic attitude which can make anyone feel the oneness, with the absence of discrimination, exploitation, oppression, but with the presence of a community that practices justice and righteousness with the truth of God and the world. Living out a *bahem* perspective makes the borderless church an inclusive and just church.

I conclude with a positive question and narrative. Who can break barriers? Who will start the action is a challenge for this liberating journey from the *bahem* perspective? In Oct 2017, CSI Synod organised a program in the CSI Synod Centre for

Theologically Trained Women and Ordained Women to share the experiences andvoice their concerns. In the closing ceremony, General Secretary announced the prospective hope for women interested in theological education when he declared that one-third of CSI scholarships for theological education will be reserved for women.

Borders of tradition and cultural systems need to be challenged without losing the witnessing power of Jesus Christ and the Church. Courage to question, challenge the oppressive barriers and to stand up to break them and envision a new church without borders, will be a great move towards a just and inclusive society where all can enjoy life in all its fullness.

Endnotes

[1] Givonni Garboni, *History and Ideology in Ancient Israel* (London: SCM Press Ltd, 1986), 77.

[2] John Bright, *History of Israel* (London: SCM Press, 1964), 84.

[3] Gen 12:6,7; "Abram came to the Oak of Moreh and there Yahweh appeared to him and he built an alter there". Gen 12:8. "Here between Bethel and Ai, Abram built an alter and invoked the presence of Yahweh". Gen 12:9. " He journeyed by stages ..."

[4] John Bright, *History of Israel*, 92.

[5] John Bright, *History of Israel*, 134.

[6] W.E. Oesterley & Theodore H. Robinson, *History of Israel* (Oxford: Clarendon Press, 1932), 52; also cf John Bright, *History of Israel*, 70f.

[7] W.E.Oesterley & Theodore H. Robinson, *History of Israel*, 52.

[8] Judges 1:16 "they went and dwelt among the people"; 1:21 "So the Jebusites dwell with the children of the Benjamin in Jerusalem".

[9] This Hebrew term means 'in/with/among them'- as per Hebrew grammar inseparable preposition plus 3rd common plural suffix. This is the common feature found within the migrants.

[10] Albrecht Alt, "The Settlement of Israelite in Palestine" in *Essays on Old Testament History and Religion* by Albrecht Alt (transl. R.A. Wilson; Doubleday: Garden city, 1968), 175-221.

[11] Joseph A Callaway, "The Settlement in Canaan", in *Ancient Israel* by Hershal Shanks, (London: SPCK, 1988), 70.

Bibliography

Garboni, Givonni. *History and Ideology in Ancient Israel.* London: SCM Press Ltd, 1986.

Bright, John. *History of Israel.* London: SCM Press, 1964.

Oesterley, W.E. & Theodore H. Robinson. *History of Israel.* Oxford: Clarendon Press, 1932.

Alt, Albrecht. *Essays on Old Testament History and Religion.* Translated by R.A. Wilson; Doubleday: Garden city, 1968.

Shanks, Hershal. *Ancient Israel.* London: SPCK, 1988.

9

The World of Jude: Paradigm for an Alternate Ecclesia

C. I. David Joy

It is important to expose, evaluate and experience fresh voices in the thinking process of alternate ecclesia in the light of the study of the New Testament. It is suggested to look into the details of one stream of the New Testament texts, namely the early Christian community and their documents with the help of one representative text. How is one to understand the attitude of early Christians to the formation of the formal and structured ecclesia? Since the composition of the early church remained remarkably plural in nature, it is proposed to analyze Jude 17-22 and 2 Peter 3:3 from the viewpoint of subaltern ecclesia which would present the picture of a borderless church as a paradigm for an alternate ecclesia. It is noted that the presence of an Eunuch in Jude seems to be an indication of the feature of the Ethiopian church and there may be insights to equip the thinking of a modern hermeneut in a deeper manner. This paper will address the issue of the identity of the ecclesial community based on Jude and 2 Peter and then will present the space of alternate ecclesia.

Jude: A Context for Reformation?

As this Consultation is part of remembering the event of Reformation along with a series of reformations including the formation of the Church of South India, it is significant to study the views of some New Testament scholars in interpreting the text with the help of the historical data of the early church. For instance, I would like to discuss the question of how the book of Jude played a role in the life and history of the Ethiopian church in the early stages. Richard Bauckham's book *Jude and Relatives of Jesus* provides essential ingredients for a contemporary borderless ecclesia as it analyses how the early church could develop a paradigm for community living based on the values of the Kingdom of God. Stephen J.Kraftchick evaluated the identity of the people of Jude based on the internal evidence regarding the identity of the audience.[1] The people of God in Jude waited for the Lord in prayer and solidarity as they were aliens and no-people in the Roman Empire.

I have deliberately tried to locate the origin of *parakois* (Aliens) by linking them with the wider and different flavors of the theology of the kingdom of God in the New Testament. In spite of quieter actions of the Early Christian communities and the Jesus movement in the second part of the first century CE, the proclamation of the Kingdom of God received a huge welcome within the people of margins, *parakois*, the community of the borderless people. My engagement with the systematic studies done by scholars namely Helmut Koester, N.T.Wright, J.D.Crossan and Gerd Theissen, offered a major question for another level of discussion. "Did all people have a right to enter early church?". Pauline deliberations and Johannine deliberations attempted to portray a church that could stand up for equality. However, the Petrine community and the community of Jude expose and touch on real problems by initiating the discussion on the identity of *Parokois* (Aliens) and the issue of divisions in the early church due to the deviations from the basic teachings of the Gospel. There was a link between the context of Jude and the church in Ethiopia. It is important to revisit history from the point of view of the subalterns and their issues in terms of the community of Jude. Ethiopian church was certainly aware of the inner dynamics of the early church including the challenges from second Temple Judaism. Scholarly opinions range from the understanding that Jude was written to a mixed audience in order to address the issues of heresy and dilution of faith.[2]

Kingdom of God- a Reformed Space

Jude 17-22 is a very powerful and well-crafted statement by the author to the church asking the followers of the Lord Jesus to wait for the Lord. Based on the historical context of early church in Ethiopia where one could see the images of Jude's community, it is a legitimate reconstruction to imagine the borderless ecclesia in view of the ideas and values of the Kingdom of God as portrayed in Jude 17-22:

> [17] But you, my dear friends, must remember what the apostles of our Lord Jesus Christ predicted. [18] They told you that in the last times there would be scoffers whose purpose in life is to satisfy their ungodly desires. [19] These people are the ones who are creating divisions among you. They follow their natural instincts because they do not have God's Spirit in them.
>
> [20] But you, dear friends, must build each other up in your most holy faith, pray in the power of the Holy Spirit,[a] [21] and await the mercy of our Lord Jesus Christ, who will bring you eternal life. In this way, you will keep yourselves safe in God's love. [22] And you must show mercy to[b] those whose faith is wavering.

The expectation for the coming of the Lord is in a way an expectation for actualizing the Kingdom of God. How can the

Christian Church encounter, challenge and address problems when surrounded by a complex socio-political world? is a major question posed by the author of Jude here. In the midst of false teachings and prophecies, the Church should situate and develop a faith that is based on the values of the Kingdom of God. A fourfold responsibility is given to the church namely, build each other up in your most holy faith, pray in the power of the Holy Spirit, await the mercy of our Lord Jesus Christ, and show mercy to those whose faith is wavering. It is clear from this text that a borderless ecclesia will surely bring forth the taste and image of the early church in today's challenging world.

Michael Jagessar in his article "Rethinking Reformation: Marginal Voices Strike Back," argues that the Reformation of 1517 should also be understood from the point of view of the people on the edges.[3] Since historiography is a major tool to rethink of Reformation, it is important to develop historiography from the point of view of the people of the margins. Keeping within the framework of the New Testament, the proclamation of the Kingdom of God could be a possible pattern to develop and experience the passion of borderless church.

The proclamation and message of the Kingdom of God enabled the early Christian communities to challenge and break the barriers and hurdles. By challenging derogatory practices, the cornerstone (church) could create a community which taught values such as respecting diversity. Such an atmosphere provided a new space for frustrated and dissatisfied people to enjoy and celebrate freedom and equality. In order to understand and estimate the realities of praxis of the early church, a post-resurrection road map is essential. It is important, mainly because of the chaotic patterns of assessments and evaluation by many groups in revisiting ecclesia in view of remembering Reformation. As we revive the alphabet and keys of an alternate ecclesia, the honest use of biblical insights seems to be vital. The image of alternate ecclesia could show an open mind in addressing the oppressive and exploitative administrative mechanisms of the Roman Empire.

The driving force of Jesus' ministry in Galilee was the proclamation of the Kingdom of God. Jesus courageously proclaims: "The time has come. The kingdom of God has come near. Repent and believe the good news!"(Mark 1:15). Michael L.Humpries' recent book *Christian Origins and the Language of the Kingdom of God* explains the indispensable theological and sociological symbols and ideas used by the writers of the New Testament to denote the summary of the proclamation of the Kingdom of God.[4] He argues:

> The Beelzebul controversy exists in two versions -- Q and Mark -- and thereby allows the study to engage the import of the kingdom language at the point of juxtaposition between two distinct textual representations. This makes it possible to deal directly with the issue of the disparity of texts in the synoptic tradition. Humphries suggests that these two versions of the same controversy indicate two distinct social trajectories wherein the kingdom of God comes to mean something quite different in each case but that nevertheless they demonstrate a similarity in theoretical effect where the language contributes to the emergence of relatively distinct social formations.[5]

There are three major considerations that emerge within the understanding of the Kingdom of God in the Gospel tradition.[6] It can be believed in straightforward expressions namely teaching, preaching and witnessing. However, in the context of Galilee, Jesus' proclamation of the Kingdom of God was indeed a new way of resistance and path of justice. Let us try to understand some important features of the way of Christ for our ministry. Donald Guthrie explains the concept of the Kingdom of God using four important theological terms: theocentric, dynamic, messianic and salvific.[7] Albert Schweitzwer further expands this point by highlighting the role of historical Jesus in actualizing the Kingdom of God:

> Let us not forget that we are dealing here with an antinomy from which only one conclusion can be drawn, namely, that what has hitherto been accounted the "historical" conception of the messianic consciousness of Jesus is false, because it does not explain the history. Only the conception is historical which makes it intelligible how Jesus could take himself to be the Messiah without finding himself obliged to make this consciousness of his tell as a factor in his public ministry for the Kingdom of God… rather, how he was actually compelled to make the messianic dignity of his person a secret! Why was his messiahship a secret of Jesus? To explain this means to understand his life.[8]

Jesus stresses the eschatological anticipation of the Kingdom of God by exposing its divine elements. "Once, on being asked by the Pharisees when the kingdom of God would come, Jesus replied, "The coming of the kingdom of God is not something that can be observed, nor will people say, 'Here it is,' or 'There it is', because the kingdom of God is in your midst."(Luke 17:20-21). Alan Richardson distinguishes its mystical and theological dimensions:

> Jesus regarded the imminent reign of God as a mystery in the biblical sense of the term. That is to say, even though the news of the near approach of the reign of God was proclaimed throughout the land, it would still remain an incomprehensible mystery apart from personal faith in God's purpose of salvation.[9]

Since this is a reflection of the dynamics of the society, it is assumed that this could be the manifesto of the first Kingdom community. Bruce L McCormack's article "With Loud Cries and Tears: The Humanity of the Son in the Epistle to the Hebrews", discusses the humanity of Jesus with the help of theology and soteriology.

He continues to argue that in Jesus Christ the pre-existent Logos is manifested and perfected.[10] It is a very momentous dimension of the revelation of God as the humanness of Jesus Christ could contact the people on the edges through an act of solidarity and sharing of struggles and burdens. Saint Cyril of Alexandria called this a kind of *theosis,* where one could come into contact with the divine nature in the act of incarnation. Advent is not only a time of celebration of hope and anticipation but also a time of pronouncement of faith. The epistle to the Hebrews, in general, offers a clear platform for comprehending the meaning and memorandum of such a manifestation of Jesus, the Christ, in Nazareth.

R.S. Barbour's famous book *The Kingdom of God and Human Society* expresses the idea that Christian engagements and participation namely social thought is designed within the framework of Jesus' proclamation of the Kingdom of God.[11] G.E.Ladd, a New Testament Theologian summarizes the understanding of the Kingdom of God in the following manner:

> An Initial manifestation of God's Kingdom is found in the mission of our Lord on earth. Before The age to come, before the millennial reign of Christ, the Kingdom of God has entered into This present evil age here and now in the person and work of Christ. We may therefore now experience in power; we may know the life; we may enter into a participation of its blessings.[12]

This is a challenge posed before us as we try to seek justice by doing justice. Thus it is noted that the manifestation of the Kingdom of God brings a mandate for us to work together to establish a just, egalitarian and participatory society.

A first step is always important. In today's context, that first step should be a step that will honestly identify priority areas of ministry. It is not a question of who gains the lead in a race to form more conceptual clarity in proposing, promoting and proclaiming an alternate ecclesia. The link between those who were waiting for the Lord in Jude's community and the praxis of the Kingdom of God offers a vision of the formative years of the early church as it struggles with its identity. Therefore, I consider a realistic debate on the question of identity is very significant in understanding the invisible effect of the early church in the first century.

New Testament interpreters have touched many issues such as poverty, slavery, gender discrimination and ethnic conflicts in the light of the Kingdom of God and cross as the experience of the way of Christ should enable us to look at things differently. In the context of secular India, especially in the locations of its multicultural and polyvalent features, a redefinition of a relevant Christo-centric ministerial leadership may be endeavored. Hans Schwartz's 2005 book *Theology in a Global Context,* uses two interesting phrases while describing the significance of Jesus Christ namely "Relating Christ to the World" and "Emergence of New voices".[13] These expressions indicate the trend in modern Christology as the modern trends in Christology will take the living context of the followers of Jesus into account when the identity of Jesus Christ is redefined. Undoubtedly, the significance and relevance of Jesus Christ in today's world can be accepted as the life and message of Jesus Christ continues to empower the marginalized and the despised in society.

Why did the people of the margins in Petrine community begin migration in Urban and Semi-Urban areas of the Roman Empire from Tribal settings? The answer is not simple as it involves many factors and components. This spectacular phenomenon enabled them to avoid extreme conflict conditions created by the Roman Empire in Asia Minor. In 1928, International Missionary

Council which met in Jerusalem declared that "the race problem, the position of women and war" should be addressed. I think, the *Parokois* to cornerstone in the Petrine community offers the same dimension for a wider understanding of the proclamation of the Kingdom of God.[14]

Conclusion

It is not very easy to locate and fix a definite framework to define the identity of the early Christian communities due to the plurality of cultural and social systems. However, this study could bring out one aspect of such an identity based on Jude and 2 Peter. Those insights could also express their links with the wider affirmation of the Kingdom of God. Thus the identity remains at the heart of the proclamation of the Gospel. I have noticed there is often a reference to the proclamation of the Kingdom of God while talking about the identity of alternate ecclesia. It is mainly because of the intent and trust of the people of the margins in terms of actualizing the values of the Kingdom of God by promoting the praxiological dimension of the church. This is clearly evident in the new mass movements and liturgical movements in the united and uniting churches across the globe.

Endnotes

[1] Stephen J.Kraftchick, *Jude and 2 Peter* (Nashville: Abingdon Press, 2002),17

[2] Gene L Green, *Jude and 2 Peter* (Michigan : Baker Academic, 2008), p.24.

[3] Michael Jagessar, "Rethinking reformation: marginal voices strike back," A Paper presented at the Queens Foundation, Birmingham UK, Dec. 13, ….(year).

[4] Michael L.Humpries, *Christian Origins and the Language of the Kingdom of God* (Illinois:Southern Illinois University Press), 2008.

[5] Ibid. p.45.

[6] C.I. David Joy "Kingdom of God", in ed., Paul Sing, *ECC Jubilee Volume* (Bangalore: ECC, 2014).

[7] Donald Guthrie, *New Testament Theology*. (Secundrabad: OM Books, 2004), 415.

[8] Albert Schweitzer, *The Mystery of the Kingdom of God: The Secret of Jesus' Messiahship and Passion* (New York: Macmillan, 1950), 2.

[9] Alan Richardson, *An Introduction to the Theology of the New Testament* (London: SCM Press, 1972), 86.

[10] Bruce L McCormack "With Loud Cries and Tears: The Humanity of the Son in the Epistle to the Hebrews," *JSNT* (2009), 40.

[11] R.S.Barbour, *The Kingdom of God and Human Society* (Edinburgh: T&T Clark, 1993),157.

[12] G.E.Ladd, *The Gosepl of the Kingdom* (Grand Rapids: WBEerdmanns, 1959),123.

[13] Hans Schwartz, *Theology in a Global Context* (Grand Rapids: WBEerdmanns, 2005), 23.

[14] *Annual Conference Statement* (London: IMC, 1928), 63.

Bibliography

Annual Conference Statement. London: IMC, 1928.

Barbour, R.S. *The Kingdom of God and Human Society.* Edinburgh: T&T Clark, 1993.

Green, Gene L. *Jude and 2 Peter.* Michigan: Baker Academic, 2008.

Guthrie, Donald. *New Testament Theology*. Secundrabad: OM Books, 2004.

Humpries, Michael L. *Christian Origins and the Language of the Kingdom of God.* Illinois: Southern Illinois University Press, 2008.

Jagessar, Michael. "Rethinking reformation: marginal voices strike back," A Paper presented at the Queens Foundation, Birmingham UK, Dec. 13, ...(year).

Kraftchick, Stephen J. *Jude and 2 Peter.* Nashville: Abingdon Press, 2002.

Ladd, G.E. *The Gospel of the Kingdom*. Grand Rapids: WBEerdmanns, 1959.

McCormack, Bruce L. "With Loud Cries and Tears: The Humanity of the Son in the Epistle to the Hebrews," *JSNT* (2009), 40.

Richardson, Alan. *An Introduction to the Theology of the New Testament.* London: SCM Press, 1972.

Schwartz, Hans. *Theology in a Global Context.* Grand Rapids: WB Eerdmanns, 2005.

Schweitzer, Albert. *The Mystery of the Kingdom of God: The Secret of Jesus' Messiahship and Passion.* New York: Macmillan, 1950.

10

The Paradigmatic Challenge of Visions of Cornelius and Peter in Acts of the Apostle for a "Borderless Ecclesia"

Joseph Samuel

Introduction

Mathilukal (Walls, borders) is a novel written by Vaikkom Muhammad Basheer in 1965 and later made into a movie starring popular Malayalam actor Mammotty. It is one of the most cherished and well-known love stories in Malayalam. Its hero, Basheer himself, and heroine, Narayani, never meet, yet they love each other passionately. Despite being imprisoned and separated by a huge wall that divides their prisons, the two romance each other. The movie pictures only this side of the prison - the Male section. The other side of the narrative, the female side, is simply a voice. They exchange their heart without seeing each other, they celebrate their love without even seeing their face…but they fall in love and it grows intensely. They exchange gifts, and their hearts, without meeting each other. Narayani then comes up with a plan for a meeting: they decide to meet at the hospital a few days later. But before that, Basheer is released, unexpectedly. For once, he does not want the freedom he had craved for. At the end of the movie, when the jailor informs the hero that he is going to be released... He says with pain in his heart and tears in his eyes… "Who wants this freedom?" The novel ends with Basheer standing outside the prison with a rose in his hand. May be for him, freedom meant love… freedom to love within the walled or bordered contexts. The movie and novel cinematograph that love can transcend boundaries. Borders/boundaries can be broken or dismantled only when this side (OUR SIDE) comes to realize the life of the other side (THEIR SIDE). This can happen only when we engage in dialogue. Life is dialogue, love is dialogue and the very being and becoming of all human existence is dialogue.

We are living in a context where the spirit of dialogism in a democracy is being hegemonically and politically annihilated by growing antagonism and militarism. The military might and brutality weaponry are employed within the nation rather than at the borders of the nation. Where exactly is the violent, excluding and bloody line of control drawn? We aggressively protect the borders within us. The fascism within. The Empire within. To break the barriers and boundaries, we need Visions, not only in our dreams but in our alphabets and in our articulations. As Peter had been paradigmatically challenged by a divine vision, we need to be intimidatingly disturbed by the vision of a borderless people of God, the multitude of god.

Text, Context, and Hermeneutics

Birth, in a sense, is a process of bordering. Reality has borders. Otherwise, we are yet to realize reality without borders. Nations are born when their borders are fixed. The body is bordered. Border-less-ness is not body-less-ness. It is our consciousness to move beyond the body and border even when we live within the body and border.

Text of any kind is bordered as a result of a historical process. We cannot theoretically say that the shift from orality to textually is one of border-less-ness- to bordered-ness. However, text as a reality, since it is born or begotten, is a bordered entity. Text, as grammatical-linguistic construction, is fixity. The text should also be seen as a continuity because as Julia Kristeva held, "any text is constructed as a mosaic of quotations; any text is an absorption and transformation of another."She argued that the literary word is "an intersection of textual surfaces rather than a point (fixed meaning) … a dialogue among several writings: that of the writer, the addressee (or the character) and the contemporary or earlier cultural context." Kristeva treated the text not as a closed structure but as a relational phenomenon: "It maintains relationships to other texts and to the one "general text," which Kristeva designates as culture.[1]

Context is the dynamism that constantly moves the text. Though we see a sense of fixity in terms of grammatical-linguistic characteristics of the text, it is the energy of the context that rejuvenates the text in relation to the meaning. In other words, the liveliness of the context defines the relevance of the meaning of the text. Specific social situations, the complexities, conflicts and bewilderments of the particular Indian situations, create and maintain borders violently. Poverty, unemployment, modern slavery, nationalism, monumentalism, freedom of people, gender – are all systemically used to create borders between people.

Ideas, Characters and Polyphonism

Michael Bakhtin suggests that dialogue constitutes an integral part of human existence and that it has been demonstrated in all the texts. For Bakhtin characters are independent and free in terms of their involvement in reproducing a *sitz im leben*. They are "not voiceless slaves… but free people, capable of standing alongside their creator, capable of not agreeing with him and even of rebelling against him." Bakhtin characterized this phenomenon by the word *polyphonism,* which means "a plurality of independent and unmerged voices and consciousnesses, a genuine polyphony of fully valid voices is, in fact, the chief characteristic of artistic creations of any kind."[2]

Early Christian and specifically Lucan world is profoundly pluralistic. If we were to seek an image toward which this whole world gravitates, an image in the spirit of the evangelist's own worldview, then it would be the church as a communion of the othered peoples, where multi-leveled-ness is extended into eternity, where there are the penitent and the unrepentant, the damned and the saved. Such an image would be in the style of the evangelist, or, more precisely, in the style of his ideology, while the image of a unified spirit is deeply alien to him.

The ideas really do become almost the vitality of the text. There is a special role to ideas throughout the early Christian narratives since each character seems to be possessed by an idea. More than this, there is an endless interaction, a never-ending quarrel between characters and ideas. Lucan narrative world in Luke-Acts is characterized primarily by coexistence and interaction of ideas and characters. The interaction between ideas and characters contributes toward changing both. Characters identify with ideas, whereas ideas receive a personal flavor.

Luke-Acts: A Particularistic Ancient Historiography

One the one hand, well-known Greek and Roman forms of literature were suggested as the generic background for Luke-Acts. Among them, one can find a proposal reinforced recently by Sean Adams to read Acts as an adaptation of ancient biography.[3] Nevertheless, it has also been pointed out the central characteristics of ancient biographies, such as the discussion of "birth, death, appearance, and remarkable character traits" is of no concern for Luke. The Book of Acts seems to be interested in its characters more for what they stand for than what their attributes are. The lack of that interest takes away the claim of biography. Ben Witherington argues this when he lays out specifics of Lucan history writing: "Luke and Acts together must be seen as some sort of two-volume historiographical work. Luke in his second volume is writing a continuous narrative about the growth and development of a remarkable historical phenomenon, early Christianity, which he believed was the result of divinely initiated social change."[4] The motivation for the Lucan form of historiography is fundamentally theological or more specifically theocentric.

Events triggered by the conversion of Cornelius leading to the acceptance of Gentiles at the Jerusalem Synod are central to the narrative of Acts. Acts 10:1–15:35 is a central section in the whole book focusing mainly on a major development in the early Christian movement—namely the reception of Gentile Christians in the Church. The first major section is Acts 10:1–11:18 centering on the conversion and baptism of a certain Roman centurion named Cornelius along with his household. Peter plays a crucial role in the events, first by being reluctant to obey God's initiative toward the Gentiles, then by convincing others to embrace the new group within the Church. The episode itself breaks into two parts. First, in Acts 10:1–48 events leading to the conversion and baptism of Cornelius are told, and then countering opposition in Jerusalem is recounted in Acts 11:1–18. Therefore, is essence, the narratological matrix of Acts portrays the ecclesiological development of the Jesus' movement into a transethnic and intersectional amalgam of communities contesting the border affirming tendencies within the ideology of ecclesia.

Faith of Dominant Others in the Narrative

The reception of Gentile Christians is not only a phenomenon recorded in the NT, but examples are also enormous in both the OT and NT, Namaan(2Kings 5), Daniel; in NT, Luke 7 (Centurion), Acts 8:24-40 (Ethiopian Eunuch), are few examples. Luke takes the *topos* more seriously on several levels. Jesus is said to pronounce the faith of the Roman soldier to be superior to that he found in Israel. Second, already implicit in the story of the Ethiopian eunuch is the reception of the Gentiles into the community of the people of God. It will become more explicit in the conversion of Cornelius' household. Following the account of Cornelius and the outpouring of the Spirit on the Gentiles, Peter understands that God welcomes all the Gentiles, not just the ones with whom he came into contact. From a singular event, Peter makes a general assumption. The Gentiles in Luke's use of the *topos* show more faith than their predecessors did. The approval of their faith by the outpouring of the Spirit leads to more radical conclusions regarding the status of the Gentiles in relation to the people of God.

Complementary Visions as "the Game Changers"

The other significant phenomenon of generic character of Acts is the presence of visionary experiences. There are two visions in

Acts 10:1–11:18. The first one (Angelophany) in Acts 10:1-8 tells of an angel appearing to Cornelius, the Roman centurion, giving him instruction about sending messengers to Peter in Joppa. The second vision is that of Peter in Acts 10:9–16 told again later in 11:5–10 about the descending vessel and the voice telling him to eat the animals in it. The two visions in the passage do not stand in isolation. As Michael Goulder noted, there is a detectable pattern present in Luke's works to interlock pairs of visions. He named them complementary visions.[5] The first instance of such visions would be the ones seen by Zechariah and Mary as told in Luke 1. The complementary visions of Saul and Ananias in Acts 9:1–19 can be seen as a further example of the same technique applied in Acts. Saul's visionary experience on the road to Damascus is brought into connection with the vision of Ananias, a prominent Christian disciple of the city. In a vision he is told to go to Saul and baptize him. The two human agents are to meet and to share God's initiative. James Dunn understands the dual visions as expressing the same truth. It is argued therefore that the same truth is established twice in visions thus contributing to a more powerful statement. Luke's artistry however does much more than legitimizing or enforcing certain contents in the visions of Cornelius and Peter.[6] It is somewhat surprising that one of the seers of vision is a Gentile, a Roman soldier. More than this, Cornelius' experience is recounted first, thus giving it a prior position. The relationship between the two parties involved is that of opposition and possible conflict. The Roman centurion was considered as unclean therefore unfit for a communion with Jews. The complementary visions place two people together as receivers of divine instruction one of which is incompatible with God and his people. The visions offer epistemological break from the dominant perceptions on "otherness" and act as point of detour for the church to go borderless and inclusive community.

Peter as Jonah's son: Intertextuality of Acts 10 and Book of Jonah.

Robert Wall proposes conceptual linguistic correspondence as a more accurate description of the parallels found in Acts 10. Wall detected parallels at the level of sequential ordering of catchwords throughout the Cornelius narrative "which go beyond mere coincidence and suggest that it was the intent of the evangelist to place the conversion of Cornelius against the backdrop of Nineveh's conversion." Wall admittedly examined the parallels at the level of words and phrases to propose that at the main turning points of both narratives one can find the same quasi-technical terms.[7]

First, Wall writes of continuity of location, Joppa and the command to go to the Gentiles given to reluctant servants of God. It would have to be added immediately that Joppa plays different roles in both narratives. According to Acts 9:43, visiting Christian communities along the coast, Peter arrives in Joppa from the South, where he stays at the house of a certain man named Simon. Jonah most likely comes from the same direction to board a ship in the city already in rebellion to God's command which he received earlier. Only Peter receives God's command in Joppa whereas the location of Jonah's encounter with the Lord is not named. Both protagonists are to go to the Gentiles to fulfill their mission.

Second, the objection of both Jonah and Peter comes to an end after God intervenes. In both cases, God's intervention is characterized by the number three. One could also strengthen Wall's argument by adding that in both cases animals are involved (fish and the many creatures in the object) in convincing God's servants. Jonah spends three days in the belly of a sea fish. Peter sees the object filled with animals descending from heaven three times (Jonah 2:1; Acts 10:16). A further link can be seen in the role of Spirit/wind in convincing both Jonah and Peter for their upcoming mission projects. According to the Book of Jonah, the Lord raised a great wind on the sea (Jonah 1:4). The Spirit has a prominent role in convincing Peter (Acts 10:19) when it tells him to go with the servants sent for him by Cornelius.

The third parallel is based on verbal correspondence as suggested by Wall. The commands issued to both Jonah and Peter contain the words "arise and go." God charges his servants to go and preach to the Gentiles using the same words (Jon 3:2, Act 10:20).

Fourth, in response to the prophetic message, the Gentiles both in Nineveh and Caesarea believed God's word (Jon 3:5; Act 10:43) and were thus forgiven. Wall takes this to be another verbal correspondence.

Fifthly, a thematic parallel is pointed out: the faith of the Gentiles results partly in hostile response. Jonah is angered according to 4:1 that God did not destroy the pagan city as he expected whereas in Acts the brothers in Jerusalem made a hostile response (Acts 11:2) to the inclusion of the Gentiles.

Finally, God convinces the doubters and opponents in a like manner in both stories (Jonah 4:2-11; Acts 11:17-18). After the worm smites the plant that had provided protection to Jonah from the sun, God raises a burning wind upon Jonah. As a result, Jonah became so angry that he wanted to rather die than to live. While making a case for receiving the Gentiles in the Church,

Peter pointed out that the Spirit descended on them: "And as I began to speak, the Holy Spirit fell upon them just as it had upon us at the beginning" (Acts 11:15). In the end, having been convinced, the leaders of the Jerusalem Church note that God gave to the Gentiles the repentance that leads to life. A clear parallel between the two narratives is the social and religious attributes of their characters.

First, both Jonah the prophet and Peter the apostle are representatives of their religion entrusted with a task: they are both commissioned by God to deliver his message. In addition, both servants show opposition to God's initiative. Jonah refuses to carry out the mission right away while Peter is reluctant to obey the command to eat the unclean animals—an action that stood for receiving the Gentiles in the Church. Peter's religious role and mission resemble that of Jonah while the apostle departs from the prophet in one regard: he is easier to convince than Jonah. The prophet remains hostile to the end, while Peter stands convinced about God's grace. It must be mentioned here that Jonah's objection is also represented by the circumcised believers of Jerusalem. Once Peter changes from opponent to helper, the role of the former is assumed by the unnamed people in Jerusalem. Both Peter and the people undergo the same development from opponent to helper while Jonah's reluctance remains. The other main protagonist in the text, Cornelius, closely resembles the king of Nineveh. They are both non-Israelite figures of authority. Naturally, the king is superior to a Roman centurion—a difference in degree. The other important correlation is their surprisingly positive response to God's word. The king repents and orders national fasting. Cornelius received a positive religious evaluation from the beginning, yet his coming to faith is still a surprise. In addition, both men of authority stand for larger groups: the king for his people and Cornelius for his household and friends and for the entire Gentile race.

Conclusion

The need to be open to and responsible for the other is something which is there in all of the great religious traditions of the world. It is there at the heart of the Christian gospel – love God and your neighbour as yourself. Christianity, then, is also a religion of openness to the other, to all others. Alterity, attention to the awareness and eventual celebration of the other and of otherness, has become commonplace. An increasing awareness that domination, control, manipulation and suppression of the other are morally wrong has also been a prominent feature of postmodern consciousness. In many quarters today, commonality and shared humanity are less to the fore in ecclesial and theological discourse. Divisions, deficiencies and disagreements occupy far too much of our energy and time. These might well be symptoms of our increasingly divided world, but they are also causal factors that further contribute to the divisions that ravage the human family today. Thus, in general, religious otherness in the twenty-first century has become not less but rather more accentuated. Entire faiths and cultures are perceived to be pitted against one another. Conflicts rage, defining the opposition through their very cultural and religious otherness. Indeed, even churches in recent times have returned to discourse and practices which are destined to accentuate otherness more than human commonality. Therefore, the paradigmatic challenge of the Visions of Peter and Cornelius in Acts for envisioning a borderless ecclesia can thus be concluded, perhaps in poetic words of a Malayalam writer Ravunny who recites:

We plant the trees in distance
Restricting their leafs to touch the other
However, we don't realize their roots
Are intertwined beneath the ground...

Yes, this Consultation challenges us to realize that we all are intertwined essentially as the people of God in our roots. Let us live on our roots and you know root is also a route - A hard path for comprehending the inclusivity of our living space as an arena of faith activism.

Endnotes

[1] Megan Becker-Leckrone, *Julia Kristeva And Literary Theory*, (London: Palgrave Macmillan, 2005), 34-38.

[2] M.M. Bakhtin, *Problems of Dostoevsky's Poetic*, Edited and translated by Caryl Emerson (Minneapolis: University of Minnesota Press, 1984), 6-7.

[3] Sean A. Adams, *The Genre of Acts and Collected Biography* (Cambridge: Cambridge University Press, 2013)

[4] Ben Witherington III, *Acts of the Apostles: A Socio-Rhetorical Commentary* (Grand Rapids: W B Eerdmans, 1998), 10.

[5] Michael Goulder, *St. Paul verses St. Peter: A Tale of two Missions* (London: SCM, 1994), 45.

[6] James D G Dunn, *Acts of the Apostles* (Grand Rapids: W B Eerdmans, 1996), 136.

[7] Robert W Wall, "Peter, 'Son' of Jonah: The Conversion of Cornelius in the Context of Canon", *The New Testament as Canon: A Reader in the Canonical Criticism*, Edited by Robert W Wall and Eugene E Lemcio (England: Sheffield Academic Press, 1992), 129- 141.

Bibliography

Adams, Sean A. *The Genre of Acts and Collected Biography.* Cambridge: Cambridge University Press, 2013.

Becker-Leckrone, Megan. *Julia Kristeva and Literary Theory*. London: Palgrave Macmillan, 2005.

Bakhtin, M.M. *Problems of Dostoevsky's Poetic,* Edited and translated by Caryl Emerson. Minneapolis: University of Minnesota Press, 1984.

Dunn, James D G. *Acts of the Apostles.* Grand Rapids: W B Eerdmans, 1996.

Wall, Robert W. "Peter, 'Son' of Jonah: The Conversion of Cornelius in the Context of Canon", *The New Testament as Canon: A Reader in the Canonical Criticism,* Edited by Robert W Wall and Eugene E Lemcio. England: Sheffield Academic Press, 1992: 129-141.

Witherington III, Ben. *Acts of the Apostles: A Socio-Rhetorical Commentary,* Grand Rapids: W B Eerdmans, 1998.

11

Imag(e)ining ἐκκλησία with John:

Call of the Fourth Gospel to Being and Becoming Christ Communities – towards a Borderless Church

Gregory Thomas Basker

The Gospel of John is known for its imagery, figurative language and symbols. The various images like "lamb", "king", "bread", "shepherd", and "vine", all point to the characteristic bond between Jesus and his disciples. Recurrent themes like Truth, Word, Knowledge, Love, and Eternal Life also serve to ratify this purpose. In this paper, I seek to interpret the Johannine allegory of the 'Vine and the Branches' (Joh. 15: 1–10) in light of the ἐκκλησία model (*ecclesia*, Church) and propose a fresh understanding of a "borderless church" in our Indian Christian context. Before we begin this rereading, it is pertinent to understand the concept of ἐκκλησία in its historical context.

Understanding *Ecclesia* As Utopia - from (Pre) Biblical Times

I would like to begin with the surmise "*Ecclesia* as utopia". In pre-biblical times, much writing concentrated upon imaginations and predictions of a mythical utopian world. For instance, in Hesiod's poem *Works and Days* (750 BCE), the Olympian gods create the human race who live in a golden age ruled by the Titan Kronus. Here, the first generation human beings live a joyful, ageless life, feasting and enjoying the bounty of the earth. Zeus is portrayed as the all-seeing God of righteousness who rewards righteousness and punishes injustice.[1] Similarly, in the poems of Virgil (40 BCE, particularly *Ecologues*), we observe the dawn of the new golden age in the utopian place called Arcadia. Again, the Hyperboreans, one of a mythical people in Greek mythology, lived for 1,000 years in a land where the sun shone twenty-four hours a day. These fantastic romances seem far removed from the concerns of Judaism and Christianity, but it is important to remember that the well known biblical themes also show remarkable affinities with such kinds of utopian visions.

In the Old Testament, there are several paradigms to represent this utopia. The Eden tradition and its associated narratives; the tradition of Israel; the Promised Land flowing with milk and honey; Jerusalem; Temple; The era of David/Moses; The reign of God also known as the restoration of Israel in messianic terms (Isa 11: 1-10). All these themes and more characterise the utopian ideal in Jewish religious thought.

Further, in the intertestamental period too, ideal communities were envisaged in early Hellenistic Judaism. The Essene and *Therapeutai* were particularly influenced by Hellenistic utopian values. The Essenes (referred by Philo, Josephus and Pliny), who originated from Palestine, were pronounced "Village-dwellers" who shared their possessions, shunned commerce, pooled any wages they earned, dined communally, shared clothing, had no slaves, rejected marriage and children, were pacifists, and had no luxuries. The *therapeutai* were a Jewish sect, who, like the Essenes, also lived austere lives in their pursuit of wisdom and yearning for release.

It is true that the origin of Christianity as a religion can be historically traced to Emperor Constantine's conversion. However, the fundamental themes and the so-called "Christian" theological ideas were already present in the human psyche from pre-biblical times, from time immemorial. The belief of a utopian world (read "kingdom of God"), the transformation of the cosmos, and redemption of humankind were always part and parcel of human aspiration, civilization and vision. Hence, utopian ideology proves to be the basis of the concept of ecclesia in the New Testament.

In the New Testament, the word *ecclesia* originated in the classical Greek institution of democracy procuring implication from the Hebrew/Jewish *qahal*. The Hebrew word *qahal* (Gen 35: 11; 28: 3; 48: 4; 49:6; Exod 12:6; Num 14:5; Deut 9:10; 10:4; Neh 8: 2, 7; Ezek 38:7, 13) represented a religious assembly of Israelites also known as the people of God. In the NT, the word "ecclesia" initially did not have any religious usage but only a secular function (Acts 19:32, 39, 41; cf. Acts 7: 38 with reference to Deut 9:10). The early church chose this term to present itself as a "new creation", a "called out community". The word actually meant a religious assembly or local assembly, predominantly applied to the church of Jerusalem, a local community. However, in due course, the word was also given a global spiritual dimension, that all are created in the image of the Divine, and equally, in the *cosmopolis*, i.e., world community. In addition to its usage to represent the Christian community of Jerusalem (Acts 8:3; 11:22; 12:1, 5; 15: 4, 22; 18:22), it was also used to designate churches in Antioch (Acts

11:26; 13: 1; 14:27; 15:3), in Lystra and Iconium (Acts 14:23), in Syria and Cilicia (Acts 15:41), in Ephesus (Acts 20: 17, 28), in unnamed cities (Acts 16:4) and throughout Judaea, Galilee and Samaria (Acts 9:31). The early church was a struggling church, not only against its persecutors but also within its own fold. It grew through the crises it underwent (Acts 8:14 – 17; 11:19-26).

However, it is interesting to note how βασιλεία (*basileia*, kingdom) became *ecclesia* (church). Initially, the Jesus movement was only a *basileia* movement. During the time of Paul, when he wrote his letters, the crucified Jesus, became the hero/protagonist of the Gospel. Jesus became the crux of the movement and not his message, which was the kingdom of God (βαςιλεια του θεου, *basileia tou theou*)! The early church started focusing exclusively on Jesus and not on the kingdom. For instance, for Paul, the Kingdom of God was realized through resurrection and reign of Christ; for Mark, the Kingdom of God was a mystery revealed to those who understood and accepted Christ (Mk.4:11-12); for Matthew, the Kingdom of Heaven was endorsed by the charge given to Peter (Matt. 16:18-19) and given to those who followed Jesus' teaching (Mt. 7:21; 5:3, 10, 19, 20; 13:52; 19:12); for Luke, Jesus was the king and following him led to heaven; John used the word Kingdom of God only twice (Jn.3:3, 5). So, this is how *basileia* came to be identified with Christ, Church and the Christian state.[2]

Imag(e)ining *Ecclesia* in John from the Vine-Branch Allegory

We know that the term *ecclesia* is not at all mentioned in John, but the Fourth Gospel contains a number of corporate metaphors for Jesus and his disciples such as "the door and the flock" (ch10), "the vine and the branches" (ch. 15), bread that is eaten (ch. 6) and the washing of the feet (ch.13). However, the idea of *ecclesia* is expressed in a highly characteristic way in the Gospel of John in the image of the vine and the branches (John 15: 1 – 17). We observe in the following a few archetypes of ecclesia-imagination of John in this passage:

a. *Unity of the believing Johannine community*

The New Testament scholar Raymond Brown rejects the general opinion that there was no idea of *community* or *church* in the Gospel of John, due to the absence of specific terminologies. On the contrary, he presents several proofs of the existence of a community (John 6, 70; 13, 18; 15, 16; etc.). He repudiates Rudolf Bultmann's opinion that the idea of church or community in John was inserted by a "Church redactor" and asserts that the Gospel of John was written by a disciple of Jesus. Pointing to the idea of community in John in the metaphor of the "vine and branches" (John 15: 1 ff.). Brown states that "abiding" in the love of Jesus (John 15: 9) and "loving one another" (John 13: 34; 15: 12) represented a love within the Johannine Christian community. In this regard, he does not differentiate between a personal union with Jesus and with the community.[3]

Further, the union between Jesus and his disciples was based on service (διακονη, service). The verb διακονέω (*diakoneo*, to serve) has a range of meanings, such as "to wait, attend upon, serve, be an attendant or assistant, to minister to, to relieve."[4] In 15:20–21 (13:16), the disciples are reminded that "a servant is not greater than his master." However, the disciples, though they are servants, are taken into confidence, as friends. With regard to John 15:20, Ridderbos believes that the servant shares the good and the bad with the master.[5] In this connection, Kemp writes:

> The reciprocal love of the disciple for his master is to be marked by humble, self denying service, (as the Greek word *diakonos*=servant shows) and by the continuous practice of serving and following

> Jesus (in Greek the two verbs are in the present continuous tense), in the same close relationship of obedience with him that he has with his Father."[6]

Brown describes the Johannine community as one, which constantly strived towards the unity of the believing community (Joh 17: 21). Moreover, Brown's interpretation presents Jesus as a victim, who fought for the poor and marginalized and gave his life for the sake of them as a martyr. Beasley-Murray's summary of the Feet-washing episode is relevant to our study.

> The paradoxical nature of the footwashing remains transparent in vv.13-20: first it is the Teacher and the Master who performs the slave's task; then the Master of his slaves and the Sender of the Messenger; and finally the reminder is given that behind the Sender, Jesus, stands none other than the Father who sent him."[7]

Therefore, the believing Johannine community had to fulfil a code in order to be true disciples. It meant that those who have believed in Jesus had to remain in him and know the truth, and be freed by the truth (8:31). In Judaism, the truth was the Law, and the study of the Law made a person free. Barrett sees the expressions, "truth" and "freedom," as primarily referring to the Christian liberation from sin.[8] The disciples are instructed that hatred and persecution of the world are part of discipleship (16:33; 15:18-20; 16:2). There are two worlds, one heavenly and one earthly and the disciples belong to the heavenly (6:27; 17:14; 18:36). The disciples, therefore, do not attach much significance to the present world but regard it as a preparatory ground for the next, heavenly life.[9] They are ready to die, given the predicament of this world.

b. Reciprocal formula of immanence

One of the main points of the vine-branch allegory is that just as the branch gets its life from the vine, the disciple gets his/her life from Jesus.[10] What makes Jesus the true vine is that he gathers a community, in which his word exerts a life-creating, purifying and dividing effect (cf.14:23f) and binds the community to himself, so that it may grow.[11] Ridderbos calls this the "reciprocal formula of immanence" where disciple "remains" in Jesus and Jesus "remains" in the disciple."[12] The fellowship described here is one of love, represented by Jesus, which the disciples should hold on to by "remaining". This allegory has been understood as the church. Thus, the Vine-branch metaphor in connection with the church, suggests a relationship of co-dependence and consanguinity.

The motif of "remaining" is characteristic of the Fourth Gospel and recurs every now and then, but here it occurs more often (seven times) and with greater emphasis than elsewhere. "To remain" connotes continuing to live in association or union with Jesus. For the first time in this passage, the content of Jesus' commands is described as the disciples' mutual love for each other. The disciples' mutual relations ought to be "as I have loved you" (vv.12, 17) and should extend to the ultimate length, namely to be prepared to die for each other (v.13).

It is noteworthy, that within the aspect of "remaining" there is also the "sending motif"[13], in that, the Father's sending of the son serves both as the model and the ground for the son's sending of the disciples. Just as the Father is present in the Son's mission, so is the Son present in the mission of the disciples.[14] Ridderbos sees a unity of the Father and the Son, a unity in which the disciples participate (cf.17:21ff).[15] It is important to note that *Jesus* is the sender of his disciples. This importance is brought out clearly in Koestenberger's words:

> The disciples are to bring glory and honour to Jesus (as well as to the Father; cf.15:8, 16). They are to do Jesus' will, perform Jesus' works, and speak Jesus' words. The disciples are to witness

> to Jesus and to represent *him* accurately. And they are to know Jesus intimately, live in close relationship with *him* and follow his example. In a word, *their* relationship to *their* sender, Jesus, is to reflect Jesus' relationship with his sender, the Father.[16]

The word ἐνεφύσησεν ("breathed", 20:22) echoes the LXX of Gen.2:7 which has God breathing into Adam. If the reference to the LXX text is direct, then symbolically, John is proclaiming that just as in the time of creation God breathed a living spirit into a human being, so now Jesus breathes into the disciples his own Holy Spirit, for eternal life.[17] But the expression can also be understood as Jesus' equipping of his disciples for the work assigned to them.[18]

Further, one can notice that there is also a parallel between the Johannine formulae of immanence and the Pauline notion of "*en Christo*". Both these models, according to Udo Schnelle, "describe the unique mutual 'existence-in' of Revealer and believers, without surrender of each one's personal identity."[19] Therefore, without this reciprocal remaining in Jesus and he in them, the disciples would fall into unfruitfulness (15:5b-6) and vitiate their relationship with him and be cut and thrown away (15:6).

c. *Mutual love 'within' the community*

Johannine scholarship has at times overemphasized the differentiation in the Gospel with regard to the centrality of love in John. In his discussion on the Johannine relation to the Catholic Church, Holtzmann highlights the difference between the "world" and his "own" (John 15, 18.19). He observes, that the synoptic emphasis on the double commandment of love (*Doppelgebot der Liebe*) did not find a place in the Gospel of John. According to him, one could notice in John a limitation and shortcoming (of love). In this regard, he refers to the fellowship-oriented influence of the Gospel of John (not in an apostolic tradition or succession but in the consciousness), which enabled one to understand the Johannine love commandment as a mutual sibling love (*wechselseitige Brüderliebe*). This love was present only within the Christian, congregational fellowship (Joh 13, 15). Hence, there appeared a specific Christian fellowship (Joh 13, 35), from whose working sphere the heretics were excluded (2 Joh 10, 11).[20]

In this connection, Rensberger claims that the Johannine community was called to love its own and not the world nor its enemies. The Eucharist is then understood as a "remaining in Jesus" and as an expression of mutual love. The Johannine community had to, therefore, love its own and protect itself from betrayers.[21]

Consequently, there is also a baptismal symbolism that can be identified here. The image of the vine and the branches symbolizes a baptismal act for Jesus' disciples, on account of which they become Jesus' brothers and can call his Father their Father (20:17).[22] According to Dodd, the gift of the spirit is the "ultimate climax of the personal relations between Jesus and his disciples."[23]

d. The Unity of being

In Indian theological exegesis, the allegory of the vine and the branches has been interpreted mystically. For instance, Bede Griffiths, following Sankara's *advaitic* teaching of the unity of being, states that Brahman bore in himself the ideas of transcendence as well as immanence, contained in himself both the living and the non-living worlds and ruled from within (*Svetasvatara Up.* 3,19.12.13.; 6, 7; 5, 11-12).[24] According to him, the idea of the unity of being was present in Christianity too, particularly in John. The mystery of being in the Gospel of John resembled Indian thought, inasmuch as it was an experience and not as in Greek thought, where it was only a concept. Griffiths postulated that one had to go beyond human limitations, in order to understand the unity of being. At this level, there were no more borders or categories of time and space and it was here that the true being, the ground of the universe, the city of Brahman, who held everything in himself, was realized. It was only in this unity of being that the "final state of fulfilment" could be realized.[25]

For Barrett, the Fourth Gospel, in spite of its many "non-mystical features" contains within it an element of mystic thought, implicit throughout the Gospel but clearly brought out in certain passages (14:6, 17, 23; 1:18; 15:1-6).[26] Evelyn Underhill writes, "had the Fourth Evangelist never known what it was to feel the sap of the Mystic Vine flow through him, his words would have lacked their overwhelming certitude."[27]Apart from Pauline Epistles, the Fourth Gospel is the only book to contain a large amount of mystical thought. In John the mystic's aim is the union between God and the soul. This idea of 'mystical union' is illustrated by Philo, by what Kanagaraj calls the "sexual mystic union" where a supreme deity has sexual relations with a 'Female Principle of nature' by which human beings are begotten and as a result, human beings can have mystical union with that deity.[28] Kaesemann, in his acclaimed study on John 17, points to the "failure" of both "historical realism" and "mystical spiritualism" in John's Gospel. According to him, it is the *Word* that dominates Johannine ecclesiology.[29]

Also, in this union, we can regularly see a "centripetal tendency" wherein unity in difference, "one in many" is always sought. Jesus' prayer for oneness (17:22-23) has been understood as a prayer for "mutual inhabitation" or "ethical harmony" of human souls with God.[30] Here, it is important to note that the mysticism centered on Jesus goes beyond Jesus: Jesus actually leads his disciples to the Father, whom he knows to be identical to him ("Do you not believe that I am in the Father and the Father is in me?" "Believe me that I am in the Father and the Father is in me" 14:10, 11a). The mystic can be best understood as a "process of sublimation, which carries the correspondences of the self with the universe up to higher levels than those on which our normal consciousness works."[31]

This unity of being is taken further by Abhishiktananda, in that he states that the union of Jesus and the father in the Gospel of John, was a proclamation of the union of all Christians. Abhishiktananda approaches this idea from a catholic perspective, emphasising the mystery-aspect of it. The greatest mystery for him was the *guha* (inwardness). Here, the union of all Christians was undisputedly demonstrated – so that "the world may believe" (Joh 17: 21) – and one needed to strive to bring all the scattered Christians together as one family of God's children (Joh 11: 52).[32]

In the same vein, William Temple explains that the true vine, which symbolized Israel (Joh 15: 1-6), was also a symbol of the modern ecumenical movement, in which all the churches, (excluding the Roman Catholic Church) got together to establish the *World Council of Churches*.[33]

Additionally, in Indian theological exegesis, the passage of the vine and the branches has been interpreted ethically, in opposition to the Brahmanical, mystical interpretation of the "Indian Christian Theologians". For instance, in the Tamil language, the Greek word μείνατε ("remain"/"abide", 15:4) is sometimes translated as *iṇ aintiruṅkaḷ* (be united) instead of *nilaittiruṅkaḷ* (remain/abide). This envisages a sense of unity since one could bear fruit only when one is united with Jesus.

Concluding Remarks

The Gospel of John exhibits a close linkage between identity formation and praxis. Symbols in John have almost always praxiological implications. Thus, the allegory of the vine and the branches presents to us a community that "does". The branches that "do not" bear fruit are thrown away, but the ones that "bear fruit" are sustained and nurtured to bear more fruit. In other words, it is in the praxis that identity is constructed.

In the Indian context, words like "community", "identity", and "politics", have negative connotations. So, in this background, the question arises, whether or not the Johannine community could be an image of the church? With its emphasis on "love one another" and not anyone outside the community, does it not place a stumbling block towards a borderless church? These are relevant questions to be raised on any study on Johannine ecclesiology. However, the Fourth Gospel categorically maintains that, when following the Jesus model, even "identity construction" has a positive connotation.

Although identity construction (in John) requires "bordering" and "othering" of "us/them, you/we", ("*we* speak of what *we* know, yet *you* do not receive *our* testimony" 3: 11; "*you* worship what *you* do not know, *we* worship what *we* know, (4: 22); "*you* were born entirely in *your* sins, and are *you* trying to teach *us*?" (9: 34), the identities are not static. They give rise to "imagined communities" through symbols and allegories (such as the vine and the branches) of a common past (Jewishness/Judaism). They build bridges between the Jews and others (e.g. Samaritan woman, Nicodemus, the man born blind) and establish newer and transnational patterns presenting Jesus as the matrix for change. In John's Gospel, we see that Jesus turns down the offer of kingship and armed power (John 6:15) and chooses the path of peace.

The word "church" is not a translation of "*ecclesia*". It is derived from *cir(i)ce* (Old English), which in turn is derived from the German, *Kirche*, having its roots in the Greek *Kuriakon doma* (house of the Lord). *Ecclesia*, which actually denoted a democratic community of equals, an assembly, became the "church". The course of history shows us how *ecclesia*, from its initial identity of a democratic, idealistic, communitarian, open, kenotic, pentecostal assembly has deteriorated into a hierarchical, kyriarchical, individualistic, power-centered, profit-oriented, conservative, non-idealistic, discriminatory, conquering, homogenous institution. The members of the *ecclesia* initially had a vision of a new social order, where human values, like love, justice, freedom, equality and human rights played important roles. However, the Institutionalized Church was bent upon maintaining its status quo, thriving on age-old traditions and values based on triumphalism. Contrary to the members of the *ecclesia*, who identified themselves with the victims, the members of the church were in solidarity with the institution, having absolutely no connecting bond among them.

Today, the Institutionalized Church is edging towards identity formation on the basis of caste, class, race and religion. Being a 'victorious' entity, it continues to be an instrument of oppression. By and large, the church wants to remain conservative, in order to protect its institutional interests, rather than present itself as a prophetic voice among the suffering.

In this situation, we are led to ask the question, whether or not a borderless church is practically possible, or is it only a utopian idea? The Fourth Gospel imagines an ecclesia that endorses a growing community that is defined by action. The church is not a static, dormant, inactive institution, but one that *acts*. In this sense, it is borderless. The church is like the branch of the vine that spreads further to pervade unexplored avenues and is ever the "borderless church", always exploring, never repressed, never self-righteous.

In India, the Dalit movement, envisaged a grassroot model as opposed to a top-down model. It confronted the state-sponsored marginalization and promoted political, social and religious alternatives. In this sense, a "church without borders" is nothing but a creation of a new society, which conforms to the Jesus model. Jesus did not found a religion but sought to awaken the consciousness of the people. He protested against the status quo and rejected the dominant oligarchy. It envisaged an egalitarian communication, which was based on love and acceptance within the movement.

The call of the Gospel of John towards an ecumenical church - "that they all may be one" (John 17:21) – is a call for a Copernican revolution, where no church is the center. There is diversity, egalitarianism and acceptance among the community of believers. Such an ecclesial model of the church imagines a missionary church, where the Lord and his disciples are like the vine and the branches. Such a 'borderless church' will be the one that includes the perspective of the poor and be in solidarity with the oppressed by identifying with them. It will be open to other religious traditions and ideologies and committed to the unity and integrity of the whole creation and the sanctity and sanity of the world, here and now.

Endnotes

[1] See M.C. West, "Hesiod" in Mircea Eliade (ed.) *Encyclopaedia of Religion Vol. 6* (New York: Macmillan, 1987) 307 – 308.

[2] Mary Ann Beavis, *Jesus and Utopia: Looking for the Kingdom of God in the Roman World* (Minneapolis: Fortress Press, 2006) 103 ff.

[3] Raymond Brown, *The Gospel According to John*. AB, Vol. 2 (Garden City, New York: Doubleday & Company, Inc., 1966) cv ff.

[4] William D. Mounce, *The Analytical Lexicon to the Greek New Testament.* (Grand Rapids: Zondervan Publishing House, 1993).

[5] H. Ridderbos, *The Gospel of John: A Theological Commentary*, Tr. by John Vriend (Grand Rapids/Cambridge: William B. Eerdmans Publishing Company, 1997) 524; also Barrett, C.K., *The Gospel according to St. John: An Introduction with Commentary and Notes on the Greek Text.Second Edition* (Philadelphia: Westminster, 1978) 370,400; Brown (*John* 2, p.68) takes "if" in "if they kept my word they will keep yours also," as "to the degree that," which according to him has a purely negative meaning. It would then be translated as "as to the degree that they kept my word they will keep yours also (they have not kept mine). According to Rengstorf, "the fact that μαθηταὶ can be parallel to δοῦλοι (13:16; 15:20) is quite alien to later Judaism". Rengstorf. "μαθητής" *Theological Dictionary of the New Testament*, 4: 448 (415-461).

[6] Kemp, I.S., & J. J. Kanagaraj, *Gospel of John, Asia Bible Commentary* (Bangalore: Asia Theological Association, 2000) 290.

[7] G.R. Beasley-Murray, "John." *Word Biblical Commentary* (Texas: WACO, Word Books, 1987) 236.

[8] Barrett, *John, The Gospel according to St. John: An Introduction with Commentary and Notes on the Greek Text. Second Edition* (Philadelphia: Westminster, 1978) 285.

[9] Most, if not all, Western interpreters find this idea hard to accept, and keep emphasizing the idea of "realized eschatology" in John. Asian readers, particularly those living in India can easily understand this concept, probably because of the socio-economic condition of their country.

[10] Brown, *The Gospel According to John*, 660.

[11] Ridderbos, *John,* 516-517; cf. Brown, *John*, 660.

[12] Ridderbos, *John*, 517.

[13] According to Dodd, *Historical Tradition in the Fourth Gospel* (Cambridge Univ., 1963) p.144. v.21 ends the passage. Vv.22-23 is a later insertion.

[14] Brown, *John 2*, 1036.

[15] Ridderbos, *John*, p.642. For Temple (*John*, p.385), the commissioning, suggests a new form that had to be taken by the fellowship of the disciples with Jesus.

[16] A. J. Koestenberger, *The Missions of Jesus and the Disciples according to the Fourth Gospel* (Grand Rapids, Michgan/Cambridge: William B. Eerdman's Publishing Company, 1998) 191-92.

[17] See Brown, *John 2,* 1037; Barrett, *John*, 474.

[18] Ridderbos, *John*, 643.

[19] U. Schnelle, *Antidocetic Christology in the Gospel of John*, Tr. by Linda M. Maloney (Minneapolis: Fortress Press, 1992) 206.

[20] See G.T. Basker, *Interpreting Biblical Texts: John and his Tamil Readers* (New Delhi: ISPCK, 2016) 166.

[21] Basker, *Interpreting Biblical Texts,* 194.

[22] See Brown, *John 2*, pp.1037-38.

[23] Dodd, *Interpretation*, p.227.

[24] B. Griffiths, *Return to the Centre*, London: Collins, 1976, 30 f.

[25] *ibid.* 16.

[26] See Barrett, *John*, pp.71-72.

[27] Evelyn Underhill, *The Essentials of Mysticism and other Essays* (London & Toronto: J. M. Dent & Sons Ltd., New York: E.P. Dulton & Co., 1920) 41. She extensively uses Johannine texts to explain mysticism.

[28] Kanagaraj, *'Mysticism' in the Gospel of John*, 74.

[29] It is our feeling that E. Kaesemann (*The Testament of Jesus: A Study of the Gospel of John in the Light of Chapter 17*, London: SCM, pp..45f.) does not give any place to the human participation in Jesus and the Father, which comes out clearly in John 17:21, 23.

[30] Kaesemann, *The Testament of Jesus*, 22-23.

[31] Underhill, *The Essentials of Mysticism and other Essays*, 6.

[32] Abhishiktananda, *Hindu-Christian Meeting Point*, (trans. Sara Grant, New Delhi: ISPCK, 1976) 1f.

[33] See Basker, *Interpreting Biblical Texts*, 179.

Bibliography

Abhishiktananda, *Hindu-Christian Meeting Point*. Translated Sara Grant. New Delhi: ISPCK, 1976.

Barrett, C.K. *John, The Gospel according to St. John: An Introduction with Commentary and Notes on the Greek Text. Second Edition.* Philadelphia: Westminster, 1978.

Basker, G.T. *Interpreting Biblical Texts: John and his Tamil Readers*. New Delhi: ISPCK, 2016.

Beasley-Murray G.R., "John." *Word Biblical Commentary.* Texas: WACO, Word Books, 1987.

Beavis, Mary Ann. *Jesus and Utopia: Looking for the Kingdom of God in the Roman World.* Minneapolis: Fortress Press, 2006.

Brown, Raymond. *The Gospel According to John*. AB, Vol. 2. Garden City, New York: Doubleday & Company, Inc., 1966.

Eliade Mircea. ed. *Encyclopaedia of Religion* Vol. 6. New York: Macmillan, 1987.

Griffiths, B. *Return to the Centre*. London: Collins, 1976.

Kemp, I.S., & J. J. Kanagaraj. *Gospel of John, Asia Bible Commentary*. Bangalore: Asia Theological Association, 2000.

Koestenberger, A. J. *The Missions of Jesus and the Disciples according to the Fourth Gospel*. Grand Rapids, Michgan/Cambridge: William B. Eerdman's Publishing Company, 1998.

Mounce, William D. *The Analytical Lexicon to the Greek New Testament*. Grand Rapids: Zondervan Publishing House, 1993.

Rengstorf. "μαθητής" *Theological Dictionary of the New Testament*, 4: 448

Ridderbos H. *The Gospel of John: A Theological Commentary*. Translated by John Vriend. Grand Rapids/Cambridge: William B. Eerdmans Publishing Company, 1997.

Schnelle, Udo. *Antidocetic Christology in the Gospel of John*. Translated by Linda M. Maloney. Minneapolis: Fortress Press, 1992.

Underhill, Evelyn. *The Essentials of Mysticism and other Essays*. London & Toronto: J. M. Dent & Sons Ltd., New York: E.P. Dulton & Co., 1920.

12

Dining with the Detested

M. John Sunder

A borderless ecclesia can be envisioned in the pericope from Mark 2: 15-17 which portrays Jesus dinning with the marginalized. The ministry of Jesus in associating with sinners was a sign not only of the remission of sins but also of the presence of the one who can remit sin.[1] It was a phenomenal breakthrough in the prevailing social norms regarding the individuals' identity and placement. Besides challenging this prevailing social norm it also paved the way for socio-religious reformation.

Contextual Background

In an anticipation of the messianic banquet, when Jesus broke bread with the outcasts, he ate with them at his table as Messiah and extended to them fellowship with God. "Tax collectors and Sinners" are linked three times (2 Kings 15-17). Both terms represent groups that were ostracized from pious Jewish society; the former for political, ethical reasons and the latter for purely religious or cultic reasons. The TEV' translation for "sinners" explains the essential issue in a single word with the word "outcasts." The note in Mark 2: 15 that "there were many (social and religious outcasts) who followed him" doubtless declares not only Jesus' associates during his earthly life, but also the early Christian community from which this gospel emerged and for which it was written.

Dining with the Detested: Cultural and Religious Scenario

In the times of Jesus, the Jews who believed in purity of blood took pride in not eating with tax collectors and sinners (Mark 2:17).The disadvantaged and the marginalized were constantly labelled as "sinners" by the religiously and socially dominant people viz., Pharisees - a sect in Judaism. Jesus used the strategy of eating with those who were socially outcast. Eating together creates a kinship among those who share the meal together (Mk 2:.15). Inter-dining was the most effective and radically powerful tool to reiterate and integrate the excluded into the community (Mk 2:17). Eating together has to become a spontaneous cultural feature in the Indian social, religious and cultural structure to break the system of caste and untouchablity[2].

The whole passage illustrates Jesus' attitude towards outcasts and strikingly brings to the fore the amply attested fact that Jesus' concern for outcasts was a scandal to the religious authorities. The table fellowship (between Christians of Jewish and Gentile backgrounds) was a problem in the early church (cf. Acts 11:3; Gal 2:12); and it would have been crucial in the matter of Eucharistic table fellowship.[3] Jesus' association with sinners was a sign not only of the remission of sins but also the presence of the one who can remit sin. The early Christians were well aware that the saving call of Jesus had been to sinners, for whom he came into the world to summon them was to be with him in the messianic banquet.[4]

The issue centers on the fact that Jesus eats with outcasts. The question of table fellowship also foreshadows and reflects a concern among early Christians (see. Gal 2:12), which explains why the story was treasured. For pious Jews who kept a *Kosher* table, indiscriminate association with those who did not was unthinkable.[5] The Pharisees protest that Jesus mixes with sinners – with men and women who have deliberately excluded themselves from the people of God. They would obviously be indignant if Jesus, who claimed to teach and heal with God given authority, identified with such people, apparently indifferent to their violation of the commandments of God. If the early Christian community set aside the norms of table fellowship with outsiders, then it was because, they believed that the coming of Jesus had created a new situation in which the division between the so-called "righteous" and "sinners" no longer existed. A new division had however been created between those who respond to Jesus and those who reject him.[6]

The NIV is quite correct to put the word "sinners" in quotation marks to indicate that it is being used with an unusual meaning. The reference is not of immoral or irreligious persons but to those who, because of the necessity of spending all the time earning a bare subsistence were unable to keep the Law, especially oral Law, as the religious authorities thought they should. As a result the Scribes despised these "sinners". Hence a better translation would be in this case is "outcasts"

In Semitic society table fellowship was one of the most intimate expressions of friendship. For this reason the religious leaders could not understand how Jesus could be a religious person and dine with "bad characters." Jesus defied many of the conventions of his society which had developed during the period of Hasmonean independence (142-163 BC) and bound them to keeping such conventions, especially its oral interpretation, as taught by the Scribes. The name properly means "Separatists" and they may have been called such, because of their separation from the common people, the "sinners" of the present passage.[7]

Probably none of the Scribes were present at a banquet attended by "sinners" and another complaint was reported to Jesus. Jesus affirmed that his mission (note: "I have come...") was to call sinners not just to repentance, as in the Lukan parallel and in a copyist addition here (KJV, NKJV), but to full repentance in the kingdom of God. The love of Jesus for all kinds of sinners, his initiative in seeking them, his giving them full acceptance, and his desire to have close fellowship with them was a new and revolutionary element in religion and moral values.[8]

Jesus eagerly shocked good, religious people by associating with such detested. He not only recruited a tax-collector as a follower, but he dined sumptuously with other tax collectors and "sinners" at Levi's home. Jesus and his companions did not "sit" at the table, as many translations suggest, but *reclined.* The verbs indicate that his was not a normal meal but a banquet, at which the guests reclined as Romans did. In accordance with Palestinian village culture, such banquets were often semipublic events; an entrance to the courtyard was left open so that villagers could enter and observe how important guest like Jesus were being entertained. It was Jesus' participation in events like this that prompted the hostile comments: "Look, a glutton and a drunkard, a friend of tax collectors and sinners!" (Matt 11:19; Luke 7:34).[9]

The Pharisees' opposition to Jesus in this passage must be seen in relation to their goals; while they campaign for greater conformity with the Law, Jesus (in their view) encourages laxity by nobbling with religious scofflaws.[10] Jesus defends himself with a proverbial saying and a vocational statement. As a physician sent by God to Israel, he must concern himself primarily with those who leave God out of account. A similar thought is expressed with a different metaphor in Matt 15: 24, "I was sent only to the lost sheep of the house of Israel." Jesus' ministry to tax collectors and sinners is presented by Mark as evidence that Jesus personifies the good news of God.

Jesus enacted God's offer of mercy (Mk 2: 17) by associating with social and religious outcasts of his time. Tax collectors were considered dishonest and also ritually impure because of frequent contact with Gentiles. Jesus' acceptance of them shattered fundamental religious convictions and social conventions of his contemporaries.

The phrase "tax collectors and sinners", used three times in this short story, combines two nouns in a somewhat odd way, as though sinning was an occupation. Mark probably means "other sinners". It is often supposed that the term was used by the Pharisees to refer to "the people of the land" i.e. all those who did not keep the Pharisaic ideal purity (which would mean the great majority of Jews). It is more likely to refer to notorious sinners who deliberately violated the Law, and who were thus treated as religious and social outcasts.[11] They ate with Jesus and his disciples. The Pharisees, in doctrine, were more progressive than the priestly party of the Sadducees, believing both in the resurrection of the dead and in angels, and in this respect they were closer to the position of Jesus.[12]

It is likely that this story was used to justify the practice of Jewish and Gentile Christians eating together, but this does not necessarily exclude the possibility that such an incident took place in the ministry of Jesus himself.

Why does he eat with tax collectors and sinners? Few of the reasons could be that it may not have been tidy or that he might have come into contact with unclean garments or dishes. However, instead the Pharisees protested that Jesus was eating with tax collectors and sinners, who deliberately excluded themselves from the people of God. Mark's first readers saw the relevance of this story for their context, for many of them had been outsiders –perhaps "sinners", perhaps Gentiles.[13] The early Christian community came to set aside the regulations regarding table fellowship with outsiders, because they became aware that the coming of Jesus had created a new situation in which there was no division between the so-called "righteous" and "sinners"

The attitude expressed in the saying seems to be as characteristic of Jesus as righteous indignation was of the Scribes. Jesus' own power to bring forgiveness is understood as greater than the power of uncleanness to contaminate.[14] The Pharisees and Sadducees are seen here operating within the frame work of social and religious notions of purity and pollution. On the other hand, the so-called sinners and tax collectors, it is their inclination to resist the religious domination and subjugation. Apart from these two groups who are engaged in juxtaposition to each other, it is the approach of Jesus which is interpreted as being involved in the ministry of striving for expanding the boundaries of kingdom of God and thus the borderless church.

Purity and Pollution

This is the raw reality of Indian society - a notion on which the people operate. This notion is based on Hindu religious writings and is very much active and continues to be exploited by religious fanatics. This notion is causing religious animosity and social disorder quite often between castes particularly the upper castes and the Dalits. This is the basis for the practice of untouchability and hence the oppression and subjugation of the outcasts. The notion of purity of race and culture sustains the psychological borders adhered to by caste Hindus. The futile exercise of keeping up this pseudo identity and image has become offensive and this process is resulting in the oppression and death of Dalits. It is a similar understanding based on which Pharisees criticised Jesus of eating with the "sinners" and "tax collectors". Jesus is engaged in showing the model of eschatological banquet in this process. It is in this engagement Jesus is showing the way for a borderless church.

Borders Within

The Indian society has to face the challenge of discriminations based on class and caste. The problem of patriarchy is still prevalent in the minds and attitude of the people in general. The social evils such as dowry deaths, domestic violence and male chauvinism continue to persist. This situation is no better in the Church life. It is the challenging task of the Christian community to counter these practices and transform the mindset of its members to resist and henceforth cross these borders within which hinder the life and witness of the community. The values of the kingdom of God are to be nourished to resist the domination of the prevalent social order which invisibly supports the borders which exploit humanity.

Towards Borderless εκκλεσια

Jesus, in his ministry aimed for a borderless society preaching about the kingdom of God: To be humble and have a child-like heart which transcends all the borders. Dining with people who became the victims of borders is a symbolic activity towards a borderless church. Apostle Paul writes of a borderless society to the Church in Galatia with this theological understanding in the first century that, there is neither Jew nor Gentile, slave nor free; male nor female for you are one in Christ (Gal 3:28). It is a challenge and imperative on our part to go beyond borders and strive for borderless εκκλεσια. May God help us.

Endnotes

[1] Wilfrid Harrington, O.P, *Mark* (Minnesota: The Liturgical Press,1991), 32.

[2] Sr. Maria Goretti, F. S. Monodeep Daniel and A. Maria Arul Raja SJ, *Dalit Bible Commentary - The Gospel According to Mark* (New Delhi: Centre for Dalit /Subaltern Studies, 2009), 42.

[3] Wilfrid Harrington, O.P. *Mark* (Minnesota: The Liturgical Press, 1973), 32.

[4] Ibid, 32.

[5] Lamer Williamson, Jr. *Interpretation Mark* (Louisville: John Knox Press, 1973), 68.

[6] Mona D. Hooker, The Gospel According to Saint Mark (London: Hendrickson Publishers, 1997), 96.

[7] Ibid, 97.

[8] Ibid, 63.

[9] Douglas R. A., Hare Mark (Kentucky: Westminster John Knox Press, 1996), 39.

[10] Ibid, 40.

[11] M. Morna D. Hooker, The Gospel According to Saint Mark (London: Hendrickson Publishers, 1996), 95.

[12] Ibid., 96.

[13] See E.P. Sanders, *Jesus and Judaism*, (Philadelphia: Fortress Press, 1985), 174-211.

[14] Ibid, 97.

Bibliography

Goretti, Sr. Maria, F.S. Monodeep Daniel, A. Maria Arul Raja SJ. *Dalit Bible Commentary - The Gospel*

According to Mark. New Delhi: Centre for Dalit /Subaltern Studies, 2009.

Hare, Douglas R. A. Mark. Kentucky: Westminster John Knox Press, 1996.

Harrington O.P, Wilfrid. *Mark.* Minnesota: The Liturgical Press, 1991.

Hooker, Mona D. The Gospel According to Saint Mark. London: Hendrickson Publishers, 1997.

Sanders, E.P. *Jesus and Judaism*. Philadelphia: Fortress Press, 1985.

Williamson, Lamer Jr. *Interpretation* Mark. Louisville: John Knox Press, 1973.

13

Jeremiah's Letter to the Exiled Community:

From Captivated Faith Community to Borderless Community

K. Sagar Sundar Raj

Transforming the borders from enmity to intercultural learning and living with other faiths is a difficult thing to imagine. Using opportunities especially in adverse situations to be a transformed community is a huge challenge. But the Bible envisages a transformed and reformed life even during times of conflict and it helps us understand and reshape our human relationships and reaffirm our faith accordingly.

Being known as a place of peace and intolerance, India has earned a global reputation for its communal harmony, coexistence and living together with many faiths. However, in recent times India's image has been tarnished by a dominant culture of the nation. A dominant majoritarian culture is constantly trying to create the façade of a mono-culture by destroying diversified cultures and the ethos of interfaith learning. Being a great example for independence through non-violence, in the last few years however India is turning towards intolerance towards minorities. The Church in India is one of the victims of this rising phenomenon, along with other minorities. In this situation, Church has to face the problem and answer threats which question its faith and mission. This is the impetus for the Church to assert its roots where it is being projected as a mission from outside. Church has to come out of its comfort zone to transform itself in order to witness in the country it exists.

The call from the prophet Jeremiah to the exiled community in Jeremiah chapter 29, to come out of its comfort zone and "seek shalom of the city" to which they were deported to was a radical move. Jeremiah's letter to the exilic community changed their understanding of an enemy nation – Babylon. The letter helped the Jewish community transform themselves to become an open community and invited them to a new attitude towards living in a foreign land. I believe this message of Jeremiah will also help us, the Church in South India, to transform the borders of Church to become Christ communities in the midst of our present challenges that place us sometimes in hostile situations.

Socio-Political Situation of the Exiled Community (Jeremiah 29:7)

Jews were captured and sent to Babylon. However the number of the people sent seems to be a reasonable figure.1 Among 4,600 exiles, many represented the political, ecclesiastical, and intellectual leadership of the country. They had the capacity to reshape future of Israel. Many scholars defend the comfortable life of the exiled community in Babylon. But this belittles the hardships of Jews who struggled in captivity at Babylon. According to John Bright they were transported to southern Mesopotamia not far from Babylon, but were not dispersed among the local population and rather placed in separate settlements.[2] Biblical and Babylonian documents reveal that the Jewish community was settled in the city of Nippur, Kabaru-canal (River Chebar) along with other conquered and exiled groups. Many feel that this kind of settlement itself was a way of working out the wholeness or *shalom* of Babylon.[3] It would not have been possible for the newly exiled community to adapt themselves to the required situation unless someone forced them to do so.

In this scenario, Jeremiah's words of direction guided them to reshape their faith and life according to the emerging and required situation. He becomes a force of transformation for them. His letter brings new force for them to become a transforming community. According to the historical and political situation of that time it would have taken tremendous effort for the exiled community to transform themselves rapidly. For this reason Jeremiah was also attacked by the Nabis who were deported to Babylon and who were proclaiming false messages of imminent return. The faith and lifestyle of the exiled Jewish community was challenged by the dominant culture of Babylon.4 However, though a minority they became effective catalysts in the midst of the community they were deported to and made to live. Moreover this adaptation of the Jewish community to be effective members of the Babylonian community also contributed to the growth of the nation of their exile - Babylon. Even in a situation where they were small in number and living amidst an alien culture, they were able to gather together as a community in order to remember Yahweh and pray for their deliverance. They probably organised within their community under their elders for self-administration, but also contributed constructively under the Babylonian imperial administration.[5]

Prophetic Call to Be a Wider Community to Transcend Borders

> "But seek the welfare (shalom) of the city when I have sent you into exile, and pray to the Lord on its behalf" (Jeremiah 29:7).

Jeremiah's letter in chapter 29 begins with God's instructions to those in exile to accept the new life situation in Babylonia and to build, live and make families there. The activities they could carry out are mentioned in Jer 29: 5–6, where they are exhorted to establishing a new home, indicating that it was fairly long term i.e. for at least two generations Babylonia should be treated as home. The advice to seek the welfare of the city and to pray to the Lord on its behalf anticipates the prayer for the government that appears as part of the Torah service for Sabbath and the festivals. The rhetoric of this verse is intended to shock as most people would have expected the words "And seek the welfare of the city" to refer to Jerusalem, not to Babylon. But Jeremiah made no reference to Jerusalem but only to Babylon. We can be sure of this because Jeremiah had been forbidden to pray for a salvation oracle for Jerusalem (Jer 14:11–12). Through this letter, Jeremiah brings out a new exilic theology of accepting others and a new culture for the exilic community by teaching them how to live with others in a foreign land.[6]

Jeremiah's letter seems to be a command. Because the words in Jer 29:7 דרש (darash) "seek," and פלל (phalal) "pray for," are in the imperative. Therefore Jeremiah commands and charges the Jewish exiles with the message that they were to modify and transform their life in their situation which created such an opportunity. He teaches them to settle there and not destroy the opportunities of learning it provided and to seek the welfare of the city and pray for it. Though Jewish community was probably preoccupied with returning due to their uneasy new circumstances and loss of everything familiar, Jeremiah changes their plans and perspective through his letter. In this changed socio-political and religious scenario, Jeremiah calls the *gola* community to be tolerant towards other nations and new cultures and "forbids them to attempt anything against the public peace while they were subjects to the king of Babylon."[7] Moreover, he advises them to consider it an opportunity provided by God.

The prophet's advice to the Diaspora community was challenging and radical in the context of extreme and fundamental views that were being spread by false prophets. But Jeremiah declines their fake and temporal comforting words and calls the exilic community to cling to the will of God which transforms them. He guides them to use the new opportunities afforded to them for living and growing. Though his prophetic message was radical and could have been considered anti-national, he delivered those on behalf of Yahweh to His people for the betterment of their future and of the nation they had been sent to. The purpose for Yahweh's people to experience in Babylon is foreseen in the letter. While delivering this message Jeremiah simultaneously asserts God's sovereign power and purpose for all nations of the world.[8]

Bearing the Babylonian burden of captivity and praying for their masters under the sufferings of the captivity was a tough task. The characteristic change expected among the Jews was to pray for the enemies who had brutally destroyed their country and their future. Jews generally prayed for the destruction of the Babylon (Jer 51:35). However now they were challenged to submit to the opportunity given by God in order to reveal the true nature of religion and true will of God:

> This was, we may believe, the hardest command of all. To refrain from all curses and imprecations, even from such as came from the lips of those who hung their harps on the willows by the waters

of Babylon (Psalms 137), to pray for the shalom and prosperity of the city where they were eating the bread of captivity - this surely required an almost superhuman patience.[9]

Captivated Faith to Universalistic Faith and Hospitality

The command from Jeremiah might have evoked many questions and doubts among the faithful Jewish community because of the intent and approach towards the enemy nation that Jeremiah advised. Jeremiah tried to eliminate doubts and confusion among people who had lost their homeland and holy city. He instilled a new spirit among them to accommodate themselves to the new pattern and culture of Babylon by showing motherly love towards the exiled community. Indeed, the prophet's letter to the exiled community helped renew their faith in Yahweh and live in Babylon.

According to the socio-historical evidences the Jewish community participated in the life and administration of Babylon and contributed to its growth. This shows that Jeremiah's call caused them to change their negative approach towards the enemy nation though the faith they had hitherto held to was challenged. Babylonian exilic situation brought radical change in the life and faith of Israelites. According to Erhard S. Gerstenberger,

> "....at the same time a kind of ecumenical Jewish Community developed which extended from Babylonia to Egypt and perhaps beyond. Between these two poles, local and universal socialization, the life of the followers of Yahweh developed in the sixth and fifth centuries BCE. The opportunities and disadvantages arose in this specific contextualization of the religious community."[10]

In this situation, captivated faith transformed into universality. The understanding about God's presence in a foreign land changed as they recognized the presence of Yahweh in their suffering and in the plans of deliverance (Isa 45:5-7). The exiled community affirmed that they were sent to exile due to divine judgment and the purpose of God. "The world is to learn from the sufferings of the exiles and from their return and restoration that the ways of God are good and the he alone has power to save."[11]

It was not a hospitable situation for the exiled community in Babylon to become *athithi* (guests). But they were called to offer *athithya* (hospitality) to the *athitheya* (the hosts)[12]. Instead of *dwesha* (enemity) to an enemy (shathru), the Jewish community was called to offer *athithya* (hospitality) to the *athitheya* (hosts). The prophetic command to seek the welfare and pray for the city was the duty given to them in order to exhibit inclusive, peace loving and non-triumphalist values becoming of the people of God. Being God's people they were called to take the place of *athitheya* (hosts) although they were there as captives and not as "guests", in a foreign land and to offer *athithya* (hospitality) to their enemies who had exiled them. This radical change in roles and attitudes gave an opportunity to the exilic community to be God's community and share countercultural values of life, love and peace in a situation where praying for death, hate and destruction of their enemies would have been what was expected. In such a reversal they were called to become *athitheya* and be hospitable even in a conflict situation.

However, this radical phenomenon rapidly disappeared from the Jewish community soon after their restoration from exile and reformation of the nation under the Torah by Ezra and Nehemiah. It is evident that during exile though their faith transformed with fresh perspectives of inclusivity in the midst of plural faiths and peoples, they became more communal and fundamental in their identity formation due to the spiritual leadership in the later years of exile and after exile.

From Temple to Synagogue, from Synagogue to Church, from Church to Where?

Surely, Babylonian exilic period caused reform in the idea of worship and centrality of Israel. Center was destroyed and scattered communities came to the fore when the exiled community was deported to Babylon. In order to remember and protect their religious traditions *gola* community met in Synagogues. The Synagogue transformed into a new place of learning and defining their faith. Synagogues spread over Babylon, later on after exile they appeared in Palestine too.

Synogogues played a key role in holding the Jewish faith intact and were also places to discuss the resurrected Christ and the spread of the gospel. In the Christian faith, the Church has taken place of the synagogue but it has forgotten for what it has been called. There cannot be barriers among its communities when it has been established in the name of Christ. Sometimes in order to "defend" its faith, the Church seems to be losing its vision. It is in this situation that the call for being and becoming a borderless Church is an imperative. The Church was meant to be an open community being known for its contributions in spreading the gospel of love, justice, shalom and integrity. This is the purpose the Church should strive hard for. Perhaps conflicts may be imminent. But the Church should not forget to embrace the other, to be open to new cultures, to share herself with and for others and be hospitable to others in order to live out being Christ Communities. Being a called out community, Church must inculcate the values of Christ.

Jeremiah's Call to be a Borderless Community: Borderless Church

The Church in India resembles the exiled community of Babylon. Undoubtedly the Church in India has contributed to the development of the nation. However, its witness and presence is questioned by the dominant powers. There are times that the Indian Church has been projected as anti-national in several ways. Amidst all such oppositions and labelling historically the Church has continued to serve for the betterment of humanity.

But in recent times, due to threats from external forces the Church seems to be creating a comfort zone for itself and for its missionary activities. In this regard, the Indian Church which tends to live within its four walls as an established institution has to change its approach towards the community that lives outside the walls. It has to transform its boundaries. Church's true nature lies in accepting the newness and revealing its identity. Here becoming *athitheya* (hospitable) even in the hostile situation is significant. New situations create new opportunities for the mission of the Church.

Jeremiah's challenge to the *gola* community is also a challenge for the changing Church in India. Church is changing because it is becoming comfortable and leaning towards mono-culture. Such a tendency may be because of the perceived and felt threats from the dominant culture. But Church should recall its calling and purpose. Jeremiah's challenge to the Church is to seek the welfare of the country and pray for it. Call to love enemies and pray for those who curse you are new laws of the early Church (Luke 6:27-28; Romans 12:20). Church always face threat from within and from outside. But being body of Christ, the Church should open the doors of *athithya* (hospitality) to everyone like Christ gave *athithya* (hospitality) to everyone to make them part of the *Kindom of God*. Love and righteousness of the Church should be evidenced in its *athithya*. When Church opens the door for everyone and gives *athithya* (hospitality) even amidst hostile situations it will be a chance to create borderless communities.

Creating atmosphere of love and care amidst the opposition and trouble is the real challenge for the church that is called not to be served but to serve.

The existence of the Church in India is questioned by many critics from the earlier days. But Church or community of Christ is in the world though not of the world. Church will become community of Christ when it establishes the values of Christ's teaching through its practice. Church was always suffering community. It always took side with the suffering. Now being a voice of the downtrodden and marginalized the Church has to reinvent its presence in the multi religious context of India. Opening our doors to opportunities for new learning with others even with so-called "enemies", will usher in a radical change in the Church.

To conclude, indeed it is a privilege to be part of Church of South India's 70 years Celebration. It has been an opportunity to be part this important discussion on the vision of a borderless Church from a biblical perspective. Church of South India's 70 year existence in India is yet another opportunity for the Church to establish the *Kindom of God* on this earth. Even amidst pain and suffering we should not forget to contribute to the nation's growth. In a rapidly changing scenario, we should not seclude ourselves from others and from the opportunities for learning and sharing that such interactions provide. We are also commemorating 500 years of the Reformation journey. These 500 years provide rich experiences that call us to renew our faith in God and to open our doors to find spaces of learning that we can utilize for spreading love and showing human care. When we open ourselves to the newness to become a wider community then we will surely be part of Christ communities which we are called out to be.

Endnotes

[1] John Bright, *A History of Israel* (London: SCM Press Ltd, 1972), 345-346.

[2] John Bright, *A History of Israel* (London: SCM Press Ltd, 1972), 345-346.

[3] Keown G. L. Scalise P. J. Smothers T.G., *Word Biblical Commentary, Volume 27: Jeremiah 26-52* (Dallas, Texas: Word Books, Publisher), 1998.

[4] Klaus Koch, *The Prophets: The Babylonian and Persian Periods*, Vol 2 (London: SCM Press Ltd, 1980), 57.

[5] Erhard S. Gerstenberger, *Theologies of the Old Testament*, translated by John Bowden (Minneapolis: Fortress Press, 2002), 209.

[6] Keown G. L. Scalise P. J. Smothers T.G., *Word Biblical Commentary, Volume 27: Jeremiah 26-52* (Dallas, Texas: Word Books, Publisher) 1998.

[7] Though the king was considered a heathen, an idolater, an oppressor, and an enemy to God and God's people, while he gave them protection, they must pay him allegiance, and live peaceable lives under him, in all godliness and honesty, not plotting to shake off his yoke, but patiently leaving it to God in due time to work deliverance for them *(The Book of Jeremiah-Matthew Henry Notes).*

[8] Kondasingu Jesurathnam, *Exploring Dalit Liberative Hermanuetics in India & the World: Based on an Ancient Hebrew Prophet, Jeremiah of Anathoth* (New Delhi: Christian World Imprints, 2015), 267.

[9] Rev. E. H. Plumptre, "Jeremiah" in *Ellicott's Commentary for English Readers* (ed. D.D. Charles John Ellicott; London, Paris, New Ayork & Melborurne: Late Lord Bishop Of Gloucester Cassell And Company, Limited, 1905) < https://biblehub.com/jeremiah/29-7.htm> (23 October 2017)

[10] Erhard S. Gerstenberger, *Theologies of the Old Testament*, translated by John Bowden (Minneapolis: Fortress Press, 2002), 209.

[11] Peter R. Ackroyd, *The People of the Old Testament* (Madras: The Christian Literature Society,1981), 119-125.

[12] These are Kannada words. Kannada is a language spoken in the South Indian state of Karnataka from where the author hails.

Bibliography

Ackroyd, Peter R. *The People of the Old Testament.* Madras: The Christian Literature Society,1981.

Bright, John *A History of Israel.* London: SCM Press Ltd, 1972,

Gerald, Keown, Pamela Scalise, Thomas G. Smothers. *Word Biblical Commentary, Volume 27: Jeremiah 26-52.* Dallas, Texas: Word Books, 1998.

Gerstenberger, Erhard S. *Theologies of the Old Testament*. Translated by John Bowden. Minneapolis: Fortress Press, 2002.

Jesurathnam, Kondasingu *Exploring Dalit Liberative Hermanuetics in India & the World: Based on an Ancient Hebrew Prophet, Jeremiah of Anathoth*. New Delhi: Christian World Imprints, 2015.

Koch, Klaus. *The Prophets: The Babylonian and Persian Periods*. Vol 2. London: SCM Press Ltd, 1980.

London, Paris, New Ayork & Melborurne: Late Lord Bishop Of Gloucester Cassell And Company, Limited, 1905. < https://biblehub.com/jeremiah/29-7.htm> (23 October 2017)

Plumptre, E. H. "Jeremiah." in *Ellicott's Commentary for English Readers* (ed. D.D. Charles John Ellicott ??????????????????????????????????

14

Breaking Borders Within and Without:

Naomi-Ruth-Boaz Model

M. Jyothi John Sunder

William Temple said, "The Church is the only institution that exists primarily for the benefit of those who are not its members". Throughout biblical history this theme has been a continuing thread. Abraham was blessed for the sole purpose of being a blessing to all the nations of the earth. Israel was called to be a light to the nations and the Church was called to extend the borders of the Kingdom of God. The church has been involved in doing this in over the centuries. However when its own members become captive to the rigid boundaries within and without, it becomes necessary for the church once again to seriously rethink about being and becoming a borderless church.

The protestant Church as it emerged and took shape from the womb of reformation, has been undergoing several changes that had far reaching influence on within the church and without during the last 500 years. The protest led by Martin Luther against the gospel being bound in the hands of the papacy moulded European secular history and church history worldwide. The bitter wars in the name of religion between the Catholics and Protestants on theological understandings, explanations and interpretations of the Bible that led to bloodshed in the 16th century have brought in more divisions and boundaries within and without the church. The wars in the name of religion continue worldwide and the boundaries continue to exist, some boundaries became stronger and some weaker.

The formation and journey of CSI embracing thirty-three big churches that existed then with the motto that "they all may be one", has culminated in 70 years now. This effort in 1947 was a breathtakingly bold step towards a borderless church. Its very name is inclusive. Since those path-breaking beginnings the agenda of its life and ministries have worked towards breaking borders within and without, to test those borders constantly, and improve ways to embrace all. Once again we attempt to do this seriously as we celebrate 500 years of reformation. Such an attempt is a hopeful sign of things to come as reviewing of boundaries will certainly lead to either removing or breaking the boundaries which are regressive and to extending or redrawing certain boundaries for its progressive future journey.

This paper attempts to understand the timely creation of borders by God and also their removal by God with a definite purpose and its implications for humanity. It also attempts to understand how human beings have drawn, redrawn and interpreted borders.

God created the world with all its complexities and differences thus creating various borders. Every single creature is different from the other. The implications of these differences among the species and between the species certainly influence all the creatures. The creation of borders/ boundaries was for a definite purpose. There are several instances in the biblical text where the boundaries were reviewed and dealt with by God and human beings that would serve as guiding principles as we deal with our borders in the process of becoming Christ Communities.

God's Timely Decisions: The Tower of Babel (Gen 11:1-9) and the Pentecost (Acts 2:5-12)

The Lord created and brought human beings, Adam and Eve, together for companionship. However, when people multiplied, the Lord saw that the wickedness of human beings was great and the earth was filled with violence (Gen 6:11-12), that grieved God. Hence God decided to bring an end to all flesh (Gen 6:13). He did so through the great flood but saved the family of Noah. Soon after the great flood God made a unilateral covenant with Noah and all of creation that he would never destroy the creatures with floods. This demanded nothing on the part of the creatures (Gen 9:8–16). After the flood, Noah's descendants increased on the face of the earth. They all had one language and began to build the tower of Babel to make a name for themselves. The Lord saw the absolute unanimity of all the people. He felt that such unity might not deter them from doing anything they purposed – either good or bad. God decided that the human beings would incline towards doing that which displeases the Lord and hence God chose to confuse their language so that they would not understand one another's speech (Gen 11:7). From God's perspective scattering people all over the face of the earth was the impending need of the hour in human history. Language borders were created by God.

Several theologians opine that the purpose of the Babel narrative is to give the aetiology of the languages on the earth but the reason for this is explained very well in the text. It is definitely for the advancement of humanity from God's view point. However, at a much later stage in history, the Lord spoke through the prophet Isaiah and made known his will that he would reverse it (Isa 2:1-5). God decisively obliterated the boundaries of languages on the day of Pentecost (Acts 2:5-12). At Pentecost people of different languages heard the gospel in their own mother tongue. That was the need of the hour then in the salvific history of the humankind.

Therefore, the time, context, and the purpose of either becoming borderless or redrawing the borders, are extremely important for the progress of the church in becoming Christ communities. The biblical idea that the people of god and the church exist for the sole purpose of being a blessing for all, should be the guiding principle to identify, review, and test carefully the borders and the borderless areas within the church in the contemporary times. The church has to be engaged in this onerous task constantly.

Naomi - Ruth - Boaz Model: A Borderless Community Within and Without

One of the perfect paradigms for becoming a borderless church could be the way a Moabite woman was embraced into the genealogy of Jesus Christ, in other words, into the very community of Christ.

The Lord delivered the people of Israel from the bondage of Pharaoh and gave them the book of the law. Obedience to the law would transform the whole community as God's treasured possession out of all the peoples of the earth and they would become a priestly kingdom and a holy nation (Exod 19: 5–6). The Lord had drawn borders for the people of Israel through the book of law and the Israelite community was expected to live within the borders of the law.

There arose a situation where it became necessary to break open the boundary of the Law for the sake of a Moabite woman. Naomi was more concerned about the welfare of her daughters in law than the levirate marriage law (Deut 25:5–10). It was the need of the hour then. Naomi took an extraordinary decision regarding her widowed daughters in law. She had thorough knowledge about the levirate law that her community was bound by. It was the prevalent norm and custom as well as religious requirement to follow the levirate law. As per the literal letter of the law, Ruth and Orpha would have to lead miserable lives with uncertain hopes. The poor widow Naomi dared to cross the border within. Naomi gave a wonderful interpretation of the levirate law to Ruth and Orpha and advised them to return to their father's homes, remarry and live happily. Naomi had redrawn the border by fulfilling the spirit of the law. The interpretation of the law should protect, sustain and enrich life.

In biblical history there were always people who thought of existing boundaries and allowed it to be broken or broke them themselves for progression and empowerment. It is always difficult to go against the existing norms and power structures. Hence it becomes imperative to understand the context of the existing situation. The Mosaic law was the context of Ruth's times. Naomi takes a bold stand towards remodeling the Mosaic law. She found a way out from the existing border in advising her widowed daughters in law to remarry. This was a very timely, practical, just and acceptable way out.

Naomi was interpreting the Mosaic law in a new way. Ruth was a Moabite yet Naomi explains the law to Ruth (Ruth 1:11-12). At a much later period Jesus Christ also interprets the law several times in the same way during his life on the earth. The law prohibited Israelites to marry aliens (Exod 34: 15–16; Deut

7: 3–4). In spite of that law, Naomi and Boaz along with their community followed the spirit of the law and thereby opened the borders for an outsider. The borders within were crossed in the case of Orpha and the borders without were crossed in the case of Ruth. Ruth entered into a new border of an honorable that placed her in the genealogy of Jesus Christ.

There might be the need for new borders and extension of old borders and erosion of existing borders for a borderless church to evolve. Borders need to be constantly tested if the presence of the church has to be dynamic. In India the church has always been borderless for those not yet belonging to it. It invites and embraces all irrespective of caste, class and gender. There has been no deterrent for anyone for entry into the Church in India since first century. In fact, theologians and missionaries struggled to find ways and means to invite all. In this process they proceeded with indigenisation of worship and development of Indian Christian theology. But, once people enter the church, they are bound by borders within the church. While on the one hand these borders may enforce responsible discipline within the church, on the other hand they might subjugate those inside it.

Ruth, an alien woman was embraced by the Israelite community that became the Christ community. Ruth also embraced the Israelite community in total. She tells Naomi with commitment, "Do not urge me to leave you or to return from following you. For where you go I will go, where you lodge I will lodge. Your God is my God and your people are my people"(Ruth 1:16). That led to the formation of the Christ community and the lineage leading to the birth of Christ. This embracing is mutual and total from within and without on the part of those who invite and those who accept.

However, our contemporary church history conveys that the prevalent Indian patriarchal culture and mindset has entered the church and still dominates the church at large. Gender discrimination is a reality in the Indian church. Although gender discrimination within CSI is overcome to an extent because of few people with broad understanding and bold interpretation of biblical texts, CSI is no exception to prevalence of gender discrimination. Gender justice and gender equality are still a distant reality for a majority of women in the church.

The very serious implications of interpreting female as a lesser being has led to great harm to women in the world in general and to women in India in particular. Female foeticide, infanticide, dowry deaths and related violence, bride burning and suicides have become specific heart rending problems in India. So ingrained is such conditioning that women dread giving birth to a girl baby. The statistics related to these problems are alarming. The church being blind and silent to this stark reality amounts to the church promoting all these problems. The gender discrimination and inequality in the Indian Church is directly responsible for destroying the lives to millions of women. The church would be positively borderless when it addresses this issue because there is neither Jew nor Greek, there is neither slave nor free, there is no male or female for you are all one in Christ (Gal.3:28). As the Indian church, CSI in particular, is in the process of progressing towards becoming Christ Community, the issues of half of its members, that is women, ought to be addressed at a greater pace at all levels in order to provide gender justice and equality to all women.

15

Kingdom of God as a Paradigm for Borderless Church

P. Victor Paul

Time and space dictates emerging challenges that need to be tackled prophetically with priority and concern for those sidelined. Those sidelined or those in the margins are those deprived of their rights and privileges. The more mission expand the more borders are also created within the mission. The church in such a context is called to be the prophetic presence not with its established boundaries but as a borderless entity. Only a borderless church can accommodate communities undergoing oppression and hardships. The paradigm of Kingdom of God reflects this possibility of a borderless church that prioritizes those on the margins. This paper intends to explore the possibility of Kingdom of God to serve the purpose of the church becoming borderless.

Kingdom of God

Kingdom of God is the very core of Jesus' ministry. It was on this central theme that Jesus developed a new radical world view. This new world view emerged as a challenge to the exploitative and oppressive structures of the time bringing much needed corrective interventions. This was visible through the miracles performed by Jesus, his narration regarding the kingdom of God through the parables and his symbolic actions that portrayed the reconciling ministry. The symbolic actions were radical as we can see Jesus' association and fellowship with the people who were considered by the dominants and the moral societal code dictators as sinners and outcasts of the society. This radical intervention by Jesus introduced God's saving love into the reach of human experience. It brought about healing and reconciliation. His association with sinners and outcasts of the society were the manifestation of kingdom that he preached and practiced.[1] Therefore Kingdom of God is the idea of God, and the term Kingdom indicates that specific aspect, attribute or activity of God, in which he is revealed as king or sovereign Lord of his people, or of the universe which he created.[2]

Kingdom of God and Eschatology

The kingdom of God demands that God intervene in society with justice and equality. This in a literal way could be attributed to Gods reign in the lives of the people. This aspect of Kingdom of God is connected to "realized eschatology,"[3] as C. H Dodd rightly argues that for Jesus the kingdom was present. Jesus taught the reality of kingdom as realized in his own ministry. This realized eschatology could be read closely with the messianic expectation of the vulnerable community. But Joachim Jeremias affirms the present time along with the future drawing inspiration especially from the parabolic teaching of Jesus thereby understanding eschatology in the process of realization or as the realization of eschatology as a continuing process. Hence as a salvific reality the kingdom of God is the eschatological blessing of salvific deeds leading to liberation. Hence we can affirm that kingdom of God is a present reality with future implications.

Kingdom of God and the Marginalized Community

Jesus' inauguration of the Kingdom was a radical outcome of the response to the situation of people who were impoverished and exploited. The religious aristocracy and the secular aristocracy feast on the fat of the land created a rural proletariat of landless and often unemployed labourers.[4] Hence it is to such a marginalized people that the Kingdom of God was proclaimed by Jesus. However kingdom itself is an imperialistic terminology, according to Carter, God's empire (Kingdom) liberates and protects people from oppressive structures, relationships and powers which usurp God's role and claim. It stablishes God's Life-giving and just order in place.[5] The Kingdom of God therefore has a special concern for the marginalized, as against the imperial and social power structures. It is to them - the poor, the exploited, the socially outcast - that the kingdom belongs; a kingdom in which they found the reversal of their lot. And the presence of this kingdom was demonstrated in the merciful and transformative ministry of Jesus especially among the poor and the desperate and is continued. Jesus' understanding of the Kingdom of God can be perceived as a norm to conceptualize a borderless Church in the contemporary world.

A Borderless Church

The contemporary world also depicts a similar situation as that of Jesus' time with emerging challenges and possibilities. In order to tackle these challenges and extract the possibilities there is a need to have a rethinking in mission and ministerial aspects. The Church as the body of Christ and sojourner in the mission of God needs to have a re-visitation of its praxis. This re-visitation calls for a church which is borderless as the suffering community is found in the borders or in the margins. These margins call for the reign of God out of their bitter experience. The margins call for a new and reviving life for which the Church needs to have a different perspective of shattering its own borders.

To be a church without borders demands radical and self-critical appraisal; It also demands a self-emptying act to cater to the needs of the margins dictated not by the center but which emerges out of the margins. This borderless church must empower the margins, resist the authoritative and oppressive authorities of the time and should, more importantly, engage with and embrace the margins to have a renewed ecclesia. This renewed ecclesia is the paradigm of the kingdom of God. It is a dynamic movement flavoring the world by becoming the salt and showing new ways of engagements by emitting the necessary light in the existing world. Hence the church by following the model of Kingdom of God transforms itself into a much needed antidote for the margins to come out of oppressive structures and also provides the aspect of hope and good news. Therefore the Church needs to be the transforming presence ensuring the continuing presence of the reign of God.

Conclusion

To be a prophetic and transformative presence one needs to affirm the very essence of the Kingdom of God as proclaimed and practiced by Jesus Christ. It has the necessary aspects of the present and eschatological hope. This paradigm is a challenge to become a borderless Church. It serves as the best model for the Church in the challenges of the time and ensures the liberation of those oppressed and marginalized.

Endnotes

[1] Dennis C. Dulling, "Kingdom of God/Kingdom of Heaven," *Anchor Bible Dictionary*, Vol. 4 (ed. David N Freedman; New York: Doubleday, 1992), 57.

[2] C. H. Dodd, *The Parables of Kingdom* (New York: Charles Scribner's Sons, 1961), 21-22.

[3] C. H. Dodd, *The Parables of Kingdom*, 115.

[4] George N. Soares Prabhu, "Jesus and Social Justice," in *Jesus For Our Times: Towards a Spirituality of Social Action* (Manila: FABC Office of Human Development, 1986), 36.

[5] Warren Carter, *Mathew and Margins* (Bangalore: Theological Publication in India, 2007), 93.

Bibliography

Carter, Warren. *Matthew and Margins.* Bangalore: Theological Publication in India, 2007.

Dodd, C. H. *The Parables of Kingdom.* New York: Charles Scribner's Sons, 1961.

Dulling, Dennis C. "Kingdom of God/Kingdom of Heaven" in *Anchor Bible Dictionary,* Vol. 4. Edited by

David N Freedman. New York: Doubleday, 1992.

Soares Prabhu, George N. "Jesus and Social Justice," in *Jesus For Our Times: Towards a Spirituality of Social*

Action. Manila: FABC Office of Human Development, 1986.

SECTION 2
Theological Perspective

16

The Hospitality of the Eucharist:
Reimagining the Borderless Church

Allan Samuel Palanna

The World with Borders

The heartrending image of Aylan Kurdi, the three-year old Syrian refugee washed face-down ashore the Moroccan coast captured by Nilufer Demir, the Turkish photographer, awoke the conscience of the world. Bob Dylan's 1962 song seemed to predict and raise crucial questions on the death of innocent lives torn between borders, both literal and symbolic, that have come to mark the present geopolitical structure of the world. Dylan sang,

> How many seas must a white dove sail
> Before she sleeps in the sand?...
> Yes and how many deaths will it take till he knows
> That too many people have died?[1]

This picture horrifically painted, both literally and metaphorically, the image of the violence of the world and offered a blatant critique of the failed policies of the governments of the world. If we were to agree with Carson's view that "every culture and every age necessarily displays *some* tolerance and *some* intolerance"[2], we also need to assess the areas wherein fences are erected that propel people to take violent means in order to maintain boundaries. Violence is a conscious choice to allow particular aspects of philosophy, ideology or faith to dictate responses that are generally coercive by nature, resorting to the use of force, both covert and overt. The classic work by René Girard, *Violence and the Sacred*[3] is perhaps one of the most significant contributions to the analysis of violence. Girard contends that human societies devise ways and means to victimize their fellow human beings due to an inherent desire for violence. The urge to do harm is a deeply seated adverse emotion that must be overcome. Therefore, Girard also analyses sacrifice (surrogate victimization) as a necessity in order to indirectly desire violence. Arthur Sutherland paints a very grim picture of the angst of present day order of life where suspicion of people has led to a slew of measures that mechanize stereotypes and filter people through the increasing reliance of technology that is invariably conceived on the basis of mistrust and hatred of the ones 'across the border'. Sutherland conveys thus:

> Our mistrust exhibits itself in a renewed interest in immigration laws and efforts to limit our borders to those who seem to be most like us. Today, protection against strangers and their supposed threat has led us to retinal eye scans, DNA swabbing, and dime-sized details of where we live and work all constantly photographed and recorded by geosynchronous satellites. Technological palliatives and silicone chips are becoming the sedative of choice for an increasingly nervous public.[4]

Churches and institutions even in India continue to wallow in such enterprises without the much needed debate on the ethics of the media and technology. Varied forms of enforced borders that are evolving make it necessary to specifically identify such forms since credible response deeply dwells on identification of such evolving forms.

India and the Bordered Other

The dehumanizing vocabulary such as "human refuse" and "human waste" indicating vulnerable communities are emerging. The 'recycling' of unwanted human communities is being talked about, reflecting a paradigm shift from the welfare model to the penalty model wherein special buffer zones and "waste" countries are identified to dump "unwanted human waste" and "strangers".[5] Much philosophical work has been done on the ontology of the other, otherness and othering. There is now a physical identification of the "other" and the "other within", the former indicating the vulnerable people outside the country and the latter indicating the vulnerable people within one's own borders. The fact that vulnerability is driven and fuelled by gross injustice is seldom considered in public opinion. This is true of India as well where the root of injustice is never dwelt upon, but rather its after effects, such as trafficking or bonded labour.

In India, the possibility of climate refugees especially seeking refuge from Bangladesh would be enormous. According to an estimate, climate refugees may cross a staggering 75 million people moving into India by the end of this decade.[6] Such a situation would invariably give rise to issues ranging from political tensions to serious abuse, forced labour and trafficking.[7] Within India, there would be deeper issues to be contended with. The fragile relationship of the refugees in north east India and the ever-growing resentment that they are facing in the rest of India is an everyday reality. Also the distinction between "hindu refugees" and other refugees is emerging. Narendra Modi's election campaign in Assam was laced with such distinctions.

> ...detention camps housing Hindu migrants from Bangladesh will be done away with... We have a responsibility toward Hindus who are harassed and suffer in other countries. Where will they go? India is the only place for them.[8]

The Bordered Church

The words "border" or "borderless" are inextricably intertwined with the vocabulary of the political map. Territorial distinctions are monitored and reinforced by maps. The usage "borderless church" may, perhaps, be an unconscious realization of the geopolitical borders that mark even the present ecclesiastical polity. It may also be a far cry from the biblical understanding of Church as Ecclesia, marking the called-out-ness of the community of disciples. However, the vision of a borderless church may be an acknowledgement of these very fault lines that need to be redrawn, renegotiated, resisted, critiqued or maybe completely erased. Such adverse socio-economic and political fault lines that characterise the present world and the Indian Church must be constantly recognized.

The exclusion status of the Dalits in India seems to be the given even after the conscientisation achieved in over three decades of sociological and theological deliberations. Sanjay Paswan and Paramanshi Jaideva analyzing the injustice shown particularly to Christian Dalits in India encapsulate this struggle of consciousness, thus:

> At the level of consciousness, every Dalit feels that he (sic) is not wanted in his country and in his church. He is no citizen in his homeland as he is denied social, political rights and economic opportunities. He is a stranger in his own church because he is denied rights which are his due as a baptized Christian.[9]

This is indeed a reality for most vulnerable communities including the tribals, adivasis and other indigenous communities.

The re-imagination of the borderless Church may perhaps call attention to the othered communities of the scriptures too. There are complexities involved in interrogating the perception of the other as recorded in the biblical texts. Reinhard Feldmeier passionately points out the abject state of being the other in the biblical world, thus:

> It (otherness) is used (in the Bible) to separate off one group from those who do not, and are not supposed to, belong to it. The term stranger is thus used primarily to express something negative: not belonging, exclusion, mixed to some extent with the denigration of this other person (a "barbarian"). The state of being a stranger is experienced by those concerned as something that is *per se* thoroughly negative. This was especially the case in ancient (biblical) times, when it was only the possession of citizenship that made someone legally and politically viable in the full sense.[10]

The Eucharist: Beyond the Bordered World

Whether the idea, the notion or the theology of the borderless Church is argued as unrealistic or unsustainable, the vision of the Eucharist as the passing away of divisions and fences that have come to define the present world allows for a re-imagination of the Church as an all-embracing table of fellowship of hospitality. The ethical obligation of hospitability is the metaphor of all moral obligations in the scriptures. Mutual openness becomes a central motif in the Judeo-Christian tradition. Moreover, Kevin D O'Gorman goes further to the point of asserting that "in the Old Testament (sic), hospitality is central to virtually all of Old Testament ethics: God, the great host invites his (sic) guests into his house, the created world, to enjoy its riches and blessings."[11] Leviticus 25:23 goes even further in recognizing the stranger status of all people before God. Therefore, theologically, it may be construed that no one can claim authentic citizenship over against foreigners, since the land finally belongs to God. The ones who reside in the land do so as a provision of God, rather than possession in the earthly sense. This conditional residence is subject to the openness to the stranger.

It is in this sense that the Christic affirmations in Matthew 25 become crucial in Christ's own self-understanding as the other. It is essential to note that, "from the point of Christian ethics, this surely and primarily entails looking beyond the physical to the spiritual reality of being, the same as 'the One who empties himself.'"[12] The incarnation finally becomes the symbol of God in Christ seeking hospitality from the world. God, thereby, chooses the character of the stranger rather than the owner in restoring creation. Therefore, it is rightly noted that "in the incarnation, God becomes vulnerable to human welcome".[13]

The Eucharist as a practice is surely multilayered. Though the gospels portray the eucharistic practices in multiple layers, the account of Paul suggests that it was part of a full-scale meal, in the home of members of the Christian community in Corinth. Rumours of the "unnatural" eucharistic meals were always in abundance which sought to destabilize the ethos of such meals as the practice threatened to destroy the carefully constructed dominant social codes governing meals/banquets in the Graeco-roman world. Dominic Crossan commenting on the table fellowship of the Jesus movement says that, "commensality was, rather, a strategy for building or rebuilding peasant community on radically different principles from those of honor and shame. It was based on an egalitarian sharing of spiritual power at the most grassroot level."[14] The eucharistic table/ meal/banquet provided an alternative affirmative ethos where societal barricades were demystified and deconstructed in the early Christian communities over against the capitalistic social codes promulgated aggressively by the empire.

However, the jagged fresco of the practice of the Eucharist in Christian history began to be marked by disputes, schisms and other bordered schemas that continued to benefit and support the dominant groups around the Christian world.[15] Paul criticises the Corinthian Christians because they have come to observe "giving thanks" as a highly individualized, privatized matter: Paul writes, "For when the time comes to eat, each of you goes ahead with your own supper, and one goes hungry and another becomes drunk"(I Cor 11:21). There were significant distinctions being made between rich and poor: "You show contempt for the church of God and humiliate those who have nothing,"(1 Cor 11:22) says Paul. Obviously, people of high standing were eating and drinking all that they could do, leaving nothing for the poor. These practices took more potent forms of discrimination through the centuries prompting Claudio Carvalhaes to enquire,

> How can the borders of the Eucharist be negotiated so that unexpected guests might participate in it? If the problem here is related to borders, what borders are we talking about? In what ways do the borders of the outside world mark the borders of the liturgical space? How do we connect the proposed new global order of justice and solidarity present in the Eucharistic sacrament to a terribly disordered, brutal, violent world? And, is it possible to think and practice the eucharistic rite as a borderless border sacrament?[16]

In Exodus 16: 11–21, the familiar incident of the "manna falling from heaven" must be read intertextually. It is significant to note that as soon as people started gathering manna more than they could hold, it decayed and rotted. It was only in sharing the manna with others that it could be sustained. The closed meaning of the Eucharist being confined to modes and practices and the open meaning of the Eucharist being to offer hospitality and fellowship for all, continues in conflictual understanding until the present. Yet, the affirmative sense of the Eucharist that has been practiced offer glimpses of reimagining this sacrament.

Archbishop Oscar Romero, through his bold life and witness in fighting injustice in the Latin American context transfigured the traditional symbol of the Eucharist into a compelling God's "No" to the dehumanization of the world. Carvalhaes records this event, thus:

> Archbishop Romero's death (assassination) at the Eucharistic altar served as a witness to the death of Christ, as the death of the poor announces/have announced/will always announce the many injustices that shape and try to define our world. However, the death of Archbishop Romero at the altar of Christ also announces/has announced/will always announce that the gospel of Jesus Christ carries this kernel of unsettlement, of uneasiness, of critique, and unrest, this always annoying and revolutionary challenge of love, egalitarianism, peace, and hospitality for the time we call now, and for any power that is. The breaking of the bread and the pouring of the wine promise a new time, now and always, a new earth and new promises of God that our tears will be wiped away and we all will be freely welcomed at the altar/table/feast of Christ.[17]

Mutuality and Vulnerability at the Eucharist

At the center of our lives is sharing and relationships. During my pastoral journey, I have seen that when relationships break down due to socially monitored divisions, bonds grows weak, individual lives are wrecked and children are scarred for life. We live fragmented lives. However, our faith is that the brokenness would be healed through the broken body of Christ. The "do this in remembrance of me" call is not only to enact the Eucharist event as "do this", but our own bodies need to be broken as Christ broke his, "do this (break your body) in remembrance of me". One of the prime starting points for embracing the other at the Eucharist may be what Amos Yong calls, the discourse of mutuality and vulnerability.[18]

Mutuality involves the recognition that the act of embracing would not only be a space for understanding the other, but in myriad dimensions, opens up possibilities for a deeper self-understanding. The transformative capacity in mutuality is possible because of a privileging of the means of understanding of the other as being higher and a necessary one for one's own understanding. The axis of the power of knowledge dramatically shifts in favour of the other. The act of embracing also engages with one's own theological imaginations and calls to question deep-seated notions of discriminative ideology being held as theology or liturgy. It offers a critique of any dominant theological or liturgical perceptions that may be held as the given. And hence, such mutuality leads to a certain sense of vulnerability. This is an obvious outcome, since one's own understanding is held up to scrutiny and may need to change in the light of the critique offered by the act of embracing the stranger. The sense of teachability is a required criterion as it allows oneself to be forever open to corrections and transformation of one's own staunchly held perceptions.

The one commandment that Jesus gave to his disciples during the Eucharistic meal was that they would love one another. This is the heart of eucharistic hospitality which is mutual trust in relationship. This is what happens at the Eucharist. God in Christ renews God's covenant to us in the breaking of the bread. The envisioning and the realizing of the borderless church can become a reality when the critical lines of conditional "hospitality" at the table constructed by the socio-economic, ecclesiastical, theological, liturgical and political borders are constantly challenged, critiqued and resisted.

Endnotes

[1] Seth Rogovoy, *Bob Dylan: Prophet, Mystic, Poet* (New York: Scribner, 2009), 42.

[2] D. A. Carson, *The Intolerance of Tolerance* (Grand Rapids: Wm. B. Eerdmans Publishing, 2012), 47. (emphasis original)

[3] René Girard, *Violence and the Sacred* (New York: Bloomsbury, 1977).

[4] Arthur Sutherland, *I was a Stranger: A Christian Theology of Hospitality* (Nashville: Abington Press, 2006), 3-4.

[5] Yosefa Loshitzsky, *Screening Strangers: Migration and Diaspora in Contemporary European Cinema* (Bloomington, Indiana: Indiana University Press, 2010), 3.

[6] Bimal Kanti Paul, *Environmental Hazards and Disasters: Contexts, Perspectives and Management* (Chichester, UK: John Wiley and Sons, 2011), 298.

[7] Paul, *Environmental Hazards*, 298.

[8] Cited in Sanjay Chaturvedi and Timothy Doyle, *Climate Terror: A Critical Geopolitics of Climate Change* (London: Palgrave Macmillan, 2015), 125.

[9] Sanjay Paswan and Paramanshi Jaideva, *Encyclopaedia of Dalits in India* (Delhi: Kalpaz publications, 2003), 171.

[10] Reinhard Feldmeier, "The 'Nation' of Strangers: Social Contempt and its Theological Interpretation in Ancient Judaism and Early Christianity," in *Ethnicity in the Bible*, Mark G. Brett (ed.) (Leiden: E J Brill, 1996), 241.

[11] Kevin D O'Gorman, 'Dimensions of Hospitality: Exploring Ancient and Classical Origins,' in *Hospitality: A Social Lens*, Conrad Lashley, Paul Lynch and Alison Morrison (ed.) (Amsterdam: Elsevier, 2007), 20.

[12] Allan Samuel Palanna, 'Citius, Altius, Fortius: Deciphering the Ethical Contours in Human Cognitive Enhancement,' *Bangalore Theological Forum*, xlv/2 (Dec 2013): 113.

[13] Christine D. Pohl, 'Hospitality,' in *Dictionary of Scripture and Ethics*, Joel B. Green (ed.) (Grand Rapids, Michigan: Baker Academic, 2011), 379.

[14] Dominic John Crossan, *The Historical Jesus: The Life of a Mediterranean Jewish Peasant* (New York: HarperCollins, 1991), 344.

[15] Tissa Balasuriya, *The Eucharist and Human Liberation* (Eugene, Oregon: Wipf and Stock publishers, 2004),.2

[16] Claudio Carvalhaes *Eucharist and Globalization: Redrawing the Borders of Eucharistic Hospitality* (Eugene, Oregon: Pickwick publications, 2013), 8. Emphasis original.

[17] Claudio Carvalhaes, *Eucharist and Globalization,* 2. Emphasis mine.

[18] Amos Yong uses these terms in the context of interreligious dialogue. However, the basic emphasis of engaging with the unknown may also be applied to the encounter with the other as being addressed here. Cf, Amos Yong, *Hospitality and the Other: Pentecost, Christian Practices, and the Neighbor* (Maryknoll, New York: Orbis Books, 2008), 80.

Bibliography

Balasuriya, Tissa. *The Eucharist and Human Liberation.* Eugene, Oregon: Wipf and Stock publishers, 2004.

Carson, D. A. *The Intolerance of Tolerance.* Grand Rapids: Wm. B. Eerdmans Publishing, 2012.

Carvalhaes, Claudio. *Eucharist and Globalization: Redrawing the Borders of Eucharistic Hospitality.* Eugene, Oregon: Pickwick publications, 2013.

Chaturvedi, Sanjay and Timothy Doyle. *Climate Terror: A Critical Geopolitics of Climate Change.* London: Palgrave Macmillan, 2015.

Crossan, Dominic John. *The Historical Jesus: The Life of a Mediterranean Jewish Peasant.* New York: Harper Collins, 1991.

Feldmeier, Reinhard. "The 'Nation' of Strangers: Social Contempt and its Theological Interpretation in Ancient Judaism and Early Christianity." Page 241in *Ethnicity in the Bible.* Edited by Mark G. Brett. Leiden: E J Brill, 1996.

Girard, René. *Violence and the Sacred.* New York: Bloomsbury, 1977.

Green Joel B, ed. *Dictionary of Scripture and Ethics.* Grand Rapids, Michigan: Baker Academic, 2011.

Loshitzsky, Yosefa. *Screening Strangers: Migration and Diaspora in Contemporary European Cinema.* Bloomington, Indiana: Indiana University Press, 2010.

O'Gorman, Kevin D. "Dimensions of Hospitality: Exploring Ancient and Classical Origins." Page 20 in *Hospitality: A Social Lens,* Edited by Conrad Lashley, Paul Lynch and Alison Morrison. Amsterdam: Elsevier, 2007.

Palanna, Allan Samuel. "Citius, Altius, Fortius: Deciphering the Ethical Contours in Human Cognitive Enhancement." *Bangalore Theological Forum,* xlv/2 (Dec 2013): 113.

Paswan, Sanjay and Paramanshi Jaideva. *Encyclopaedia of Dalits in India.* Delhi: Kalpaz publications, 2003.

Paul, Bimal Kanti. *Environmental Hazards and Disasters: Contexts, Perspectives and Management.* Chichester, UK: John Wiley and Sons, 2011.

Rogovoy, Seth. *Bob Dylan: Prophet, Mystic, Poet.* New York: Scribner, 2009.

Sutherland, Arthur. *I was a Stranger: A Christian Theology of Hospitality.* Nashville: Abington Press, 2006.

Yong, Amos. *Hospitality and the Other: Pentecost, Christian Practices, and the Neighbor.* Maryknoll, New York: Orbis Books, 2008.

17

Orulai:

A Counter Eucharist to Excluding Ecclesia

Christy Gnanadason

After 70 years of pilgrim journey, the Church of South India has decided to deliberate on re-thinking the prospect and purpose of ecclesia. Why is the church being invited to rethink about its presence after 70 long years? Is it an invitation to critically re-look into the purpose of the journey travelled thus far? Or is it an invitation to be conscientised and engage creatively to be relevant to the growing contextual challenges? Whichever of these reasons it maybe, the need is for the church to realize its presence in relation to being more dynamic than static. In other words, the church is obligated to return and plunge into the context or the life-world of the people. Martin Luther King Jr emphatically asserts:

> There was a time when the church was very powerful. It was during that period the early Christians rejoiced when they were deemed worthy to suffer for what they believed. In those days the church was not merely a thermometer that recorded the ideas and principles of popular opinion; it was the thermostat that transformed the mores of the society.

The purpose of the church is to reverse the world of domination, discrimination and exploitation to a world of divine values such as love, justice, peace and equality with its liberative and transformative mission. According to Acts 17:6, the early church was engaged in turning the world upside down.

However, the church, gradually succumbed to the politicality of divisive powers and principalities of the world, than subverting them. The presence and prominence of Christ in the church has been hijacked by the evils of exclusion in the form of caste, class, colour, gender, love of power, so on and so forth. Thus, it is a dire need to re-think and re-define the purpose of ecclesia, "the church", in the growing imperialistic context.

Ecclesia Redefined

The word "church"comes from the old English and German word *Kirche.* The ancient Greek equivalent for the word *Kirche* was *Kuriakos* or *Kuriakon.* The word *Kuriakos* has its roots with *Kurios,* which means "The Lord". *Kuriakos* means related/pertaining to the Lord, or belonging to the Lord. The Greek *Kuriakos* in old English form was eventually used as '*cirice*' (Kee-ree-ke), then '*churche*' (Kerke), and finally 'church' in its traditional form.

The Greek word *Kuriakos* seems to appear only twice in the New Testament. Firstly, it appears in 1 Corinthian 11: 20 where it refers to "the Lord's Supper", and secondly, it is found in Revelation 1: 10 while referring to the Lord's Day. Gradually, through the organised religion "church" was replaced by "ecclesia". The word ecclesia appears approximately 115 times in New Testament. According to Acts 19 "ecclesia" is a town council – a civil body in Ephesus. The Greek word "ecclesia" is defined as "the called out". According to the Encyclopaedia Britannica: Ecclesia was the name given to the governmental assembly of the city of Athens, duly called out by proper officers and possessing all political power including even juridical functions. Similarly, Oxford English Dictionary asserts ecclesia as a regularly convoked assembly, especially, the general assembly of Athenians. The two most respected word resources in English language avows ecclesia as a civil body called out for a purpose, which is more political. It could be understood that New Testament scholars deliberately used ecclesia for church in order to counter the idea of the Roman civil body, and defined church as a Christian civil body called out of the Roman and Judean system to form a counter community having Christ's body as its foundation. Further, Church means a politically autonomous body of Christians under no king but Jesus. For the early church Jesus was the Lord, not Caesar. They dethroned Caesar and enthroned Christ and hence they were arrested, crucified and martyred. Therefore, ecclesia is Christ's civil body that invites one to be crucified and martyred in confronting the civil body's politics of exclusion.

Ecclesia: Excluding or Emancipating

The early Christian Church was steered by the inspiration of the risen Lord whose life angered and threatened the religious and political leaders of his time. Jesus' life and teachings confronted the world of injustice, oppression and hypocrisy having God's justice, love, truth and power as countering values. It further, rebelled against the religious and political empires of his times. Hence, these empires, conspired to end Jesus' revolt and crucified him. The disciples of Jesus, who walked and worked along, were very convinced with Jesus' teachings and wanted to take it further fearlessly. As a result, they were also subjected to harassment, surveillance, torture and murder. But, the disciples could not be silenced. They embarked on the journey of proclaiming the truth about life and witness of Jesus on one hand, and on the other, they spoke truth about the society and its exploitative powers. In Acts 4: 8–10, Peter boldly accuses the rulers and the elders for crucifying Jesus.

The early church, further, laid emphasis on the communitarian life wherein no one was claimed to be exclusive nor cornered as excluded (Peter and Cornelius, Acts 10). Acts 2:42–47 portrays a community that had everything in common and sold their property and possessions and distributed among the needy. The sharing of their earned or accumulated wealth was part of their liturgical act of worship, teaching, fellowship and breaking of the bread (Acts 2:42). The early church challenged the Apostles to get rid of their private property as a prerequisite to be part in the community of Christ. Therefore, the early church was more an emancipating church than an excluding church. But, gradually, the doctrinal emphasis of the church saw a consequent decline in church's emancipatory power or transformative power. As Walter Brueggemann asserts, the creeds and doctrinal tradition of the church has flattened all the images and metaphors of liberation and transformation and boxed the church into a nice little formulation.

Eucharist

The two significant sacraments or Christian liberative tools are Baptism and Eucharist. On one hand, baptism was a warning call to the "brood of vipers" to repent and embrace the Kingdom of God, and on the other, it was an invitation for the victims of unjust religious laws and political rules, to experience new life free from all oppression and exploitation. Similarly, Eucharist was a symbol that called one to commemorate the struggles and sufferings of Israelites under Pharaoh's imperialistic reign and commissions to participate in God's liberative movement which involved patriarchs, judges, Prophets, Jesus and the disciples. However, these liberative tools (Sacraments) of Christianity have lost its redemptive history and have succumbed to ritual rationale of exclusion and exclusivism. According to Aloysius Pieris, the Eucharist which was offered in the catacombs of Rome by Christians due to the fear of persecution, later became a symbol of triumphant Christianity when it was celebrated on the high altars of Roman Basilica. Gradually, Eucharist lost its significance of being a metaphor that disclosed the trials and tribulation of vulnerable, and became a triumphant metaphor that justified triumphalist empires. In other words, the table that was filled with the "weighted community"[1] has been reversed into the table of "weight imposing community"[2] and became the ritual of exclusion. Therefore, the Eucharistic table, is no more a beacon of hope to the weighted community, rather, it is a weight imposing table that crushes the hope of vulnerable community partaking in the broken and liberative body of Christ.

Case Studies

The following case studies will help us to understand few nuances of the transition of understanding from Eucharist as a liberative table for the weighted community to the exclusive table of weight imposing community.

Eucharist - Purity and Pollution

One of my colleagues researched on the code of purity-pollution from the book of Leviticus, laying emphasis on ritual practices followed during menstruation. She conducted an empirical study and interviewed a minimum of 100 women of different age groups, social and economic back ground. One of the questions related to women participating in the Eucharist while on their regular periods. Shockingly, 60% of women abstain from participating in the Eucharist due to their regular cycles. When they were asked for the reason, many felt that their participation could pollute the process. Majority of women have internalised the process of exclusion and have voluntarily refrained and excluded themselves from being part of Eucharist. The success of a dominant theory is to promote the tactics of exclusion as normal and acceptable by all. The continuous efforts taken by the dominants to keep away the vulnerable from the liberative process gradually becomes a norm. The patriarchal society and church have consistently pressed upon women's regular cycles as something which is polluted and polluting, and have instructed women to keep themselves away from public gathering and inter-dinning to prefer so-called purity over and against pollution.

In one of the congregations I serve in, on Youth Sunday, three young people, including a girl, were asked to preach from three different texts. It was the first time a lay woman was seen in the altar. This enraged few elder men and they have spoken ill about it after the worship. The content of their argument (I was told) was about menstruation. Similarly, in a church, a lay woman (for the first time) was invited to assist during communion. This became an issue for gossip among the congregation, mostly men.

In another experience, we celebrated Eucharist in a church on Maundy Thursday. This church has the practice of serving communion in individual cups. However, on special occasions we use common cup for Eucharist celebration. After a week an elder of the church approached me and said that his son did not participate in the communion on Maundy Thursday. When I asked him why, he responded, since the communion was served in common cup, he did not partake as he had consumed alcohol.

Eucharist – In Memory of Exclusive Caste

In one of the Seminaries students were celebrating Dalit Liberation Sunday. The entire worship was organised in a way commemorating the Dalits and their life-world. The liturgy, songs, sermon, creed and intercessory prayers were written focusing on Dalits experience of pain, pathos and protest. When it came to the celebration of Eucharist, the celebrant narrated Jesus' solidarity with the oppressed community and compared it to a Dalit martyr and blessed the communion elements. This triggered a huge commotion after the worship. A clear caste divide among the students and faculty was witnessed. The argument was how could a person of a particular community, who is unknown to a larger section of people substitute Jesus and his death. Jesus as a martyr cannot be substituted with any other martyr. It was also argued among students how the body and blood of a Jew could be compared to the body and blood of a Dalit. To resolve the issue a seminar was organised to deliberate on Eucharist from different major perspectives. The presenters did not give clear and outright perspectives and were diplomatic in their conclusions. However, one presenter broke the shackles and affirmed that Jesus, the one who confronted the evil structures of exclusion, invites everyone to participate in his fight for justice and equality. According to the presenter, those who lose their life while affirming life in a life threatening context join Jesus in proclaiming God's life and liberation in the world. Further, she emphasised on menstruation, which is considered to be impure, as the blood that rejuvenates women and engages them in the process of life-giving and life sharing mission of Jesus and his death..

The given case studies unmask the masks of patriarchy, caste and moralism that govern the Eucharist. The table, which is open and ethical in nature, has been reversed as the closed table that confines to the ritual of exclusion propagated by dominating and discriminating evils of caste, patriarchy and moralism. The Eucharist, which was countering the politics of exclusion in Jesus' time, has succumbed to the politics of exclusion and has kept away people from the body and blood of Christ, which is liberative and transformative. Therefore, it is timely to retrieve the significance of Eucharist, which combats all forms of evil that hinders the communion of people, especially the vulnerable community.

Orulai

Rev Dr. Theophilus Appavoo, widely known as *Parattai* was taking TECCA (Theological Education for Christian Commitment and Action)[3] classes in a village. One fine morning a girl student who had come early to class started conversing with Parattai. The conversation goes like this:

> Parattai: *Yaen Ma, Enna Saapta Kaalaila* (What did you have for Breakfast?)
>
> Girl: *Kanji Kudichaen Aiya, Aama Neenga Enna Saaptinga* (Porridge Sir, How about you?)
>
> Parattai: *Naan Idly Saaptaen Ma* (I had Idly Ma)
>
> Girl: *Yenna Aiya, Namma Oray Kudumbum Nu Sollringa, Oray Thagapannu Sollringa Aana Vera Vera Saapadu Saapidromay* (What is this Sir, we claim ourselves as children of one father and also pray as one family, but our food seems to be different).

This conversation challenged Parratai and encouraged him to probe into this as a serious query of theological engagement. As a result he came out with a concept called "*Uravu Murai Thiruvizha*" (Festival of Relationship), which encouraged the villagers to come together and start cooking on *Orulai*, the same food. He explained *Orulai* with a story titled *Karadipatti*. *Karadipatti* is an imagined village in which people's individual mud *Ulai* was broken. People tried rebuilding it but it kept breaking again and again. While they were celebrating a village festival, the spirit came upon a villager and spoke to them saying, "All villagers come together, build one

*Ula*i and start cooking one food". Therefore, the villagers came together and started cooking in *oru* (one) *Ulai*. This is how Parratai came up with the new concept of *Orulai* and theologizes it with Jesus's Lord's Supper which lays its emphasis on One Body i.e. one food, but same food.

The Tamil Nadu Theological Seminary (TTS), encouraged students with an exposure called "Night Experience" in the village as a common villager. The students were challenged to know the life-world of the people, their struggles, their celebrations, so on and so forth. As the students returned to the seminary they raised pertinent questions on how does one theologize the life-world of villagers and how do we express solidarity with them and their struggles? This paved way for *Orulai* celebration in the seminary. To remember the life-world of the labouring community, the TTS community, comes together once in a month and cooks *Kanji* (Porridge) the food of the working class, and the whole community, without any disparity between faculty members, administrative staff, maintenance staff and students, participate in *Orulai* and eat the same food.

Orulai – Inversive Eucharist

Eucharist reminds us of God's historic intervention in confronting Pharaoh's empire and asserting God's liberative solidarity with the struggles of the Jewish people in their fight for freedom. It also discloses Jesus' memory of his work and witness that identified with the poor and their suffering. Similarly, *Orulai* discloses God's participation in the life-world of the excluded communities which unmasks the world's politics of hierarchy and exclusion on one hand, and on the other, reveals the politicality of the excluded that continuously confronts the excluding politics. Orulai affirms the inversion that God initiates through the victims of exclusion.

Orulai – Inverts Patriarchy

The patriarchal society has imposed certain gender roles in which women are expected to restrict themselves within the private sphere (household work like cooking, cleaning, washing), whereas, men can play a vital role in the public sphere (administration, decision-making, governance). Men have the freedom to work in the private sphere too, if they chose to do so. But, women are constrained from playing any roles in the public sphere. The case studies expose the selective places where women can and cannot be.[4] Since, *Orulai* is cooked and celebrated in the public sphere, women engage in border-crossing[5] from private sphere to public sphere. Further, in *Orulai*, it's obligatory that both, men and women, engage in cooking. The cooking work is mutually shared between men and women.

Orulai – Inverts Purity-Pollution

Dalits and women are victims of the construct and ideology of purity-pollution. Dalits and Dalit women are permanent victims of purity-pollution whereas women are victims of it at certain times and in certain places. There are certain places, especially the shrines, that are solely reserved only for men and no women can enter such places (For example, Sabarimala Temple). The given case studies expose politics of exclusion in the name of caste and purity-pollution. Even theological seminaries succumb to such exclusive politics. Further, due to politics of purity-pollution, food is perceived as a dividing force. The thought of inter-dinning is completely eroded among people. Places and parties are narrowed to particular communities. Food is also classified and condemned as food of dominant caste and oppressed caste. During menstruation, women are not allowed to be part of public gatherings or enter "holy" place of worship and they are isolated even inside their own homes sometimes in separate enclosures with separate cots and utensils set apart for their use. It is in such divisive and exclusive context that *Orulai* attempts to break the importance of purity-pollution and prove its illogicality. In *Orulai*, the excluded communityies are encouraged and empowered, not only to participate but also to host. The evil of exclusion is countered and confronted through *Orulai*, paving way for inter-dinning, not with different food but with same food, the food of the working class.

Orulai – Inverts Inequality

Ambedkar opines of the Indian caste system as a "Graded Inequality". Predominantly, in the Indian context "inequality" is found in every walk of life. Beginning from the place of birth to the place of death, inequality is inherent. The sad part is that religions endorse inequality and encourage the beneficiaries to sustain inequality through different means. The Brahmanical religion paints the very birth of man in a hierarchical structure that propagates the superior and inferior status quo. Further, every religion practices inequality between male and female. Separate worship places for women, use of sexist language in the scriptures, wage discrimination, so on and so forth. Mostly, in churches, it is men who first participate in Eucharist followed by women. Seldom do men and women participate together. *Orulai*, by giving prominence to same food combats inequality. *Orulai*, is not just an open table but it is an open ground. It accommodates everyone be it male, female, transgender, disabled, rich, poor, drunken, dominant, oppressed, or menstruating. It does not stop anyone on any unequal grounds to be part of the same food. It breaks the binary of celebrant and participants and affirms everyone as celebrant and participant. Participants in *Orulai* are challenged not on moral grounds but on ethical grounds.

Conclusion

Ecclesia, the body of Christ, which emerged in countering the political body of Roman Empire that suppressed people's freedom, gradually lost its liberative and transformative purpose. Eucharist, for Jesus, was the supreme symbol of self-offering unto death for the liberation of humankind. He was killed because he championed justice and truth, and sided with the excluded and the exploited. He took an unflinching stand against injustice and deception... as a result he endured intense suffering of mind and body to bear witness to his message that God is love and love demands justice, truth, dignity and equality. Hence, participating in Eucharist, demands participation in the fight for dignity and equality. It challenges the Eucharistic community to come out of their closets of exclusion and exclusivism and participate in one bread and one cup which is the same food i.e. *Orulai*, to pull down the walls of graded inequality and affirm God's grace of life, filled with dignity and equality. As Church of South India re-thinks Ecclesia, may God of life, life in abundance and equality, help the church to re-member the dis-membered.

Endnotes

[1] Weighted Community, according to Mark Lewis Taylor, is vulnerable community victimised due to socio-politico, religio-cultural and economic exploitation.

[2] The dominant community who are at the helm of oppressing and exploiting structures.

[3] A Laity Theological course initiated by Tamil Nadu Theological Seminary, Madurai, Tamil Nadu, with the purpose of imparting basic theological education to the people of God in regional language, especially Tamil.

[4] In general pulpits and altars are considered as not meant for women, as these places are the places of public and political discourses in the religious realm.

[5] The term Border sharply captures the dominant tendency to establish fences or boundaries based on binary. Border-crossing, is a pedagogy that conscientizes the bordered to identify and be critical of the borders and creatively engage in crossing the Borders.

18

Uniqueness of Christ:

Towards a Borderless Church

Mervin Shinoj Boas

Borderlessness: Theological Paradox Towards Infinite Vs Finite Being

Constructing new borders in order to overcome the existing borders is the present theological task we are engaging with. Crossing border in order to reach out to another border is the reality here. We can never be with the reality of Borderlessness because the concept of borderlessness is constructed with specific borders. We construct borders. Then we try to cross the same by constructing another border. It is an ongoing process that never ends with borderlessness. This is a theological paradox which is based on the nature of finite being. Borderlessness is the position of infinite being. God is understood as infinite being. Therefore, only God can be in the position of borderlessness. Church is created by created beings. Created being can only be a finite being. Finite being is limited by borders. Therefore, since church is a created one it is limited with borders at any cost at any time.

Though we have a metaphor regarding Church as the body of Christ it is a paradoxical thought since Christ is formless. A formless being is infinite and cannot have any physical body. Body is finite since it is a created being. An infinite being cannot have finite body. God is formless since God is infinite. This feature does not fit into the frame of the Church since it is created with specific form with particular borders. We cross any border by holding another created border. Journeying with new borders to cross the existing borders with an intention to towards borderlessness is the reality of the theological paradox we are engaging in. However, the reality of border is static in nature whereas the concept of borderlessness is fluid in nature. It means that comprehensiveness is the methodological frame of the concept of borderlessness. Therefore, it is very much a postmodern notion with open boundaries but with specific borders because finite being cannot have infinite nature.

Concept of Uniqueness: Universality Vs Particularity

The concept of uniqueness was constructed with universal features by ideas of modernity. It is vehemently criticised by the postmodern position by incorporating particularity within the frame of uniqueness. Postmodern notion allows one to have global features with the concept of uniqueness but it is strictly based on particular frame. It is because postmodern notion of thought does not promote binarism in the ground of universality and particularity. In this regard S. J. Samartha should be considered as a postmodern theologian. One of the main theological contributions of Samartha is related with the Uniqueness of Christ. He takes a theological position that Christ is unique, no doubt at all, just as Krishna is unique and Muhammed also is unique. Constructing the concept of uniqueness with extra ordinary claims is strictly negated by Samartha. Extra ordinary claim is a trouble maker in the multi religious context of India. Everyone is unique with particular identity. If anybody tries to globalize this it brings identity clash or crisis. Let Christ be Christ with own particular nature. There is no theological mission with us to compare the uniqueness of Christ with the uniqueness of Krishna or Muhammed or any other divine figure in our context. Globalizing the uniqueness of Christ with extra ordinary claims with a purpose of defeating the uniqueness of other divine figures is quite dangerous in a multi religious context.

The postmodern position is that God can be universal but always with particular uniqueness. For example, the concept of love of God is a universal concept but the features of that love are very particular on the basis of the context. Love should be borderless but the expression of love is embedded in a specific context with very specific nature which strictly has borders. Love is infinite but materializing love is limited with a particular context which is limited with particular time and space. Therefore, context is finite since it has the border of time and space. Thus infinite should have finite frame to be revealed. This is the significance of incarnation of God. In short, the phenomenon of God can be universal but revelation of God is particular and contextual. Revelation happens in a particular context. Context is very much limited with particular time and space. Uniqueness of Christ is related with the revealed nature of God. Revelation is particular. Therefore, Uniqueness is also particular. That is why, everyone is unique. It happens with Christ also. Uniqueness without any extra ordinary claim should match with the identity of Christ. Thus, uniqueness is not in crisis but goes with any other uniqueness with friendly nature. Here, uniqueness accompanies uniqueness and lives together. Uniqueness does not contradict any other uniqueness since each uniqueness has its own specific borders.

Here, having border is a meaningful position in this regard. Christ is unique but does not negate any other uniqueness. The issue of globalizing the uniqueness of Christ is problematic. Let us therefore stay away from that dangerous theological agenda.

Borderlessness: An Existential Interrogation

The concept of borderlessness is constructed with infinite features. Infinite being does not have any existential crisis because of its formless nature. That is why we believe that God is the ground of existence. Paul Tillich nourishes this thought well. The existence of God is beyond time and space since God is an infinite being. But, the existence of created being or finite being faces existential crisis always since finite being is bounded with particular time and space. Tillichian thought promotes that only God has independent existence whereas finite being has only dependent existence. Independent reality cannot be in crisis due to its power to be *beyond.* Dependent being cannot be like this. Thus, it is always with existential crisis. Since, Church is a created one it does have existential crisis all the time. But the philosophy of borderlessness does not allow one to have any existential crisis since the concept of borderlessness is infinite in nature. Thus, there are some unreal features within the realistic frame of borderlessness. This may be a theological challenge we face in the journey of borderlessness.

Borderlessness: Re-signifying the Notion Between the Self and the Other

Modernity comes up with an argument that the Infinite being is the Self and finite or created being is the Other. Thus, Self is a necessary being. It does not mean that the Other is an unnecessary being but it is a *relative being.* Only the Self can provide organic presence to declare organic solidarity with organic commitment. The Other can only be a beneficiary of this. That is the border of the Other constructed by the Self and keeping the Other always as a slave or a dependent being. The Other is constructed for being under the custody of the Self. That is why postcolonialism does not promote the concept of custodianship. Here is the question of the power or potentiality of the Self. As per the concept of power constructed by modernity it allows the Self to acquire power with a fancy agenda to help the Other. The Self gains power to help the Other. This is the package of modernity. We are still with this package. Gaining power to empower others is the business of the Self. Thus, Self remains as the Master of the Other and maintains the Other always under its own custody. This is a power game of the Self. This strategic dynamism of the Self is vehemently questioned by both postmodernism and postcolonialism. The Other has its own power to empower itself. The only issue is, the Other should have its own space to materialize its own power. Furthermore, postmodernism does not support the quest to find the Other outside of the Self and vice versa. It argues that there is no Self without the Other. Self includes the Other and vice versa. That is the organic notion between the Self and the Other. God the Self comprehends the Other, i.e., the created beings. Postmodernism does not stop with this but goes beyond with a concept that there is no significance of God if there is no created being. This is exactly what Raymundo Panikkar articulated through his concept "Cosmotheandrism." God is significant but only with the existence of human beings and this cosmos. Here, the Other is incorporated with the frame of the Self and vice versa. Therefore, the features of infinite being as borderless incorporate the features of border within its own frame. Therefore border can be borderless through accepting fluidity of the borderlessness in order to reconstruct the frame of the border. This can be the hope of the borderlessness.

19

Rethinking: a Reflection

V. Paul Robert Kennedy

Rethinking is felt necessary because human beings are constantly on the path of change from generation to generation. God is the same Bible is the same, whereas interpretation of God and the Bible changes from generation to generation. God in OT has given Law for his people; salvation was seen in the light of Laws and Commandments. In NT, Law remains as Law for his people but salvation is seen in the light of grace which was demonstrated through His Son Jesus Christ. God in OT has shown his grace and mercy only to his chosen people. In Jesus it was extended to all people including his creation by drawing for himself everything he has created on this earth. Whoever sincerely turns to God and affirms the dignity of life for all life on earth, he/she is acceptable by God. This can be seen in the story of Cornelius. So it is important to rethink our theological stands. Rethinking wave of theological and ethical perspective began in Europe in 16th Century and we can trace its beginnings in the Indian context in the 20th century. We are now part of the spark of rethinking as begun in CSI to Rethink Ecclesia.

Rethinking Movement in 16th Century in Europe:

The reasons behind the Reformation in the 16th century are many. Church's increasing power and wealth contributed to the bankrupting of the church as a spiritual force; abuses such as the sale of indulgences (or spiritual privileges) by the clergy and other charges of corruption undermined the church's spiritual authority. Reformers attacked the popular superstitions in the church and urged the imitation of Christ as the supreme moral teacher. Pope was attacked by reformers saying Pope had no authority over purgatory.

Luther began by criticising the sale of indulgences, insisting that the Pope had no authority over purgatory and the catholic doctrine of merits of the saints had no foundation in the Bible. The Reformation incorporated doctrinal changes such as a complete reliance on Scripture as the only source for proper belief (*Sola Scriptura*) and the belief that faith in Jesus, and not good works, is the only way to obtain god's pardon for sin (*Sola fide*).

The core motivation behind these charges was theological, though many other factors played a part, including the rise of nationalism, the western Schism that eroded loyalty to the papacy, the perceived corruption of the Roman Curia, the impact of humanism, and the new learning of the Renaissance that questioned much traditional thought.

Luther's main arguments were that Scripture alone is authoritative (Sola Scriptura) and that justification was by faith (Sola fide), not by works. Luther's Reformation stood on the following five slogans: 1. Christ alone 2. Grace alone 3. Scripture alone 4. Faith alone 5. God's Glory alone.

Though the Reformation was initiated by Martin Luther, it was continued by Huldrych Zwingli, John Calvin and other protestant Reformers in 16th Century Europe. It is usually considered to have started with the publication of the 95 theses, by Martin Luther in 1517, and lasted until the end of the thirty years war in 1648. It led to the division of western Christianity into different confessions (Catholic, Lutheran, Reformed, Anglican, Anabaptist, Unitarian).

Although there had been earlier attempts to reform the Catholic Church, such as those of Jan Hus, Peter Weldo, John Wycliffe, and Girolamo Saronarola, Luther is widely acknowledged to have started the reformation with the 95 theses.

Rethinking Movement in 20th Century Indian Context

The Rethinking process in Indi was initiated a highly activist group that met intending to do things right. Rather than merely talking about what was previously wrong. They expressed serious objections to existing Christian theological thinking and praxis and sought alternate models and methods.

Rethinking Group - R. C. Das

Since the year 1911, there at various centres in North East India and at a retreat conference serious attempts were made to indigenise as fully under the circumstances as possible the mode of Christian worship, social life and intellectual process in interpreting the Bible in an Eastern way both for the enrichment of our life for ourselves as Christians and for the Hindus so that the beauty and power of the personality of Jesus Christ may be intelligibly presented, naturally understood and accepted.

Rethinking Group – The Madras Christo Samaj

The Madras Christo samaj is one of the organisational expressions of the striking group of South Indian Christians who have generally become known as the "The Rethinking group". P. Chenchaiah and V Chakkarai were the leading figures. This really was a dialogue group of Christians and Hindus who discussed together and prayed to gather over various concerns.

These remarkable men and their message continue to be discussed wherever there is any serious discussion of Indigenous Christianity in India. They remained loyal to the church and dreamed of impacting the church towards contextual faith and life.

Setback for Rethinking Group

Rethinking has had a meagre impact on Christianity in India. It is observed that institutional Christianity in India has shown that it is easily able to resist and outlast Rethinking efforts at reform. A new Rethinking effort aimed at changing the churches too failed. Herbert E. Hoefer pointed this out in his fascinating study of churchless Christianity. Can Christianity really be absorbed into this totally different religio-cultural environment? Certainly it cannot be done by the church but it has already begun among the non-baptised believers. I disagree therefore, with those who hold the church to blame for lack of progress in developing indigenous church forms. The real move forward an indigenous Christian faith can never come from the Christian community. It must grow out of the "Churchless Christianity" with the help and encouragement of the church (Hoefer 1991: 207-209).

Role of Missionaries and Hindu Converts:

Looking over the men and movement discussed above some striking trends are apparent. Few missionaries played significant roles in rethinking Christianity, although there were notable exceptions like E. Stanley Jones. There were also few Indians from Christian families involved. Rethinking processes within Christianity in India was largely dominated by converts to Christianity from

Hindu homes and by these striking individuals who refused to convert but affirmed themselves as Hindu disciples of Jesus Christ.

Reasons for Setback

Dr. Bruce Nicholls, a pastor of the Church of North India observed that Evangelicals in India are blind to the radical implications of their "Bible as sole authority" theology, as they blindly promote traditional western church methods and theologies as adamantly as high church protestant and traditional Roman Catholic teachers.

Rethinking Movement in 21st Century: Church of South India:

CSI Synod organised a Consultation in "Rethinking ecclesia from 'Prophetic Diakonia' Perspective" as part of the process towards a borderless church by being and becoming Christian communities. It was an exercise of introspection and Rethinking Ecclesia, in the context of 500th anniversary of Reformation and 70th anniversary of the Church of South India. Discussion was initiated on the subjects: 1.Ministry from Biblical and Theological Perspective. 2. Practice of Ministry within the Church and 3. Rethinking Mission in line with mission task of Jesus, the Nazareth Manifesto. There were total of 12 presentations on life-affirming activities in the community facilitated by different community organisations, People Movements and Networks which indicated to the presence of "the church" was already in the midst of community rather than within the walls of the Church. This Consultation on the Prophetic Diakonia perspective affirmed that wherever people worked alongside people's movements and for the struggles of people, they were already "being church" and "the church" was present out there in the margins of society where such prophetic diakonia was being carried out without any Christian labels.

As CSI's commemoration of Reformation 500 and CSI 70, the Church of Couth India is organising seven consultations on "Rethinking Ecclesia: Being and Becoming Christ Communities" from seven different perspectives: 1.Biblical perspective 2. Theological and Ethical perspective. 3. Liturgical and Missiological perspective. 4. Prophetic Diaconal perspective 5.Empowerment and Educational Perspective. 6. Healing and Reconciliation perspective. 7. Global Ecumenical Perspective.

The second of the seven consultations looked into the theme "Rethinking Ecclesia" and brought together 25 CSI theologians and ethicists for a comprehensive reflection and discussion on sub-themes such as:

> Sacraments - as defining borders or a call to be a borderless mission.
>
> Baptism and the Borderless church
>
> Eucharist and the Borderless church
>
> Uniqueness of Christ and the borderless church
>
> Christian Identity and the borderless church
>
> Minority and marginality and the borderless church

Rev. Dr. D. Rathnakara Sadananda, General Secretary of the CSI presented a paper titled "From mission compounds to Borderless Church" and the Moderator of the CSI spoke on the importance of Eucharist which still instils hope for the broken communities and is able to liberate people from various bondages.

Need for Rethinking Ecclesia in Today's Context:

Although Reformation in Church history had been inevitable, the reasons at each given point in time were very particular in nature. Rethinking Ecclesia is the need of the hour as we introspect ourselves in the present context.

I have tried to reflect on some of the reasons for such a Rethinking at this point in time. The Church is placed in the world for its transformation but in reality, worldly values have crept into the life of the Church. Church is understood that it exists for its non-members but in reality, it lives for it selves. Pulpit preaching is always directed towards the salvation of the human being whereas salvation for the whole creation is neglected. There is a disturbing alienation of our own culture, music and the Indian ways of worship and an uneasy, uncritical practice of including more of western Christian practices resulting in Christianity still being considered to be "foreign" religion even though Christianity in India is as old as Christianity itself. Building the Church buildings (concretisation of physical structures) is given more importance instead of building communitarian life. Church has become more programme oriented rather that giving importance to being people oriented. Church has become more of hierarchical in nature, rather than being horizontal in nature due to the wrong understanding of the Truine God whom we worship as one God in three persons. The three persons are equal and, in the same manner everyone in the church are also considered to be equal, irrespective of colour, creed and caste but in reality this is neither believed nor practised.

Conclusion

Although it is true that Rethinking in the form of the Reformation was successful in Europe in the 16th century and made its presence felt all over the world in ecclesiastical circles by transforming thought patterns and affecting the minds of people positively, it is true that the Rethinking Movement that emerged in the 20th century in India could not make their thought patterns come to reality successfully in the minds of the people of God. This may be because of several reasons and I share a few here. In the 16th century, the thought patterns of then reformers mainly revolved around biblical and ethical perspective, giving importance to both in equal manner. Whereas in 20th century more importance was given to liturgical and ministerial practices i.e. more of indigenisation in all spheres of Christian life and foundation was not laid concretely on biblical aspects. As a result such Rethinking thought patterns did not take real roots in the Christian community.

The Church of South India has taken up this cause on the theme "Rethinking Ecclesia: Towards Borderless Church", based upon biblical truths. Biblical basis for borderless church can also be traced in many biblical narratives. The Good News was brought to Jews by Jesus first and later it was widened to include gentiles. Many parables elaborated by Jesus were about how the called ones rejected the good news and same was received by those outside the borders. John 10:16 clearly mentions the sheep which were not in the sheep fold. God the Father is not willing to allow anyone to perish instead he wishes everyone to be saved. Cornelius was bestowed with the Holy Spirit even before he was baptized. The Bible acknowledges that anyone on this earth who fears God and engages himself/herself in doing good is accepted by God. Jess even acknowledged bandits who were crucified on alongside him at Calvary, was and promised the one who believed that he would enjoy paradise. This took place without a prerequisite of baptism. So with these many traces and trajectories for the idea of the borderless church in the Bible, an in depth discussion could definitely yield a new paradigm where the people who truly believe in the gospel that brings fullness of life for all can be part of the God's Kingdom and bring glory to God's holy name.

20

Baptism and Borderless Ecclesia

S. Philip Richard

When I was serving a congregation near Tiruttani, 65 km from Chennai, I was constructing a compound wall to safeguard the Church and its properties which were valued at some lakhs., but I had to face stiff opposition from within and from outside the church. I posted this concern on my Facebook page requesting my friends for prayer support. A friend of mine who was then serving the NCCI, commented, "Why can't you think of a church which does not have a compound wall, Church which do not have boundaries – a borderless church."

A pastor is not only called to serve a congregation, to conduct worship and to deliver sacraments to believers but is also placed geographically as procurers and caretakers of properties for the church. Thus Borderless Ecclesia is an ultimate challenge for both pastoral ministry and for an institutionalized Church.

In the present socio-economic and political context, the Indian society, once lauded as a tolerant society is now treading inversely and the whole understanding of secularism is at stake. For past two decades one can observe the growing influence of *Hindutva* and Hindu fanaticism in this sub-continent. *Hindutva* aims at showing the Hindu identity as a unifying identity transcending caste, relational and sectarian differences within Hindu society.[1] It aims to practice 1) birth and growth in Indian Territory; 2) belonging to the Indian race, i.e., possessing 'Hindu Blood;' 3) appreciation for and practice of all the customs and traditions of Hindu faith, acceptance of India as one's fatherland and holy land and acceptance of Sanskrit as the common language; 4) allegiance to one of the religious traditions that emerged from India (Hinduism, Buddhism, Jainism and Sikhism).[2] Remarkably for years these ideologies have been inculcated or inoculated by subtly camouflaged organisations with or without political affiliations. Recent political conduciveness and backup have helped these organisations to push their ideologies furthermore ardently in the Indian value system.

At this juncture there is an urgent need for the Church to reorient and revitalise itself, so that the Christian faith is meaningfully realized in the public domain. The present Indian scenario also calls the Indian Church to revisit its traditional practices and doctrines for a meaningful presence in the society and one among such is the doctrine and practice of baptism

Baptism of the Present

Traditionally, baptism is a ceremony of initiation into the Christian fold. For Wheeler Robinson, "Baptism is the door of entrance to the Church."[3] It is the beginning into the full liturgical life of the Church in which other sacraments may also be partaken of, first and foremost among these, the Eucharist.[4] It is a Christian practice of and for the Christian Church. More importantly, it is also one of the most debated doctrinal practices in the history of the Christian Church and each Church has its own doctrine and practice of baptism. Surely churches have been lingering to their principles to safeguard their believer's interest. Through baptisms, mission societies for centuries have purported new headcounts in the church as development. Thus baptism is demoted to a mere act of successful evangelism and as an end result of missionary work. Notably it excluded "the others;" becoming a clear demarcation between the Christians and others. For "the others" baptism is merely an act of conversion and Hindutva counters it with *Ghar Wapsi* (Back to home) or *Shuddhi.*

In a way, baptisms and conversions have become a hindrance to the proclamation of Christ in our country and even the diaconal activities of the church are looked on suspiciously as a means of conversion. Both are seen as offensive, as betrayal and alienation, harmful to the nation having undesirable political and economic implications. Till now no concrete strategies have been devised by the Church to eliminate this aversion to conversion.

If this is the perspective on baptism from outside the Church, then what is the significance of baptism for those baptised inside the Church? They are - members, communicants, subscribers, during the harvest festival they become auctioneers and bidders, every three years they become contestants and voters, serve as communal factions, and some become pastors and so on. Surely none of these relate to the body of Christ or the witnessing community of Christ for which we are "called out."

Thus baptism of a borderless ecclesia necessitates the present day church (within and outside) to revisit the doctrines and practices of baptism and calls the Christian community to be a befitting witness in the secular India for an amicable living in all spheres.

Baptism – A Biblical Schema

By rereading biblical passages one can redraw the biblical view of baptism. It aims not for deconstruction but a careful reconsideration of the practice of baptism. It starts with Moses the law-giver and his name itself. "Drawn out of water," It is an inverse of "drowning or immersed in the water," which symbolizes that nothing can overcome God's act of liberation, and signifies an ardent survival towards liberation. When the waters of Red Sea and Jordan River split and stood as a wall, it displayed the pinnacle of God's might and God's grace on the Israelites towards liberation. The liberated were spared by the waters and the dominant were overpowered by the waters. The waters of Jordan did not exclude the *baptizo* (*tevilah or way·yiṭ·bōl)* of Naaman to receive God's grace of healing and cleansing even though he was a non-Israelite. The water flowing from the temple as illustrated in Ezekiel 47 was not a stagnant pool within the temple walls but flows to all directions, giving life to varieties of creatures, irrespective of species.

In considering baptism in the New Testament one has to demark the baptism given by John and the baptism of Jesus and his disciples. As mentioned in all four gospels, baptism of John was a baptism of repentance for remission of sins. John's baptism is not merely an intensification of proselyte baptism as practiced by the Jews; it signified a new beginning and initiation within a community. His baptism was accepted mainly by Jews who were already within the Covenant. Thus it was not just a change of status, but a moral reformation within the fold through confession of their sins.

Though Jesus himself was baptised by John, it is clear that the baptism of Jesus and his disciples was not (only) by water but with the Holy Spirit and fire, as professed by John the Baptist himself. Jesus during his ministry allowed his disciples to baptise even more numbers than John the Baptist. More importantly, Jesus even evaded the man who had an infirmity for thirty-eight years to be immersed in the "divine stirring" pool of Bethsaida.

Thus water was not a significant medium to receive the grace of healing. The thief on the cross was never baptised but had the privilege to go to paradise along with Jesus. There are also other instances in the gospels of those who were saved without baptism: the paralytic man (Matthew 9:2), the penitent woman (Luke 7:37-50) and the publican (Luke 18:13-14). It is also important to note that the Great Commission in Mathew 28:19 calls only for making disciples for Christ not members for a community.

Coming to the practice of the Early Church as recorded in the Acts of Apostles, it is difficult to find a single pattern though receiving the Holy Spirit is a norm in all the events. Apostle Peter at the close of his Pentecostal sermon directs, "Repent and be baptised every one of you in the name of Jesus Christ for the remission of sins, and you shall receive the gift of the Holy Spirit." In the case of Cornelius and his fellow hearers, the Holy Spirit fell on them before they were baptised and in the case of the disciples at Ephesus it was different again. They had received John's baptism but knew nothing of the Holy Spirit. After Paul's explanation they were baptised into the name of the Lord Jesus, but only after the confirmation that they received the Holy Spirit. Paul's own experience had been the reverse. Ananias laid his hands upon him and he received his sight and was filled with the Holy Spirit, after that he was baptized.

But in Acts 8 there is a turning point where Philip preaches in Samaria, the people eagerly listened and accepted the gospel. They were baptised by Philip, but later Peter and John came and prayed for those baptised. It is clear that they laid their hands on them and they received the Holy Spirit. Signifying the Early Church moving towards three-fold ministry and accordingly the practices of preaching, baptism, confirmation, receiving the Spirit, fell into the hands of the ministers of Church. So was baptism towed in due to institutional church constraints and was it only an outcome of and for institutionalized Christian Church?

Also while developing a theology of baptism, Apostle Paul affirms that, "For Christ sent me not to baptize, but to preach the Gospel," making it more clear that the creative word supersedes the symbolic act. Thus both Old and New Testament is open enough with varieties of understanding and practices of baptism and one cannot narrow it down to one significant standpoint, thus opening a wider and a critical understanding on the practice of baptism.

Baptism– A Theology Otherwise

The question whether baptism is an obligatory rite to be accepted in the Christian fold is always debated. While most theologians vehemently nod to this view in their writings, some have left it as an open ended option for the believers to decide. The Early Church Fathers believed that,

> in atypical situations like death, unbaptised believers, who do not have adequate space to be baptised, are 'almost' members of the Church by virtue of their belief and explicit desire to be the members of the Church; they would receive the graces of baptism by the power of the Holy Spirit even though they did not receive the sacrament.[5]

St. Augustine, in his treatise on baptism against the Donatists, speaks of the catechumens, "burning with love for God." If they are martyred for the sake of Christ, they "receive the crown even without baptism."[6] He asserts that,

> a good catechumen is better than a bad man (sic) who has been baptised. For, the Centurion Cornelius was better when he was not yet baptised than was Simon the magician after he had been baptised, for the former was filled with the Holy Spirit even before baptism while the latter was full of the evil spirit even after baptism."[7]

Further, Augustine also distinguishes between the sacrament of baptism and the turning of the heart to God. He teaches that,

> if either of these conditions cannot be secured, the other will be insufficient. For example, a baptised child is saved without turning its heart to God, should it die before coming to the age of reason; and a man *(sic)* who turns his *(sic)* heart to God is saved without water baptism, provided he in no way despises the sacrament. For such persons, the position of the heart is essential in order to belong to the Church. The unbaptised persons whose hearts are overflowing with love of God can have a certain relationship with the Church, the Mystical Body of Christ."[8]

Luther in the *Small Catechism* puts it thus:

> Truly water cannot do it, but the Word of God, which is with and on the water, and the faith which believes such Word of God in the water. For without the Word of God the water is simple water, and not baptism; but with the word of God, it is Baptism."[9]

But for the Zwinglians,

> "Divine-human power and some other, such as that of water baptism, can neither be distinguished as two effective factors working on the same plane, nor as such can they be allowed to meet, without making it uncertain on whom or what in such a mixture (*Mischesgtalt*) one should believe. To believe in Jesus Christ and in water consecrated by His presence is a dangerous thing and is not confirmed by any necessary relationship between the two.[10]

Thus though the theologians were conservative in preserving the need for baptism; they also made options, opening new avenues for alterations from traditional considerations according to the context.

Baptism- A Rite of Initiation or Transformation

In the present scenario baptism has become a legal condition for the entry into the church which functions as a communal group. It has become an impediment rather than welcoming people unconditionally. Pandipeddi Chenchiah considers baptism as an unnecessary ritual[11] and expresses that "Christianity took a wrong radiant when it left the kingdom of God for the Church. Christianity is a failure because we made a new religion of it, instead of a new creation."[12] Therefore it is clear that in the present scenario, Christianity locates itself as a pathetic religious sect ruled by high western dogmatic traditional practices and needs a radical reformation if the Church has to speak meaningfully in the present pluralistic setting.

Thomas Mar Athanasius asserts that, "Baptism is the reality of the new life given in the midst of the present world."[13] For Karl Barth, "Baptism is no dead or dumb representation, but a living and expressive one."[14] This suggests that in baptism it is the not rite that matters but the transformational experience of which baptism is an expression. Thus Borderless Ecclesia asserts that baptism is not merely a rite but an act of expression, so that Christian faith is meaningfully expressed in the society as praxis. Thus it insists not on the rejection of the sacrament of baptism, but sees it as the reconsideration of the "Christian understanding" of Baptism. It demands baptism not to be a rite of Initiation but a radical transformation within the Christian community towards justice and equality. It calls from '*religio*' or '*creedo*' centric baptism to relational and human-centric baptism. In a way it calls not the "others"(those of other faiths) but Christians to transform themselves to accept and to be accepted by the "others" who occupy the chunk of "secular" society. It demands self-retrospection within the Christian community especially on our own baptism. Walter Brueggemann uses the term "othering" to remind us of the importance of not seeing the "religious other" as a counter-object but rather as "the risky, demanding, dynamic process of relating to one that is not us."[15]

Thus baptism of Borderless Ecclesia deviates from the traditional notion of considering "others" as objects of evangelism. This envisages the "others" as the subjects for Christian transformation and space providers for human relationship. Furthermore, it asserts "the gospel receivers" becoming "gospel transformers or givers" to the present Christian community. In this context baptism becomes more an inward and outward movement in the spheres of Christian living, whereby it calls every Christian to look for an inward transformation and for an outward expression or praxis.

Baptism – Mission Redefined

Baptism and conversion ultimately point to a community gathered by Jesus Christ where his redemptive work is carried forward. Without such community there cannot be any mission. A Churchless Christianity is self-contradictory, but at a deeper level mission without baptism points to God's presence and activity in the community.[16] It is good to observe that in a typical Indian situation people of other faiths in large number do accept Christ but do not join the Church, since baptism is understood as an initiation into a new sociological identification with its allied problems of caste, marriage of children, reservations, etc. More importantly one must recognize that in this peculiar Indian situation concerning religious response, one's personal religious conviction need not violate one's cultural identities.[17]

Moreover Indian Christians are vehemently criticised for being uprooted and alienated from their own cultural values and not from their sociological identifications which is always tagged with caste, class, and gender discriminations. Borderless Ecclesia affirms that in the name of baptism, for the sake of taking new religious identity, converts should not be forced to abandon their own cultural identity, especially for those, whom cultural identity is more important than their religious identity.

Also in the context of mission, Borderless Ecclesia calls us to rethink baptism not in terms of conservative preservation of historical traditions, congregational piety or upholding church structures,[18] but affirms the active presence of Christ in other faiths. For Samuel Rayan, the context of mission in India is marked by three major factors – the coexistence of many living religions, of massive poverty and massive wealth resulting in profound social imbalances and unrest, and the awakening of the oppressed multitudes and the stirring up of the repressive measures by the ruling class.[19]

In their milieu many know the Institutionalized Church and few know Jesus Christ. Pragmatically the Indian Church has to accept these views as its weakness. Here it is appropriate to mention the views of Raymond Panikkar, who asserts that, while Christianity has a mission to Hinduism (others), Hinduism (others) also has a mission to Christianity. For Pannikar, "the mission of Christianity is not making Hindus into Christians, but to make them better Hindus through a sharing of their God experience in Jesus Christ."[20] Therefore Baptism should not be seen as an end product, a goal, but as an affirmation and a starting point of the movement towards fullness of Christ, who is already present in all religious faiths. In short Borderless Ecclesia aims mission towards affirmation of Christ's active presence in all the faiths and qualitative transformation within the Christian community, not just a numerical and quantitative expansion of Christian community.

Furthermore, during the missionary era, Christianity was a popular religion among the downtrodden people, who flocked to convert themselves to a new order of religion which promised equality and social justice. But to their dismay they tumbled on to another form of discrimination with and within a new identity. The mission societies vividly ignored addressing the issues of sociological discrimination due to caste, class, gender, language, and region. This led to social exclusion within the Church, setting a wrong signpost for the "others." Unfortunately there were no serious attempts made to do away with this social malady in the Church and the present day church is no different than a Hindu caste community, in a way more ardent than the Hindu caste community to be bound by caste. Adding to it, the new converts to church through mission work are never treated as equals by the "traditional Christians". The converts meet with terrible experience of isolation within their own community as well as in the Christian community. Thus baptisms just became a legal condition for entry into the Church, without any social transformation, but assisted as yet another communal group, ultimately losing its way to be a witnessing community of Christ.

Baptism of Borderless Ecclesia profoundly bids the Christian community to renounce all these discriminations within the Church fold in order to be a witnessing community of Christ in the society at large. Traditionally baptismal (liturgy) renunciations calls only to renounce idolatry, all the works of the devil, the pride, vanity of this world, impurity, strife, covetousness, and all other works of the flesh. Borderless Ecclesia revises these traditional renunciations, as well as demands to renounce caste, class, gender and other discriminative identities prevailing in the society. It calls for a separation – the separation from Exclusiveness and Divisiveness, as suggested by Marcus Ward.[21] Since Christ has broken down "the dividing walls," through baptism humanity transcends all divisiveness in Christ and baptism is therefore a sacrament of inclusiveness, since Jesus identified himself with the sinful humanity. So also S. J. Samartha defines mission as "God's continuing activity through the Spirit to mend the brokenness of creation, to overcome fragmentation of humanity, and to heal the rift between humanity, nature and God."[22] Thus baptism of Borderless Ecclesia intrinsically redefines mission as a dynamic process of transformation within and outside the Church and a "*diapraxis*" towards an egalitarian and just society.

Baptism – Contra Extra Ecclesiam Nulla Salus

Down the centuries the Christian stand concerning the "others" (those of other faiths) has been expressed by the famous axiom "there is no salvation outside the Church" - *Extra Ecclesiam nulla salus.* One cannot disremember the Church Fathers who ardently expressed this stance in their writings. For Irenaeus,

> The Church is the entrance to life; all others are thieves and robbers. On this account we are bound to avoid them… We hear it declared of the unbelieving and the blinded of this world that they shall not inherit the world of life which is to come… Resist them in defense of the only true and life-giving faith, which the Church has received from the Apostles and imparted to her sons."

and Augustine expressed,

> No man (sic) can find salvation except in the Church. Outside the Church one can have everything except salvation. One can have honor, one can have sacraments, one can sing alleluia, one can answer amen, one can have faith in the Name of the Father and the Son and of the Holy Ghost, and preach it too, but never can one find salvation except in the Church.

and also Aquinas who said,

> There is no entering into salvation outside the Catholic Church, just as in the time of the Flood there was not salvation outside the Ark, which denotes the Church.[23]

These views clearly suggest that the Church was and is unable to look beyond its boundaries, and for centuries Christian missional and ministerial strategies were set according to this ecclesio-centric attitude.

Borderless Ecclesia compels us to revisit this axiom as it is in the context of heresies and schisms that the axiom *Extra Ecclesiam* makes its appearance. It first appeared in the writings of Origen and was later developed by Cyprian and addressed to the Gnostics and not to the "others"(those of other faiths). The two warned them that their disobedience to legitimate ecclesiastical authority puts them outside the Church and that, "there can be no salvation for anyone except in the Church." So the immediate context of the axiom *Extra Ecclesiam* is about the heretics. Cyprian adds that a Christian who separates himself /herself from the Church frustrates his/her promise made at baptism. Thus the axiom is never connected to exclude those of other faiths but addresses only the issue of Christians who have apostatized from the Church, falling into heresy or disbelief. It is wise to note that there is no mention of the fate of those who had never heard the gospel. Thus for Cyprian one who leaves the Church loses his chances of attainting salvation. Even though he emphasises that the separation from the Church community separates one from salvation, Cyprian did not mean to lay down a theory on the eternal fate of all baptised and non-baptised persons. Cyprian moves on saying "Outside the Church there is no martyr," the aim is to affirm that those who leave the Church or those who divide the Church make themselves outside the realm of salvation. Therefore, while the slogan *Extra Ecclesiam* is in its origin a call to the Christians, it was applied primarily to heretics and schismatics in order to keep the church in unity and did not apply to those belonging to other religions.[24] But in the course of centuries, this axiom has been very often used and misquoted to exclude the those of other faiths or those non-baptised, consequently making the Church invite and accept people to its fellowship not just with the experience of salvation, but only through the sacrament of baptism. For the Church, one cannot be a believer or a Christian without being baptised and traditionally the Church considers baptism a starting point of a Christian living.

Borderless Ecclesia affirms *contra Extra Ecclesiam nulla Salus,* since salvation can be found outside the Church and is not confined to the Church alone as suggested by *Historico-Eschatological Mission concept* which was widely used in the writings of Jürgen Moltmann. This concept stresses the oneness of history and salvation history (*Heilsgeschichte*) cannot be separated from the world history (*geschichte*). World as a whole is saved and one cannot reduce God's salvific act to the restricted sphere of the sacred and sacramental, because the world as a whole is the operational field of God's salvific acts and not merely any exclusive part like the sacramental. Also Karl Rahner's *Anonymous Faith of Anonymous Christians* proclaims, "a man*(sic)* who even as a 'pagan' already possess the blessings of salvation can be called as a 'Anonymous Christians,' since he *(sic)* constitutes the essence of what it is to be Christian; grace of God which laid hold of in faith."[25] Karl Barth, basically a Christian exclusivist in his *Christomonistic Exclusivism* even suggests that, "salvation has revealed in Christ, even while denying that salvation is to be found in 'Christianity,' the latter being, like any other religious tradition, representative of the human attempt to reach God."[26]

For Indian theologians like S. J. Samartha, baptism is not a criterion for receiving the gift of Holy Spirit. He refers, "to a Hindu who receives many blessings from the Hindu divine *Sakthi* (Power or energy) by attending Christian charismatic services."[27] Thus he radically illustrates the presence and activity of the Holy Spirit outside the Church. M. M. Thomas goes even further and invites the Church to be a "Christ-centered secular fellowship with the others" and to explore the possibility of giving Eucharist to the unbaptised Christians to foster belongingness and fellowship.

He states that, "the question of giving to the unbaptised Christ-bhakts in their religious communities, a sense of full belonging to the spiritual fellowship of the church including participation in the sacrament of the Lord's Supper needs exploration."[28] He adds that, "the New Humanity is that which responds in faith and receives the liberation of Jesus Christ as Lord and Saviour, do not require baptism."[29]

Also practically there were many initiatives to establish Christian fellowships like that of the "Indian Church of the only Saviour" (*Nattu Sabai*) and "The Hindu Church of the Lord Jesus" in Tirunelveli in 1858 for those who kept their social distinctions and abandoned baptism. Another movement was started in Andhra Pradesh by Suba Rao who was virulently anti-baptism and called himself a "Hindu devotee of Christ."

Therefore baptism of Borderless Ecclesia overlooks the traditional view of *Extra Ecclesiam nulla Salus* and affirms the presence of God's salvific activity outside the realms of the Church. It challenges the present day Church ventures to see possibilities of fostering belongingness, fellowship and mutual understanding among the Christians and the "others," and presents Church as a more inclusive and open community for the "others."

Conclusion

Borderless Ecclesia, therefore, calls the present day church to develop new channels of fellowship which will mutually enrich both Christians and those of other faiths as being "Children of God" and "Disciples of Christ." Borderless Ecclesia demands that baptism should serve as "an inclusive function of incorporation into the fellowship in Christ," and not serve just as a tool to add to a numerical presence in the Church. It affirms that God's grace is present in those who have not celebrated the sacraments due to circumstances but have God's salvific experience. It expects a deep renewal of the present day Church through a renewal of Christian understanding on linearity of mission, baptism and conversion. Borderless Ecclesia facilitates baptism as a new vision of the society patterned on relationship with People, God and the cosmos. It annihilates the splitting tendencies and practices of caste, creed and gender, within and outside the Church in the society. Baptism of Borderless Ecclesia promotes the growing need for a *diapraxis* and an attitude of sharing and listening. It transforms people not as objects and subjects of mission but as friends for mutual caring and co-living.

When Donald Trump in his presidential election campaign pledged to build a million dollar border wall in the Mexican borders, Pope Francis sharply replied. "A person, who thinks only about building walls, wherever they may be, and not of building bridges, is not Christian. This is not the gospel."

Endnotes

[1] Nathan, "Minority Rights and Secularism," *The New Leader* Vol.116, No.17, September 1-15, 2003, 29.

[2] V.D. Savarkar, *Hindutva,* 1923, 73, 81-82.

[3] H.Wheeler Robinson, *Baptist Principles* (London: Kingsgate Press, 1938), 25.

[4] Gordon L Health & James D. Dvorak, eds., *Baptism: Historical, Theological and Pastoral Perspectives* (Oregon: Pickwick Publications, 2011), 5

[5] Hiurdaya Swamy Sakarias, *Belonging to the Church without Baptism of Water* (Delhi: ISPCK, 2009), 276.

[6] Hiurdaya Swamy Sakarias, *Belonging to the Church without Baptism of Water…*, 276.

[7] Hiurdaya Swamy Sakarias, *Belonging to the Church without Baptism of Water…*, 277.

[8] Hiurdaya Swamy Sakarias, *Belonging to the Church without Baptism of Water…*, 277.

[9] Ernest A Payne, *The Teaching of the Church Regarding Baptism* (London: SCM Press, 1954),20

[10] Ernest A Payne, *The Teaching of the Church Regarding Baptism*...,23.

[11] Godwin R. Singh, *ed., A Call to Discipleship*: *Baptism and Conversion* (Delhi: ISPCK, 1985), 193.

[12] Godwin R. Singh, *ed., A Call to Discipleship*: *Baptism and Conversion* ...,12.

[13] Godwin R. Singh *ed., A Call to Discipleship*: *Baptism and Conversion* ...,10.

[14] Ernest A Payne, *The Teaching of the Church Regarding Baptism*...,26.

[15] Walter Brueggemann, *The Covenanted Self: Explorations in Law and Covenant* (Minneapolis: Augsburg Fortress, 1999), 1.

[16] *Godwin R. Singh, ed., A Call to Discipleship*: *Baptism and Conversion*...,7-8

[17] *Godwin R. Singh, ed., A Call to Discipleship*: *Baptism and Conversion*...,7.

[18] Herbert E. Hoefer, *Churchless Christianity* (Pasadena, William Carey library, 2001), 158.

[19] *Godwin R. Singh, ed., A Call to Discipleship*: *Baptism and Conversion*..., 8.

[20] Raymond Panikkar, *The Unknown Christ of Hinduism* (London: Longman & Todd, 1977), 29.

[21] Arthur Marcus Ward, *The Outlines of Christian Doctrine* (Madras: Christian Literature Society, 1955), 156.

[22] S.J. Samartha, *One Christ – Many Religions* (Bangalore: SATHRI, 1994), 170.

[23] Hiurdaya Swamy Sakarias, *Belonging to the Church without Baptism of Water*..., 276-277.

[24] Hiurdaya Swamy Sakarias, *Belonging to the Church without Baptism of Water*..., 277-278.

[25] *Godwin R. Singh, ed., A Call to Discipleship*: *Baptism and Conversion*...,148.

[26] Karl Barth, "The Revelation of God as the Abolition of Religion," in the *Doctrine of the Word of God,* Vol.1. of *Church Dogmatics,* translated by G.T.Thomson and Harold Knight (Edinburg: Clark, 1956), 17

[27] Stanley J Samartha, "The Holy Spirit and People of other Faiths," *Ecumenical Review,* 42/3-4, 1990, 255.

[28] M. M. Thomas, "The Church - The Fellowship of the Baptised and the Unbaptised?," as cited in Prasanna Kumari, ed., *Liberating Witness: Dr. K. Rajaratnam's Platinum Birthday Anniversary Commemoration,* Vol.1 (Madras: Gurukul, 1995), 13.

[29] Andrew vhWingate, *The Meeting of the Opposites? Hindus and Christians in the West* (Oregon: Cascade Books, 2014), 20.

Bibliography

Barth, Karl. "The Revelation of God as the Abolition of Religion." in the *Doctrine of the Word of God*, Vol.1. of *Church Dogmatics.,* Translated by G.T.Thomson and Harold Knight; Edinburg: Clark, 1956.

Brueggemann, Walter. *The Covenanted Self: Explorations in Law and Covenant.* Minneapolis: Augsburg Fortress, 1999.

Health, Gordon L & James D. Dvorak, eds., *Baptism: Historical, Theological and Pastoral Perspectives.* Oregon: Pickwick Publications, 2011.

Hoefer, Herbert E. *Churchless Christianity.* Pasadena: William Carey library, 2001.

Nathan. "Minority Rights and Secularism," *The New Leader* Vol.116, No.17, September 1-15, 2003.

Panikkar, Raymond. *The Unknown Christ of Hinduism.* London: Longman & Todd, 1977.

Payne, Ernest A. *The Teaching of the Church Regarding Baptism.* London: SCM Press, 1954.

Robinson, H. Wheeler. *Baptist Principles.* London: Kingsgate Press, 1938.

Sakarias, Hiurdaya Swamy. *Belonging to the Church without Baptism of Water.* Delhi: ISPCK, 2009.

Samartha, S.J. *One Christ – Many Religions.* Bangalore: SATHRI, 1994.

Samartha, Stanley J. "The Holy Spirit and People of other Faiths." *Ecumenical Review,* 42/3-4, 1990.

Savarkar, V.D. *Hindutva.* 1923.

Singh, Godwin R. *ed. A Call to Discipleship: Baptism and Conversion.* Delhi: ISPCK, 1985.

Thomas, M. M. "The Church - The Fellowship of the Baptised and the Unbaptised?" in *Liberating Witness: Dr. K. Rajaratnam's Platinum Birthday Anniversary Commemoration.* Edited by Prasanna Kumari, Vol.1; Madras: Gurukul, 1995.

Ward, Arthur Marcus. *The Outlines of Christian Doctrine.* Madras: Christian Literature Society, 1955.

Wingate, Andrew vh. *The Meeting of the Opposites? Hindus and Christians in the West.* Oregon: Cascade Books, 2014.

21

Debriefing Baptismal Entitlements and Engaging Borders

Rohan Gideon

> A border theology must address [the] 'impossible within,' which constitutes the love and hate drama of 'isolation and intimacy... desolation and creativity, repulsions and attractions'. I would like to suggest a theology of 'not quite' to articulate the grief, loss, and tensions of border subjects[1]

The debate on the mode and theology of baptism had not got fiercer than it was in my BD batch of 21 students that graduated from the United Theological College (UTC), Bangalore, in 2002! My batch comprised of representatives of at least eight denominations including a rare representation from Salvation Army. On one hand, I am still proud of my batch for the way we handled power struggles during some student body elections. Some of us sought to be elected but then backed off. Some of us thought we should talk through the situation and identify the right person for the available posts. Some even volunteered to take up responsibilities and were warmly welcomed. We waded through difficult waters of UTC's ecumenical politics quite successfully, I should say!

But one course that tested the unity of our class was "Baptism and the Unity of the Church" taught by Jayakiran Sebastian. The classes used to be highly charged and competitive (more than during election times!) because of this fetishized sacrament called baptism! The majority of us lost our arguments to two Pentecostals and a Baptist! However, at the end of our course we came out enriched with flexible notions that we should attribute to baptism. Here flexibility means understanding the practices and theology of baptism not just through reading biblical verses that directly refer to the word baptism but nuancing deeper contents, the "impossible within" through which denominations work together with multiple ways of understanding baptism. One of the important lessons that have remained with me is that the practice of baptism should not become a liability to the church. In the words of the editorial of *Religion and Society* which was dedicated to issues of baptism:

> If baptism is to be retained in Indian Christianity, the churches that retain it should be constrained to find in it (or for it) a meaning that is strongly supportive of Christian life and faith. Otherwise its liability to the Gospel in India can hardly justify its continued practice.[2]

In this paper I highlight the constricted notion the church has of baptism as offering privileged entitlements and ensuing powers. This notion, I argue, can be interrogated by Jesus' teaching and practice of baptism as a life style that contested Roman Empire's expansionist notions. I argue that Indian cultural entitlement that comes through caste and class tie up weirdly with the theology of the Great commission to promote unwarranted borders. I conclude by exploring baptism as praxis that questions privileged entitlements.

A thought on privileged entitlement will be in order here. Mark Lewis Taylor, a theologian and activist, has this to say on how privileged entitlement comes about:

> In the main, it is a problem for those who have access to colonizing and powerful orders, because of some cultural entitlement made possible by their access to wealth, ethnic identity, gendered being, educational opportunity, or other cultural/political regions of power.[3]

The tangible culmination of the Great commission is proposed to be baptism, an external manifestation of an internal faith. This formula of the commission ending with a baptism erases borders in a way to obliterate the multiple cultural identities of the baptized. However, I also argue that sometimes borders are warranted to shun the practice of co-option and obliteration as I will explain through a methodology of Dalit theological discourse. Therefore, this paper projects diverse notions on the issues of borders and theologies while debating baptism.

Baptism and Entitlement

We should begin with the note of caution that Jesus gives James and John, the children of Zebedee and his unnamed wife regarding the definition of baptism (Mark 10 and Matthew20). This story has impacted me deeply as it reflects the mind-sets that claim undue ecclesial entitlements in the name of membership through baptism. We are familiar with the story of Zebedee's family's presumption that being part of Jesus movement readily assured them positions of power. Therefore they unhesitatingly claim prime positions for themselves, probably assuming that at a later point they would succeed Jesus in managing this movement or an established organisation by then. In Mark 10: 35, James and John, the sons of Zebedee come to their teacher and almost demand of him, "we want you to do for us whatever we ask."

The conversation continues:

> [36] *"What do you want me to do for you?" Jesus asked.*
>
> [37] *They replied, "Let one of us sit at your right and the other at your left in your glory."*
>
> [38] *"You don't know what you are asking," Jesus said. "Can you drink the cup I drink or be baptized with the baptism I am baptized with?"*
>
> [39] *"We can," they answered.*
>
> *Jesus said to them, "You will drink the cup I drink and be baptized with the baptism I am baptized with,* [40] *but to sit at my right or left is not for me to grant. These places belong to those for whom they have been prepared."*

Jesus' last response that James and John will be baptized with the baptism that he was baptized with compels us to rethink the sacrament of baptism. Jesus alerts them that baptism is not just a one-off ceremonial act but a life style that might not assure accolades and prestigious power. Neither is it a sacrament as it has now turned out to be.

While the above passage does not offer names of those who are eligible to sit on the right and left of Jesus, it does suggest that baptism is not meant to enhance cultural and political entitlements through memberships in societies; rather it calls to sacrifice them in the process of empowering the disentitled as Jesus showed through this definition of baptism. Not just that. Once baptized, Jesus offers an alternative notion called the Kingdom of God to that of the entitled Roman kingdom.

I have shared these above thoughts in my sermons. My experience of sharing these thoughts with congregations and theological faculty has elicited a common response, which is: "Wow! Jesus has offered us an alternative idea of baptism." Is that really so? Rather, what in fact we should be asking is: "Why do we think that Jesus' words were an alternative?" It is most likely because we are steeped in the notion of baptism as an institutionalized sacrament that fetches us a place and identity in a church which will not be much different from a club membership which offers classist entitlement.

How does the critique of entitlement facilitate the discussion on our theme for our context? The theme 'Borderless Church' calls to question the audacity with which many churches attempt to expand their borders towards homogenizing the church. Such an audacity can be seen as empiric. Taylor critiques the sense of entitlement when colonisers with expansionist motif co-opt and subsume the lesser voiced communities therefore subordinating the other.[4] Taylor's critique is relevant for the theme of baptism too as baptism has been conventionally driven by and strongly embedded into the theology of so-called Great Commission which is closely associated with baptism. This explanation of entitlement and power helps us understand why a critical acceptance of baptism places us a bit away from the dangerous imperialist notions.

Interrogating the Entitled Great Commission and Ensuing Baptism

The Great Commission is a contested idea. Even those of us who deny to be motivated by it need to be alert that an uncritical acceptance of the sacrament of baptism would make us colluders with such motifs. A very brief critique of the Great Commission would help revisit the act of baptism and the notion of expansion that has undergirded the identity of the church.[5] It would not be inappropriate to observe a theological defect here! Neither in Mathew 28: 16ff nor in the parallel texts (Mark 16: 15–18; Luke 24: 44–49) did Jesus say that he was giving his followers a "Great Commission" as it has turned out to be in missions' history of

Christianity. Rather, we are certainly aware of passages where Jesus has given a *Great Commandment* or the *Greatest Commandment* (Matt 22: 35–40; Mark 12: 28–34) through which he summarily captures Mosaic commandments. These commandments of Jesus' have not found as powerful a place in Christian mission as the Great Commission. The greatest commandment does not call for baptism and therefore is traditionally thought of as lacking a climax expression in Christian missional practices.

A significant fallout of a naive and overwhelming acceptance of the phrase *Great Commission* creates unsolicited binaries. Such binaries have propelled the churches to preach and to make disciples over against a mission to love God and neighbours. Prefixing 'great' to the commission generates an agency—both in the sense of an organisation and as a capacity to act and establish a discourse—that has deeply established in history a patron- recipient binary of not just in the wider act of mission but also in the act of baptism. The implications of such binaries are deeper than just finding answers to rectify binaries. In short, there has been a history of irreversible colonial missions based on baptism as expressed through the *Great Commission* where Christianity raided many cultures both militarily and culturally to make disciples out of the so understood non-Christian and non- Western *heathens*.

India has been deeply impacted by Christian missions, where Christian missionaries from Denmark, Portugal, Britain and other European countries came to establish themselves as legacies of their empires. They intended to preach, in the words of William Carey, to *Mahometans and pagans*[6]. Responsively, Indian theology exhibits both acceptance of and resistance to Christian mission. Dana Robert notices that twentieth century has witnessed "the great geographic expansion of Christianity since the conversion of Europe". Therefore those who are critical of the expansionist motifs of missions believe that the "Great Commission should no longer be emphasised as the center of Christian mission because the age of expansion is over"[7] precisely for employing baptism as a vehicle for expansionist notions. Those who abide by the Matthean mission strategy give themselves a clear mandate to preach (and invariably to convert), thus considering everyone else they encounter uncritical hearers of the gospel. The agency rested with the expansionists making the borders disappear only to aggressively co-opt communities. Therefore, baptism became the sign and expression of the expansionist theologies.

However, the present mission context clearly urges a necessity for an alteration from customary grand suppositions about preacher – hearer or baptizer-baptized dichotomy, and a recreation of approaches for non- imperial relational basis.

A Model to Interrogate Expansionist notion of Borders

As mentioned earlier, Indian theology has offered alternatives to the expansionist mode of initiation/baptism. Dalit theology proposes ways of handling the issue of borders. I bring this debate on borders by Dalit theology because the majority membership of the Church of South India is dalit. Therefore, it is appropriate to draw insights from these debates on borders to emphasise the notion of suffering or pathos that Jesus unequivocally highlights as a defining concept for baptism.

Dalit Theology proposes closed boundaries in the contexts of co-options and treacherous inclusivity. To explain it briefly, Arvind Nirmal, in his attempt to promote the exclusive agency of dalits or in other words methodological borders, presents pathos or the oppressed experience of dalits as the formative factor of their agency. He insists that

> a Christian Dalit Theology will be produced by dalits. It will be based on their own dalit experiences, their own sufferings, their own aspirations and their own hope. It will narrate the story of their *pathos* and their protests against the socio- economic injustices they have been subjected to throughout history. It will anticipate liberation, which is meaningful to them. It will represent a radical discontinuity with the classical Indian Christian Theology of the Brahminic tradition. [...] This also means that a Christian dalit theology will be a counter-theology. I submit that all people's theologies are essentially counter-theologies. In order that they should remain counter theologies, it is necessary that they are also exclusive in character. This will be a methodological exclusivism.[8]

For Nirmal, "pathos" or the inner most pain constitutes liberative agency. This agency could be expressed best within a strongly bordered community. Sathianathan Clarke also exhibits a strong movement towards an exclusive position when he says:

> Other communities can participate in doing dalit theology but must recognize their respective distance and respectful relatedness to the distinctiveness of Dalit pain- pathos.[9]

Clarke reiterates Nirmal's argument but within the parameters of a dalit exclusivist position. Therefore, Indian liberative theologies convey cautiousness while envisioning a borderless ecclesia. Identity specific discourses tell us to be cautious of being co-opted again while there is also a sense of seeing a potential to break open strong borders.

Baptism as Praxis

In communities where exclusive borders are rigorously sought to best express the community views and where the dominant too wish to reinstate conventional borders, Taylor's recommendation of authentic advocacy offers helpful suggestions to explore the theology of baptism as praxis. Taylor's proposal of authentic advocacy calls for a participatory action and "self-contradiction" of the entitled advocates, the powerful and the privileged who should let go of control and domination. Taylor offers four modes for authentic advocacy: acknowledging the problem and trying to journey along the route of the subalterns that advocates attempt to represent, participating and being embodied in a praxis of resistance more locally, the dominant risking their own freedom and wholeness and not of the subaltern other, and acknowledging the numinous space and embrace the "mystical dimension at the heart of political struggle in relation to subaltern people."[10]

Having seen that Jesus' baptism contained anti-expansionist stance of the then empire and that the current notions of baptism too is expansion-driven through the Great Commission, I wish to explore the practice of baptism as praxis. Maria Arul Raja offers two significant insights on praxis for liberation theologies to complete the process of liberation. They are a) identifying liberative aspects and, b) furthering the liberative aspects through praxis in the light of scriptures. A liberative aspect is incomplete unless translated into a liberative action.[11] It is here that we understand baptism as a liberative action. This exploration, while not negating the baptism as a sacrament, sees it even outside the realms of sacrament. It involves challenges: There is a challenge of two-space dilemma: Initially, the sacrament of baptism has the challenge of identifying two spaces: a space that retains the sacramentality of baptism which confirms the identity of the baptized in a community and at the same time a space that identifies the Jesus model of baptism which is taking a plunge into contextual realities.

Also openness to praxis opens up negotiable spaces. As observed in liberation theologies in India, the advocates of the subaltern thoughts delicately, if not impeccably, recognize that grassroot activism within bordered space is crucial and that activism challenges the notion of an established space. These borders raise alerts to any dangers of dominant entitlements that borderless ideologies could unduly claim.

This exploration may not be novel, but needs to be reclaimed within the theology of baptism. This is in the spirit of the Church of South India's resounding response to the famous *Baptism, Eucharist and Ministry* text adopted by the Faith and Order Commission of the World Council of Churches at its meeting in Lima, Peru, in 1982. This is how the CSI' thoughts have been worded:

> While making public declaration of one's own commitment to Christ as Lord and Saviour, it was understood by the others that [a] person became separated from the community and was lost to the culture. The church proclaims the need for baptism as a testimony but does not exclude people who are not baptized from the fellowship of the church, and continues to have pastoral care for such people.[12]

Reclaiming this tradition of being rooted in the communities while being strongly rooted in the baptismal exposition of Jesus provides strong driving forces to engage with borders that always surround us.

Endnotes

[1] Kwok Pui-Lan, "A Theology of Border Passage" in D. N. Premnath edited *Border Crossings: Cross Cultural Hermeneutics* (New York: Orbis Books, 2007), 113.

[2] J. Jayakiran Sebastian, "Baptism and the Unity of the Church Today" in Michael Root and Risto Saarinen edited *Baptism and the Unity of the Church* (Geneva: WCC Publications, 1998), 198.

[3] Taylor, "Subalternity and Advocacy as Kairos for Theology," in *Opting for the Margins: Postmodernity and Liberation in Christian Theology*, ed. Joerg Rieger (Oxford: Oxford University Press, 2003): 24.

[4] Mark Lewis Taylor, "Subalternity and Advocacy as Kairos for Theology," in *Opting for the Margins: Postmodernity and Liberation in Christian Theology*, ed. Joerg Rieger (Oxford: Oxford University Press, 2003): 23-44.

[5] Rohan Gideon. "Children's Agency and Edinburgh 2010": 195-213.

[6] "An Enquiry into the Obligations of Christians, to use means for the Conversion of the Heathens (1792)" William Carey. http://www.gutenberg.org/files/11449/11449-h/11449-h.htm

[7] Dana L. Robert, "The Great Commission in an Age of Globalization," in D. Jeyaraj, R Pazmino, R Petersen, eds., *The Antioch Agenda: The Restorative Church at the Margins. Celebrating the Life and Work of Orlando Costas* (New Delhi, India: Indian Society for the Promotion of Christian Knowledge, 2007). 7-8

[8] A. P. Nirmal, "Towards a Christian Dalit Theology" in A.P. Nirmal and V. Devasahaya, eds., A Reader in Dalit Theology. (Madras: Gurukul, 1985) 58-59.

[9] Clarke, "Dalit Theology,"22.

[10] Taylor, "Subalternity and Advocacy," 17.

[11] Maria Arul Raja, "Living through Conflicts: The Spirit of Subaltern Resurgence," in Vidya Jothi Theological Review, vol. 65 (June 2001): 465-476.

[12] Max Thurian edited *Churches Respond to BEM Vol. II: Official responses to the "Baptism, Eucharist and Ministry" text* (Geneva: WCC, 1986), 74.

Bibliography

Nirmal, A.P. "Towards a Christian Dalit Theology" in A Reader in Dalit Theology. Edited by A.P. Nirmal and V. Devasahaya. Madras: Gurukul, 1985.

Pui-Lan, Kwok. "A Theology of Border Passage." in *Border Crossings: Cross Cultural Hermeneutics.* Edited by D. N. Premnath. New York: Orbis Books, 2007.

Raja, Maria Arul. "Living through Conflicts: The Spirit of Subaltern Resurgence", in Vidya Jothi Theological Review, vol. 65 (June 2001)

Robert, Dana L. "The Great Commission in an Age of Globalization." in *The Antioch Agenda: The Restorative Church at the Margins. Celebrating the Life and Work of Orlando Costas. Edited by* D. Jeyaraj, R Pazmino, R Petersen. New Delhi, India: Indian Society for the Promotion of Christian Knowledge, 2007.

Sebastian, J. Jayakiran. "Baptism and the Unity of the Church Today." in *Baptism and the Unity of the Church.* Edited by Michael Root and Risto. Geneva: WCC Publications, 1998.

Taylor, "Subalternity and Advocacy as Kairos for Theology." in *Opting for the Margins: Postmodernity and Liberation in Christian Theology*. Edited by Joerg Rieger. Oxford: Oxford University Press, 2003.

Thurian, Max. ed. *Churches Respond to BEM Vol. II: Official responses to the "Baptism, Eucharist and Ministry" text.* Geneva: WCC, 1986.

22

Dalit Synergies for Borderless Solidarity

Praveen P.S. Perumalla

> "Are we not *Mala* that our fellow *Mala* brothers and sisters are not mindful of us?"

Theological and sociological reflections on the themes "Borders" and "Margins" are engaging with the marginalised communities of a caste society. The present discussion on "borderless" is to explore borders contiguous with the forces of caste, dominant social and economic structures, corresponding philosophies, etc, that restrain selective communities to the margins of society. This article searches for synergies created by the Dalit communities of Telugu language States a midst of marginalisation and alienation, metaphorically referred as borderless.

Dalit synergies is one of the many which affirms life in fullness. It is assumed that the Dalit synergies are a creation by the Dalit communities in their struggles to withstand the dominant caste borders and through which Dalit solidarity is a possibility to sustain. In difficult times of caste domination and exploitation, the Dalit communities' recourse to historical memory and its subsequent practice for strength. The question mentioned above is a question posed by a Dalit woman belonging to a *Mala* Dalit community from Vishakapatanam in the State of Andhra Pradesh.[1] It is a question in reference to their historical memory and practice a midst of caste domination.

There are few households of *Mala* Dalits in the Dalit hamlet. The living conditions of this place can be summarised by a theological word "hell" (a place to throw city garbage and waste), a place filled with filth; without proper approach road, without any sanitation and inadequate drinking water facilities; a herd of pigs and stray dogs roam wildly harming people. In spite of extremely poor living conditions, the *Mala* Dalit households had been living in that place for over a period of time. For their living they narrate stories of God (not Biblical stories but mostly from Hindu mythology) and stories of the *Mala* community Origins to the Dalits in their respective hamlets and villages year after the year. In return, they are awarded with some grain, cloths and money by the respective Dalit community. They also work as daily wagers in unorganised sector. Beside narrating stories of God, each household has a story of their own sufferings which is full of pathos; but nobody has time to listen to their stories. There stories powerfully portray shrinking spaces for Dalit solidarity.

A widower in that Dalit hamlet, who is a professional story teller, has a young girl child. This girl studies at a government High School. Most of the time the widower is on tour from village to village narrating stories of God and *Mala* community origin. One day it so happened that he fell down from a tree and broke his back. Ever since, he is bedridden. Consequently, his daughter is compelled to give-up school education, join as a maid servant in the nearby apartments, and she looks after her disabled father. Added to the agony, their living place (habitat) is claimed as private land (claim of land ownership) in the backdrop of growing market for the Real Estate Business in Vishakapatanam. Because of which the whole community is under the threat of losing living space. The faith background of this Dalit community is affiliated to Christianity. Every home has a Bible and a picture of Jesus. They regularly worship at a local church. The so-called evangelical theology of the local church seems to segregate spiritual from the mundane world struggles of its members and it fails to show any solidarity with the worshipers. In the absence of any sign of solidarity from the church, from the State and Civil Society, not even from the fellow *Mala* community living elsewhere, these *Mala* (Dalit Christians) remember their historical memory of being part of the *Mala* Dalit consortium. The question posed by the woman of the respective Dalit hamlet is a question of belonging to the *Mala* consortium that invites for a solidarity move. When the dominant castes alienate the Dalit communities from their basic necessities, the Dalit communities look forward for solidarity from their own fraternity in order to weaken the strong walls of the caste system. The above question guides the query to know what kind of Dalit synergies that the Dalit women are counting upon?

Dalit Synergies for Dalit Church: Borderless Challenges

In order to understand Dalit synergies, I will start with Christian missionaries in a way to understand significance to go borderless for the Indian Church. The time frame is 19th century British missionary work in South India. The theological understanding of the Gospel commission to "Go" (Matt28:19) is collaged with the (capitalist) Church administration[2] that in no way corresponds to the everyday struggles of the Dalit who joined into Christianity. There are expectations and demands to comply with from the missionaries, and any failure to comply with the expectations and demands is interpreted as falling short of Christianity.[3] An important aspect of the Church administration is introduction of money economy through wage- structure. The paradox is that the Dalit who joined into Church operate outside of the money economy, in barter system of that time. In the absence of adequate wage, the evangelists and pastors of Dalit origin are said to be working for their subsistence either in a farm or as a medicinal man on other than sunday. But the missionaries are said to be objecting to it for the reason that the spiritual leader should not engage in secular works.[4] In order to resolve financial burden on evangelists and pastors, the missionary Church administration expected good contributions to the Church (of course in cash) from the its members (Dalits in the Church).[5] But, it resulted in disappointment. The Dalit in the Church are daily wage labourers working in the fields of the landlord for their sustenance. In the backdrop of so called falling short of missionary expectations, they are blamed by the missionaries for not contributing to the Church but, contributing to the "itinerant Hindu beggars" (story tellers).[6] The missionary compulsions on the Dalits, who joined into Church, is so demanding that some Dalit evangelists left the ministry.[7] The borders in missionary Church are based on false assumptions generated out of not listening to the language and meaning systems of Dalits. To become borderless Church in India, it requires an understanding of Church of the respective communities and not of any mission agency. It further requires narration of Christianity story from the marginalised community point of view than the missionary point of view. The contributions to the "itinerary Hindu beggar," as it is said by P.Y. Luke and Carmen, is still an open question for the missionaries. Whereas, it is "brotherhood synergy" for the Dalits who joined into Church.

Dalit Brotherhood Synergies for a Borderless Church and Society

The 'brotherhood' of *Mala* and *Madiga* Dalit castes is a key to understand synergies for the borderless Church and society. Let us go into anthology of Dalit brotherhood in Telugu region. Both the States of Andhra Pradesh and Telangana recognises Dalits as a total of 59 sub-castes. Out of these 59 some are affiliated with the *Mala* sub-caste and together they are called *Mala* Dalits; some are affiliated with the *Madiga* sub-caste, together called as *Madiga* Dalits. A study about the relationship between the Dalit sub-castes belonging to *Mala* and *Madiga* reveals Dalit synergies for solidarity. Following study elucidate Dalit brotherhood.[8]

There is *Mala* brotherhood and *Madiga* brotherhood. Each of them holds an affiliation with six more sub-castes and a total of seven Dalit sub-castes put together are known as *Mala* and *Madiga* Dalits. The *Mala* sub-castes are *Ayuru, Jangam, Mala, Nathakani, Maati, Gurram.* The last one in the consortium is *Velamala,* who is accepted as son by the rest. Similarly, there are seven Dalit sub-castes in the consortium of the *Madiga* namely *Sindi, Dakali, Madiga, Nulkasandu, Gosika,* and two more. The word Dalits refers to all the sub-castes put together and the word sub-caste denotes single unit within the consortium of Dalits. A *Mala* or *Madiga* Dalits denote consortium of the respective affiliated sub-castes. The origin myth of each Dalit consortium units them in kinship relations. At the same time, each sub-caste is unique in skill and contributes to consolidate total units from time to time. They do observe unwritten rules on conjugal matters. It is only the *Mala* and *Madiga* sub-castes engaged in agricultural works full time.[9] Some sub-castes are story tellers. They narrate the origin of the consortium, stories of the gods, etc., among the Dalits of respective Dalit consortium. Year after the year these story tellers perform cultural programmes in the evenings and in the day time they organise an informal sharing about Dalit every day struggles from across the villages. In return the story tellers are awarded with rice, cloths and some money.

A Dalit related caste visits the homes in early hours, pronounces words of benevolence (in liturgical sense- words of benediction) and in return some rice or cloths are given to them by the respective Dalit households. Such an interaction between the sub-castes is one of the solidarity markers of keeping in-touch with one another daily as well as seasonally. Based on the above narrations on Dalit brotherhood, which is very complex, it can be inferred that the Dalit brotherhood is a relation of interdependency that goes along with sharing material goods for subsistence of each sub-caste. It provides required space for emotional and material care, and social solidarity.

An exhaustive work documenting on each Dalit sub-caste is yet to be done. Not mindful of complexity involved in the study of Dalit communities, the Christian missionaries had labelled an important unit of the Dalit consortium namely "story tellers" or "Benediction pronouncer" as "itinerant Hindu beggars,"[10] when these Dalit units are a source of building resilience amidst of caste domination. Moreover, the Christian missionaries had further titled Dalit sub-caste of the village in a generalised term as "village Dalits"[11] but, they couldn't demonstrate the dynamics of Dalit brotherhood in solidarity. The Dalit brotherhood is constructed on myth created by themselves using Hindu religious sources. Such a myth explains the origins of Dalit brotherhood of *Mala* and *Madiga* and also *Mala-Madiga,* which is not discussed in this paper. Such stories do provide space to build solidarity net-work among the Dalits, which is characterised by resilience in response to the caste domination; to escape from tyranny and find asylum among the Dalit communities; and to return in disguise, move forward in solidarity of Dalit brotherhood. The Dalit brotherhood is about belonging to one another as communities knitted by kinship relations.

The question raised by a Dalit woman, as stated at the beginning of the paper, is a claim on belonging to the kinship relations. Such a claim reminds of Dalit obligations towards the fellow Dalit sub-castes in the hour of life taking crisis. A revisit of Dalit memory in the light of above question is a call to recapitulate life affirming myths, solidarity initiatives, and creatively move forward building Dalit solidarity a midst of caste dominant forces. The following is yet another aspect of Dalit synergy.

Dalit Labour Synergies for a Borderless Church and Society

Dalit labour constitutes yet another important space to learn about Dalit synergies for borderless Church and society. The word labour in this article denotes both wisdom as well as knowledge that connects with appropriate technologies. These *Mala* and *Madiga* sub-castes are known for their labour power, particularly in the field of agriculture. Their labour distinctiveness complements each other's labour leaving no room for competition, which is a strong indicator on labour exercised outside of market system. Such labour is grounded on subsistence which is characterised by cooperation and complementarity. Culturally the *Mala* and *Madiga* sub-castes address one another as "brother in-law" that indicates playfulness in relationship instead of rigid rules. It further reminds of belonging to the myth of brotherhood that knits them. Take for instance water management system in Telugu region before the introduction of major irrigation systems. The idea of water management goes along with the knowledge of water bodies, local eco-systems, appropriate technology, selection of crops and land management according to seasons. The *Mala* and *Madiga* sub-castes are known for their labour in water systems. Knowing the strengths of these sub-castes, the rulers of Telangana region under the Nizam's Domain had recognized them and attached them to the government department of revenue. Whereas, the dominant castes had been deliberately placing them under the category of agricultural wage-labourers and never as tenants registered by the government. The consequences of underplaying Dalit labour synergies are exclusion of Dalit communities from benefits of land reforms in newly independent India whereas, the backward castes are beneficiaries. The socio-cultural activity of the *Mala* and *Madiga* sub-castes, leave alone the activity of their affiliated sub-castes, can't be distinguished from their socio-economic activities. To segregate Dalit cultural activities from their respective economic activities is characteristic of caste politics of negation and exploitation. Both cultural and economic activities of Dalits are intertwined, unlike with the industry, where economic is obviously indifferent to cultural.

From above discussion few highlights follow, 1). Dalit labour synergies locate its origin outside of the modern market system, therefore outside of communalising political. 2). Dalit labour synergies continue to harp upon the Dalit brotherhood synergies which provides mutual cooperation. 3). The Dalit sub-castes complement each other through their specialised knowledge in agriculture and coordinate with each other for the sake of making a living under the iron cage of caste system. 4). Yet their labour is not made visible by the caste communal politics.

A vision for a borderless solidarity necessarily requires overcoming the capital and caste nexus that sinks into caste communal politics. It further requires locating labour in much broader sense than working for a wage that includes a discussion on wisdom, knowledge, technology, ecosystems, economy and cultural meaning of each and every form of labour. Such an approach has all potency to include every labour without discrimination and exploitation.

Dalit Synergies: Are they Vulnerable before Dominant Market forces

The market system under neo-liberal globalisation known as "Multi-level Marketing" (MLM), popularly known as "network marketing," is one important sector that projects as democratic but, it poses threat to the vison of borderless Church and society. The MLM technique has developed strings to co-opt the potency of the people that is grounded outside of the market system and through which markets are advanced.[12] In the process of co-opting potency of a community that includes cultural, economic, social aspects along with their faith expressions, they are either transformed to suit the purpose of generating new markets, increase profits or destroy the community potency. For instance, the Dalit brotherhood and Dalit labour synergies are not originated within the modern market system and they don't subscribe to market logic of profit making. But the dominant ideology of the market system transforms the culturally bonding relations into partners in MLM business and introduces cut-throat competition between the members of kinship relations. Further it moves the communities away from their synergies of solidarity. The so-called scientific discussions portray what belongs to the communities as "social capital" therefore, it counts under one form of capital. To allow such market centred knowledge and approaches to encompass over what belongs to the people, such as Dalit synergies, is not only agreeing for change in the meaning systems and corresponding practices, it further makes communities and their resources vulnerable. Therefore, the way forward is to work with the Dalit synergies and take them forward as relevant for our times as resource for borderless solidarity. A discussion on Dalit synergies for solidarity is not to glory in the past and not to call for a backward walk. Instead, it is a call to move forward working with the resources for solidarity in more creative and appropriate ways. In such a context of co-opting and destroying forces, to withstand them the Dalit synergies serves as an important locus to infer and to strengthen borderless solidarity initiatives.

Nurturing Dalit Synergies: A Movement Towards Borderless Theologies

An important yet, a grey area in relation between the missionary Church and the Dalits joining into Christianity is "induced guilt." While critically examining the question on Christian practice among the "village Christians," it is said " 'weavers were the first converts to Christianity in Karimnagar and Siddipet, but they (weaver caste) returned back to Hinduism because Malas joined in Christianity."[13] There are many such incidences of backward castes embracing Christianity in different parts of Telugu region and abruptly leaving it, blaming the *Mala* and *Madiga* Dalits joining into Christianity. There are other occasions of rejecting baptism to the *Mala* and *Madiga* Dalits blaming them for lack of conceptual approach to the Christian faith and practice. Some labelled the Dalits Christians as "rice Christians" questioning their integrity in joining into Christianity. Keenly observing different anomalies in missionary Church approach towards the Dalits, who joined into Christianity, Pandit Lekh Ram (1858- 1897), an 'Arya Samaj

Sanathan Dharmi,' says that the Christian missionaries are of no use to Dalits, Adivasis and Women for they behave indifferently in the presence of the upper castes and differently in the absence of the upper castes.[14] According to him, the Christian missionaries are creating strong borders through imposed practices, demanding faith requirements. Instead of visiting the works of Arya Samaj and Hindu reform movements from Christian apologetics point of view, it is appropriate to take them as a critique on Christian missionary anomalies if they are critiquing Christianity in India. A pertinent question emerges after learnings from the blame game of the Christian missionaries on one side and critique of the Christian missionary approaches by the Hindu reformist categories on the other is responses from the Dalit resources to the Brahmanical construct of Dalit image. In spite of limitations on the part of the Christian missionaries, a transcending approach is paved by a quarter of the Christian faith as Welfare Approach.

Welfare – democracy Approach in Nurturing Dalit Synergies

Luke and Carman are accusing Dalit Christians for adhering to the so called "Hindu practices," but they are endorsing welfare-democracy approach of the Church in relation to Dalits who joined into Christianity. It points to the times where Dalits joining into Christianity is debated by different quarters including political. The appointment of "Mass Movement Commission" in 1918 to study the nature of Dalits joining into Christianity and its report are important in redesigning Church ministries, governance.[15] Dalits joining into Christianity has to do with more of a Dalit appreciating Christianity amidst of draught in 1896-1900.[16] A number of welfare measures are said to be designed based on the commission report which is summary below.

> The recommendations of the commission was to make room for the participation of lay persons in mission works; the need

> to develop self-governance, the need to form a Panchayat in each congregation, for summer schools for the village elders; recommendations to improve the financial condition of the village congregations, endowment of pastorates with a few acres of 'glebe land,' the funding of agricultural loans, the formation of co-operative credit societies; for vocational, as well as normal training schools; and need to educate the villae congregations through regular meetings at different administrative levels such as sectional and circuit levels.[17]

The Welfare- democracy Approach by Anglican Mission,[18] Baptist Mission, etc., also needs to be explored as they did contribute towards borderless amidst of caste domination borders. The need of the hour is to take further the kind of welfare- democracy approach that suites the Church to be Dalit Church without borders. It requires a Church of the welfare category supported by democratic principles and not a Church of the market and otherworldly.

Church Lands in Nurturing Dalit synergies

Similar to many mission societies, the Methodist Mission Society is convinced of need for a strong resource base in order to serve the marginal communities (Dalit joining into Christianity). The ruler of the region namely Nizam could exercise control on huge tracks of land, infrastructure for the elite of the region whereas, the missionary Church could procure large tracks of open land, build required structures that includes Churches, educational institutions, hospitals, hostels, etc., with the contributions of the Universal Church crossing the national borders, to be in the service of the Dalits joining into Christianity. The Dalits seems to be convinced of missionary Church commitment in spite of anomalies with a sense of 'belonging' a midst of caste exclusion and caste borders. The Indian Church is required to take note of Dalit appreciation of "Church mission to land," and continue the mission to land befittingly. To be borderless, it is important to keep both people and resources together against the segregating forces of market and dominant castes.[19]

Ecumenical Networking Nurturing Dalit Synergies

The Ecumenical Christian works in different fields is an important dimension that nurtured Dalit synergies. These fields include missionaries for medial, educational and other professions. The Dairy written by Dr. Arley Munson *Jungle Days*[20] explains the problems of pre-natal and post-natal deaths suffered by the women of Telugu speaking region, Medak in particular, and she responds to the life killing patriarchal forces of the time as a medical missionary. One of the impressive aspects of her diary is about purpose in choosing to study medicine. She decided to study medicine and place herself to be at the service of the vulnerable pregnant women of Telangana region. She makes use of the good offices of the than MMS for the said purpose. Such biographical stories need to inspire every generation and it further needs to proclaim Christian commitment at the service of Dalits, Adivasis and women choosing to go borderless. Can we think of presenting the ecumenical works of the Christianity as a life time commitment for Dalit, Adivasis and Women through museums and other forms of communications?

In similar line of thought, the Ecumenical networking in nurturing Dalit synergies through education is in place. This time I choose to refer to the works of the "British and Foreign Bible Society" which later called as "The Bible Society of India" very briefly. The British and Foreign Bible Society has come down to Secunderabad from Madras (presently Chennai) in the form of "Secunderabad Auxiliary," of course first as a book depot, on the invitation of the MMS way back in 1930's. The Telugu region

Christianity is predominantly of Dalit origin is an important aspect to connect with the Bible Society of India work in nurturing Dalit synergies through the Bible in Telugu language. The year 2018 marks Bicentenary of publishing Telugu New Testament and 80 years of Bible House, Secunderabad. Remembering the pioneers in providing Telugu Bible, who crossed the national borders, linguistic and cultural borders, the Church to go borderless requires to move in to secular spaces incorporating the Dalit, Adivasi and women terminologies in Biblical narrations. The very long standing theme "people of the Book" is a reminder to move forward sharing the Bible as "Book of the people" with a vision to go borderless.

Last but not the least, the Henry Martin Institute (HMI) for Islamic Studies is yet another milestone in nurturing the Dalit synergies through Ecumenical works. The visionary leadership through endorsing significance of Church moving as borderless is evident in bringing HMI from elsewhere in Asia to Hyderabad, a city and region known for Dalit educational movements, both of secular as well as ecclesiastical. Thanks to the forethought of the MMS leadership, which is carried forward by the than leadership of the CSI Medak Diocese in locating HMI in Hyderabad in its long historical journey from Jerusalem, Pakistan and via different cities in India. An important contribution of the HMI to Christian theology as nurturing Dalit communities is through dialogical approach between Christianity and Islam, and offering Urdu, Arabic language courses. Historically it is the Dalits of the region that embraced Christianity and Islam in response to the caste domination in the region. Catering to Muslim community and Christian community is taking community concerns. The HMI enabled to move further the Dalit Christian theological categories to dialogue with other religions, which is unthinkable in a caste society. We remember the Rev. T. J. Chinnayya, a Dalit Pastor and a scholar in giving leadership to HMI in the capacity of Director. Only few of many Ecumenical contributions are mentioned for lack of space.

Way Before Us....

The above discussion on Dalit Synergies for borderless solidarity grounds us to remember our celebrated stories and traditions to move further. The Christian theological categories including Church is reminded of its nature to move forward; a movement to be a community centred faith celebration. It requires to be one with the Dalit communities, not as a "mission field" to plough, but to learn and grow together; recognise potency to liberate and strengthen; integrate people and resources. In uncovering the Dalit synergies for borderless solidarity, we discover God closer than ever before.

Endnotes

[1] The data is collected by the author in person in the year 2017.

[2] An Ecclesiastical department of the State was instituted by the British government to look after the Church administration in construction and maintenance of the Church buildings. These documents are under the custody of the Government Achieves in Chennai.

[3] Cf. P.Y. Luke and John B. Carmen, *Village Christians and Hindu Culture: A Study of a Rural Church in Andhra Pradesh, South India* (London: Lutterworth Press).

[4] Ibid. p, 117- 119.

[5] The Methodist Mission Society reports from respective regions and Dioceses will be of great help to understand the administration of the missionary Church.

[6] P.Y. Luke and John B. Carmen, *Village Christians and Hindu Culture: A Study of a Rural Church in Andhra Pradesh, South India* (London: Lutterworth Press), p, 117- 119.

[7] Praveen P.S. Perumalla, *No to Trodden Path, A Response to Network Marketing* (Delhi: ISPCK, 2007), p. 89-90.

[8] The discussion is adopted from the Unpublished doctoral thesis by P.K. Praveen Prabhu Sudheer, " Land Alienation of Dalits in Arnakonda Panchayat of Telangana : A Socio- Theological Enquiry" for the Department of Christian Studies, University of Madras, 2014.

[9] The study is based on Arnakonda village only in the District of Karimnagar, Telangana State.

[10] Cf. P.Y. Luke and John B. Carmen, *Village Christians and Hindu Culture: A Study of a Rural Church in Andhra Pradesh, South India* (London: Lutterworth Press).

[11] Ibid.

[12] Cf. Praveen P.S. Perumalla, *No to Trodden Path, A Response to Network Marketing* (Delhi: ISPCK, 2007). For a detailed discussion on the topic as a theological work the above work can be consulted.

[13] P.Y. Luke and John B. Carmen, *Village Christians and Hindu Culture: A Study of a Rural Church in Andhra Pradesh, South India* (London: Lutterworth Press), p. 18.

[14] Kenneth W. Jones (ed), *Religious Controversy in British India: Dialogues in South Asian Languages* (Albany: State University of New York Press, 1992), p. 72-74. The works of Pandit Lekh Ram are available with the Hyderabad State Archives which are consulted by Rev. Dr. David Singh. Curtesy to Dr. David Singh lectures.

[15] P.Y. Luke and John B. Carmen, *Village Christians and Hindu Culture: A Study of a Rural Church in Andhra Pradesh, South India* (London: Lutterworth Press), p. 15, 18-24.

[16] Cf. Praveen P.S. Perumalla, "Will you walk yet, another mile?" in Vinod Victor & Amritha Bosi Perumalla (eds), *Preaching in the 21st Century: Towards a New Homiletics* (Delhi: ISPCK, 2013), p. 119-121.

[17] Ibid. p. 121.

[18] Bishop Azariah of Dornakal had consulted the document and took appropriate steps for the Anglican missionary Church. Cf. Chandra Mallampalli, *Christians and Public Life in Colonial South India, 1863-1937* (New York: Routledge Cruzon, 2004), p. 182-187.

[19] Cf. Praveen P.S. Perumalla, "Re-visioning Mission in the Context of Alienation of Church Lands," in Dexter S. Maben (ed), *Borders and Margins: Re-visioning Ministry and Mission* (Tiruvella: Christava Sahitya Samithi &United Theological College-Bangalore, 2015), p. 129-139.

[20] Cf. Dr. Arley Munson, *Jungle Days* (Columbia: The University of British).

23

Re-locating Mission in the Context of Margins

Vincent Rajkumar

We are living in a time of fundamental change as it affects the shape and structure of Mission engagements. This change can be traced to the beginnings of the modern missionary movement. In the history of Christian mission there has always been a challenging task in the process of translating the faith into new languages and cultures. For a few brief centuries as Christians struggled for identity within the religious matrix of Judaism and the secular and multi–religious context of the Roman Empire and Hellenistic culture, the church's missiological imagination was what gave it identity and inspired its theology. In the seventeenth and eighteenth centuries, as theology was influenced – consciously or unconsciously – by the rationalism of the Enlightenment, the mission dimension of theology became even more isolated from mainstream theological thinking. On the other hand, dogmatic or doctrinal theology in particular became more and more a "technical and scholarly enterprise," claiming the status of an academic, "scientific" discipline. This mission programme, carried on mission activities especially "evangelizing" the "aboriginals" of Asia and Africa. In the modern sense the mission was always the mission to "the lost sheep". Sociologically speaking, the mission envisaged by colonial modernity was empowerment programmes in order to "lift up" the "weak" and the "vulnerable" to the modern/ civilized/ developed civil life. In the process, mission, of course, was not always marginal to the theological enterprise.

During the modern ecumenical movement, the understanding of mission underwent a crisis and emerged in stages between the two World Wars. The European experiences of colonial expansion, social dislocation, economic depression, and political uncertainty forced theologians to confront the impending crisis in Western civilization and as a whole and to rethink the mission afresh... They responded, appropriately enough, with a "theology of crisis," which also came to be known as a dialectical theology. For many decades, this was the mainstay of the mission theology taught in seminaries. Its inspiration was the thought of Karl Barth, Emil Brunner, Reinhold Niebuhr, but a wide range of other theologians shaped its development as well. They exerted a profound influence on ecumenical thinking about theology and mission for two generations. This idea represented a shift in the way in which mission was conceived, at least among mainline Protestants, beginning in the late 1940s. The shift was expressed in the understanding of the *missio dei*, the idea that mission is God's mission, not ours.

From then on, the missionary theology faced a radical change of paradigm, involving the transfer of the emphasis from an interpretation of the mission inside the autonomous anthropology, to its understanding as a work of God. The basis for this mission understanding is that in the biblical account, we encounter a God who opts for the poor. God does not opt for the poor out of paternalistic compassion but in order to make clear that God stands in solidarity with those who are sinned against, the victims of all systemic injustice, those who are taken advantage of, and those made vulnerable. Indeed, the mission of God as Jesus understood and pursued was a mission of realizing the reign of God with those considered the last and the least, sinners and outcasts. In the process, he rejected power and privileges, identified himself with the poor, took upon himself their vulnerability and allowed himself to be broken and crushed. The mission of the church, at this time then began with the mission of God that Jesus lived out among the poor and the marginalized, and so ought to be their mission too.

The early Christian communities who had the first hand encounter with Jesus of Nazareth following the living example of Jesus, fought against the prevalent and pervasive evils of the day, such as the imperial Roman domination, social injustice, false pride, legalism, and the hypocritical religiousness perverted by the so-called religious leaders of that time. Against the evils the society, the poor Christians, the uneducated, the untouchables from Bethany and the neglected villages in and around Jerusalem and Galilee, empowered by the event of the Pentecost developed prophetic engagements against the imperial domination. The experience of the Pentecost empowered them to express their resistance against the power of mammon and abuse of power in hierarchy, by developing the practice of common ownership of property, sharing of wealth and solidarity. The solidarity they expressed with the poor and the people at the margins became a threat to the empire and its social, political and economic structures. This new way of engaging in missions has the potential to transform not just how we do missions, but to challenge our understanding of what it means to be in mission.

Thus, relocation of mission to the margins is not a choice but it is the divine mandate. Here the mission is all about crossing boundaries. Like Jesus, whose ministry crossed the boundaries of religion, culture and class the early Christian community crossed boundaries that even Jesus could not have imagined when it admitted Gentiles and respected their customs. Indeed, I believe that it was in this willingness to move beyond itself under the guidance of the Holy Spirit that allowed the early Christian community to become aware of itself as something clearly distinct from its Jewish roots, as a discrete *ekklesia* or the church, and thus mission took a decisive and distinct hue. Furthermore, it is in continuing to cross boundaries that the community maintained its identity as the church. Whether the boundary is that of another culture, another religion or another way of envisioning things, that of the "otherness" of another person or moving out of security in an option for the poor, crossing boundaries is what it means to share in the dynamic life of the God whose very nature is to go beyond and to gather in. This implies that God's mission is beyond the confines of the churches' interests of stability and expansion but is directed towards the transformation of the world through the values of justice and love. Such a transformation is not possible through mere acts of charity but only by exposing the sinfulness of the world and confronting the forces that deny life and justice to them and others.

Today, influenced by the capitalist and colonial ideologies, Christians often think that people at the margin have nothing to offer to/for the growth of the Church and it's mission. Such an understanding has often resulted in viewing people at the margins as objects or recipients of Christian mission. Many philanthropic or humanitarian initiatives are also guided by such attitudes. Such an understanding has also failed to acknowledge the potential of people at the margin. Therefore, the church is not able to realize what it means to be involved in God's mission. Even if people at the margin do not have much material and financial resources to offer, people at the margin, through their lives and everyday resistance practice solidarity and they have immense potential to revitalise the mission of the church. They testify to the sinfulness of the world, acting as the conscience of society that needs to be held accountable for its complicity and silence. God opts for the people at the margin, not because they are weak by choice, nor because of paternalistic compassion, but primarily because their lives point towards the urgent need for repentance and transformation. They challenge us to work towards new patterns of inclusiveness, sharing and transformative action.

Here the mission from the margins implied a shift from a church-centered mission to a mission-centered church. So today we need to situate ourselves with those on the margins of empire, and there reconsider the meaning of the *missio dei* for today. Mission from the margins is associated with peoples that have been marginalized by the various oppressive ideologies associated with it. Mission from the margins suggests that the cutting edge for mission today, and as it has been throughout the history of the Christian churches, comes from movements emerging outside established Christian centers. But understanding mission from the experiences of the people sometimes causes fundamental shifts in our perspectives on mission. Mission from the margin urges people not simply to move from the margins to centers of power but to confront those who remain at the center by keeping people on the margins. In a world where people are treated as commodities and are also mistreated on account of their identities such as gender, ethnicity, colour, caste, age, disability, sexual orientation, and economic and cultural location, we are challenged to cross boundaries to build up persons and communities in ways that help them to experience God's gift of life.

Further, the Mission in today's context needs to be understood as a common united mission towards transformation of society by all religions. The mission partners need to be people of all faiths, and mission is not one religion's propriety and no one religion has superiority over and against the other. People of all faiths need to be "together in mission". In order to address some giants like the empire, people of all faiths need to come together irrespective of their religious affiliation to join hands and be collective in opening the roofs of the systemic injustices perpetuated by the altars of globalization. An important dimension of this question is how Christians should engage in mission in religiously plural contexts, a subject of intense debate in all the churches. Preman Niles and others have introduced an understanding of Christians as "the people of God among all God's peoples." This offers us a new language and a way forward in discerning the incarnative mission in relationship to people of other religious traditions, and in enabling us to cooperate with them in furthering the reign of God over all of life.

Thus, the Mission from margins is not ours, it is of God. Mission is about God's invitation to humanity to share the dynamic communion with him and his people in the margins to work towards healing, transformation and creating a new humanity. Here the church becomes an event. Church happens here as fellowship, solidarity, care, compassion, justice and the restoration of lives of people. The model of the church here is no more the household with fortified walls and exclusive claims of supremacy and purity, rather, the alternative model of the church is happening in the community and in the margins. Margins are the abode or home of those who are denied entry into the center because of their caste, class, race and sexual orientation. Hence the margins invite us to experience the happening of the church in the most unexpected places. Through its participation in these transformative actions at the margins the church receives and upholds its identity.

24

Reviewing History - Tackling the Future

Basel Mission 200 – International Symposium 2015

From Mission compounds to a borderless Church - Living in harmony in a multi-religious context: Contribution of the Basel Mission in the light of conversion and religious tolerance debates in India today

D. Rathnakara Sadananda

Towards Sarva Dharma Samabhava...

In India, to which the Basel Missionaries came around 180 years ago, secularism is a modern, political, constitutional principle, that involves two basic propositions: 1. people belonging to different faiths and beliefs are equal before the law, constitution and governing policy; 2. there can be no mixing up of religion and politics. It follows that secularism asserts the right to be free from religious rules and teachings in the public sphere and that within a state, religion is neutral. Secularism refers to a belief that human activities, decisions and designs should be unbiased by religious influence.

If you look at our India, we call ourselves a secular country, but all people are not really equal before the law. We do not have a common civil code; we are deeply religious; our religious adherence has never been a private affair; it always spills over into the public spaces; and our religions have a distinct 'presence' in the public sphere. Secularism in India has attained a very different shade of meaning, colour and implication. India has never been a *dharmanirapeksha* or religiously neutral country. Religion is very central to the life of the Indians. The age-old philosophy as expounded in Upanishads is '*sarva dharma samabhava*' which means equal respect to all religions. In India secularism has never been interpreted as *dharmanirapeksha*, but always as *sarva dharma samabhava.*

In India secularism is more a political than a philosophical phenomenon. It is more of a power sharing and political arrangement between different religious communities. India is secular in the sense that the Indian state would have no religion; though the people of India would be both individually, and as communities free to follow any religion of their birth or choice. India remains politically secular, but otherwise its people are deeply religious.

In India we ought not make a contradiction between religious and the secular, but between secular and communal, for we do not see any struggle between secular and religious power structures; but between secularism and communalism. The communal forces in religions mainly fight for a share in power, normally using their respective religions. According to the Indian constitution article

14.25 all citizens enjoy the same rights without discrimination on the basis of caste, creed, gender and religion. According to Article 25 all those who reside in India are free to confess, practice and propagate the religion of one's choice, subject to social health, law and order. Thus, even conversion to any religion of one's choice is a fundamental right.

The communal politics which thrives on igniting communal tensions on the one hand, and the politics of appeasement, looking at distinct communities to further their political power on the other, have dealt a death blow to the secular fabric of our nation. The *sarva dharma samabhava* has been diluted to the extent that communal forces in the so-called majority openly ask the minorities not only to respect the *Dharma* of the majority, but that the minorities should also learn to 'earn' the goodwill of the majority. The attempts in the not so distant past, to either reconvert Christians into the hindufold and/or cleanse the whole village from Christians with a ritual called *Shuddhi* have become the lowest points in the history of interreligious coexistence in our land. One should note that the majority as painted by and contended to, is not monolithic. It is a mosaic made up of different religious beliefs, traditions and practices, divided into castes and sub-castes, with Dalits and Adivasis forming a formidable community, not really belonging to and indeed cast out by the majority. And thus, in reality India is a nation of minorities.

We should therefore understand conversion, in the light of Indian understanding of secularism. Conversion is not just a change of religion, but the transformation of a person or a community. In Indian understanding and perception, *dharma* is more than a religion. It is the true religion, *saddharma* a vision of justice and righteousness, which transforms every person as a true human being. *Dharma* should and *saddharma* really does allow human beings to flowerforth. *Saddharma* is and should be the secular space we envisage and proclaim.

A secular society should respect mutual differences and at the same time provide equal opportunity for all members of the state to achieve their full potential. Equality can be achieved only through the recognition of, and response to different contextual needs of different sections of the society. In such an intervention, neutrality is hopelessly inadequate. The diversity of cultural membership, the inherent oppression present in the society, especially towards the weak and powerless, Dalits and Adivasis challenge us to redefine freedom in terms of taking sides and preferential option. Secularism as *Sarva dharma samabhava*, should enable citizens to respect plurality, religious plurality, cultural plurality and at the same time give equality and equal opportunity to everyone.

It is interesting to see where the Basel Mission heritage and ideology fits in with the secular fabric of India and what pointers the Church may derive today. What was the narrative of the Mission society, its missionaries, and post-missionary period Christian leaders of the Basel Mission tradition? What was the level of 'acceptance' or dialogue that they were able to achieve and are there any implications, or even challenges for present day Christianity and the Church in India?

Towards an exploration into the theology of Dialogue

The Basel Mission sent its missionaries to India in 1834 with a challenge by Count Otto Victor von Schoenburg-Waldenburg, who offered the Basel Mission Switzerland 10,000 Taler to establish a catechist seminary in India. The very purpose of a catechist school was to establish an 'indigenous mission' in India. The Catechist School was founded by Hermann Moegling in 1847 and became a seminary in 1863. Except for a period between 1914-1927, that is, during and after the 1st World War, the seminary has continued to train pastors for the Kannada-speaking regions. In 1947, the Basel Evangelical Mission Theological Seminary got affiliated to Serampore College and became part of the all-India theological education fraternity. In 1967 it became Karnataka Theological College, an ecumenical venture with the responsibility of training pastor theologians for the whole of the state of Karnataka. All through its historical existence, this theological faculty not only imparted relevant contextual theological education, but also gave and moulded the theological vision of the community. It also epitomised the community's identity in the context of secular, multi-religious India.

It is pertinent to note that the Basel Mission came to India in the year 1834 with a pietistic mind-set to proclaim the Gospel of Jesus, of the coming Kingdom of God, of liberation and salvation, envisioning an eschatological community of equality and justice. They came to a caste-ridden India. South Kanara is one area in South India where the Basel Mission left an indelible imprint. Sturrock in his Manual on South Kanara observes that the whole population, with the exception of Muslims, Christians and Jains, called themselves Hindus, and were divided into more than 600 separate caste divisions.

The first and largest group of converts of the Basel Mission in South Kanara were the Billavas, toddy tappers by caste. Being considered as Shudras, they occupied a lower position in the caste hierarchy and were ardent '*Bhutha*' worshippers. The rest were sprinklings from other communities such as Mogeras (Mogaveeras), Moilies (weaver caste), Ganigas (oilmaker caste), Achary (carpenter caste), Kelasi (barber caste), Kumbara/Odari (potter caste), Vishwa karma (goldsmith caste), who like Billavas belonged to the lower strata of the society. Further, while on the one hand, the Basel

Mission faced a serious problem when the converts were ruthlessly expelled from the caste system, became jobless, homeless and economically helpless for having embraced Christianity, on the other, the missionaries objected to the Billavas' toddy trade, as the mission objected to everything connected with alcohol, as it was unacceptable to the moral ethics of the new religion.

Thus, missionaries created safe havens for new converts and called them "Mission Compounds" by which they were uprooted from their culture and given instructions into a new culture, a new way of living. At some places missionaries enabled the new Christian converts to become agriculturists and farmers, the only major difference now being that they paid their yearly lease money/agricultural produce not to the 'landlord' of the prevailing feudal system, but to the mission. In some other instances those who gave up their caste-based professions were rehabilitated with honour by teaching them new trades such as weaving, book binding, printing, watchmaking, tailoring, working together in tile factories or foundries. The method of rehabilitation though had positives too; such as erasing their former caste distinction based on professions. They began their lives afresh as Christians and followed a new calling.

This paper is a very modest attempt to explore the journey of the BM Christians from mission compounds towards becoming a borderless Church, by enumerating the theological developments exemplified by three important theologians: One - Herman Moegling, the founder of the BM theological faculty in Mangalore, Channappa Uttangi, a pastor who studied at the faculty at the turn of the 20th century, and Stanley Samartha, the first Indian principal of the faculty, in order to explore nuances of the inter-religious, inter-cultural theology developed in the Basel Mission community in India.

Hermann Moegling (1811-1881) - *Bridge builder between cultures*

Hermann Moegling is the pioneer who brought a newness to the Basel Mission communities in the first half of the 19th century. He was born in 1811 in Gueglingen, Germany and had his university education at Tuebingen. Taking into account his expertise in languages and his missionary zeal, he was sent to India by the Basel Mission as their missionary. He arrived in Mangalore in 1836. As soon as he arrived, he started learning Kannada with the help of a Munshi. The views expressed in his diary as he embarked on an exploratory journey of his mission field in India, tell us how committed he was to the cause of the Gospel. He strategized and planned as he preferred to choose areas of initial operation, he visited and surveyed every temple, every place of the *bootha* (ancestral) cult, looking for openings and opportunities. He sounds like a well-trained soldier. Gospel propagation was conceived as a war to win the souls of wretched sinners for the Lord. In 1837, only a year into his arrival with little knowledge of Kannada, he went to Hubli-Dharwad to take up missionary work. While in Hubli, he wrote the religious text *Hrudaya darpana* which typically and pictorially depicts the 19th century mission strategy of rejecting and replacing the other culture and religions.

However, on his journey he met with people who received him with warm hospitality. He had an intensive and cordial interaction with the Lingayat *Moorusavira matha* and *Kalagnanis* a prophetical sect within Lingayats who showed initial enthusiasm. He got deeply involved in an intellectual, religious dialogue that, unknown to him, became an epithet of Indo-German inter-cultural exchange and learning. And when he started schools in Hubli, Dharwad, Mangalore and Kodagu, he received the support of willing collaborators. For Moegling, education was the right to information. Even when he went to Coorg in 1852, he opened schools to impart education to those who were denied the right to learn and were condemned to the margins. His envisioning a village to rehabilitate the socially and culturally discriminated working class was Moegling's attempt to give them education and human dignity.

In 1843 he started publishing a newspaper called *Mangalura Samachara*, the first Kannada fortnightly in lithography and then had to transfer its publication to Bellary with a new name, *Kannada Samachara*, thus for the first time conceptualising and visualising the dream of Kannada Nadu (Land of the Kannada-speaking people). He is today known as the father of Kannada journalism for his pioneering work in Kannada Journalism. The newspaper, in his opinion, was a window through which light shines into, and which also opens up and extends horizons. He conceived the newspaper as an instrument of social change and transformation, informing people of local happenings and giving them a global vision.

In 1847 he founded a theological school, to train and equip indigenous missionaries in their own culture and language. He made it compulsory for students of theology to learn Kannada texts of religious and cultural importance. His love for religious and cultural texts in Kannada, his readiness and openness to unearth and learn the treasures hidden in Kannada culture and heritage gave the impetus for the collection of ancient manuscripts in Kannada. By collecting old palm leaf manuscripts, unearthing religious texts and Kannada poetry from old houses and *mathas* (temple complexes) and transcribing texts that were in the oral tradition, Moegling thoughtfully converted them to lithography. The ancient knowledge and wisdom hidden in classical texts, thus far controlled and known to only a select few, and the common people's philosophy enshrined in oral folklore were released out of dark, covered bushels and were brought to light. Indeed, it was an "*asathoma sadgamaya*" (from darkness into light) moment in the history of Kannada literature. Thus, Moegling opened the Kannada *gnana gangothri* (source/origin of knowledge and wisdom in Kannada) to everyone to read and be enlightened and brought them into public discourse.

The Basel Mission was not enthusiastic enough to support Moegling's publishing venture. They could not grasp the depth and width of Moegling's vision. Casamajor, a retired British judge was the financial security on which Moegling leaned as he collected medieval and modern Kannada prose and poetry and published it under the banner of *Bibliotheca Carnatica*. The lithographical edition of Moegling's *Bibliotheca Carnatica* contains the following volumes: *Jaimini Bharata* (15th century); *Torave Ramayana* (15th century); *Dasara Padagalu* (15th-16th century); *Haribhakti Sara* (16th century); *Ravaneshwara Digvijaya* (18th century); *Kumaravyasa Bharatha* (15th century); *Basava Purana* (15th century); *Channabasava Purana* (16th century) and *Kannada Gadegalu* (Folklore).

> *Bibliotheca Carnatica* enabled other missionaries to learn and appreciate the richness of Kannada language and culture. It helped them to learn Kannada in its grammatically correct and pure form, to study classical texts in Kannada, and to do culturally- and religiously relevant theology. Most importantly, *Bibliotheca Carnatica* not only introduced to the Kannada world Kannada poetry and prose that was unknown till then, but also helped in recording the various stages in the development of classical Kannada between 15th to 18th centuries. *Bibliotheca Carnatica* was therefore the maiden printed text in Kannada language, and thus had enormous historical significance.

The very fact that Herrmann Moegling also translated some of these Kannada texts and poetry into the German language, especially parts of *Jaimini Bharata*, which in his own words was in order to introduce the Europeans to the cultural and religious richness of India indicate the conversion of sorts of a Basel missionary, implying that conversion is a dynamic process. In Moegling we have an early model of intercultural and interreligious exchange and bridge-building.

Channappa Daniel Uttangi (1881-1962) - *Bethlehem Beckons Banaras*

Channappa Daniel Uttangi was an eminent Kannada litterateur, folklorist and an authority on *Lingayat* religion. He joined the Basel Mission Seminary between 1904 for four years of theological studies. For a critically independent thinker such as Uttangi however, the Seminary was a captivity of sorts. He focused his attention, almost on his own, to an in-depth study of Indian and Western philosophies and religions. He also mastered languages such as English, German, Greek and Sanskrit.

Uttangi was well grounded in his context; hailing from a *Lingayat* background he wanted to have an in-depth knowledge of the *Lingayat* religion. He wanted to see, perceive and understand Christ from his own Indian religious ethos and tradition. Uttangi knew that the truth is multi-dimensional and that one must be open to the aspects of truth as revealed not only in one's own religious tradition, but also in others. Uttangi became the bridge of love between Christianity and *Lingayats*.

Uttangi used the method of comparative religions to understand and interpret the precepts, concepts and beliefs contextually and relevantly; for example, he explained the Christian discipleship using more common *Lingayat* concepts of the one who puts knowledge into action (*Jangama*). Christian spirituality cannot be a static one (*sthavara*) but needs to be like a dynamic flowing river. *Jangama* and that true spirituality (*bakthi)* would lead the disciple to the sublime integration (*aikya*) of word and deed. This allowed people to understand the teaching of the Church in a familiar terminology and philosophical framework.

Bethlehem beckons Banaras is Uttangi's treatise where Bethlehem and Banaras become symbolic metaphors for the kind of philosophical and linguistic conversation between Christianity and the *Lingayat* religion. His other work called *Christianity and Lingayata Dharma* is a comparative study of three strands of love - God's love towards humans, human response to God's love and love for one another in a faith community. Uttangi's interaction with *Lingayats* helped him to rediscover, reaffirm and contextually reinterpret the religious concepts of justice, equality of human beings, equality of men and women, freedom of conscience, dignity of honest labour, as service to God.

As an evangelist he never confined himself to the four walls of the Church. On the one hand he continued his quest for deeper knowledge of other religions, on the other, he developed close contacts with learned men of literary, religious and cultural circles. Uttangi was called to occupy the Chair of All Kannada Literary Congress twice, a unique honour given to a Christian pastor. The mission establishment, including by a section of the Christian community, misconstrued his sympathy/support for nationalism, the Gandhian movement, "*Swadeshi*", self-rule and indigenisation of the Church and openness towards other religions.

In 1924 Uttangi published his magnum opus 'Vachanas of Sarvajna' which was a fruit of years of his arduous labour. In fact, the study of Sarvajna had led Uttangi to acquire great in-depth knowledge of the *Lingayat* religion, its history and philosophy. The people of Karnataka hailed Uttangi for making the 14th century great sage and saint namely, *Sarvajna* a house-hold name, once again.

Anubhava mantapa was an academy of mystics, saints and philosophers of the Lingayat faith in the 12th century. It was the fountainhead of all religious and philosophical thought pertaining to the Lingayats. Uttangi's research article on the "Historical authenticity of *anubhava mantapa*" resting on the firm rock of theism, gained him the affection of the Lingayats.

One of the remarkable works of this period was his service rendered to the Harijans of a remote village called Kanavalli. Facing all the resistance and odds, and all the time appealing to and persuading the caste Hindu community to support him in the name of Basavanna and Gandhi, Uttangi brought a remarkable transformation in the lives of those Harijans, who were steeped in poverty and illiteracy and socially ostracized. The ideals of Jesus, Gandhi and Basavanna were basically Uttangi's inspiration behind this remarkable work. The way he used the spiritual resources from the Christian faith, Basavanna and Hindu sages and saints in his struggle against casteism in Kanavalli village makes it crystal clear that for him inter-religious dialogue was faith in action, living out the spirituality of combat in a religiously-pluralistic society.

Uttangi always understood himself as "*Christa kinkara*" (servant of Christ). He found Jesus' life fascinating and he adored him as his Lord and Saviour. Christ had captured Uttangi totally. This, however, did not prevent Uttangi to be open towards other faiths and learn from them and understand Christ from their perspective. The remarkable aspect of Uttangi's inter-faith endeavour was never an academic/theoretical exercise, but always a life-affirming encounter.

Uttangi was a non-conformist revolutionary who defied dogmatic rigidity, orthodoxy and exclusivism, who fought for freedom in matters of faith, freedom in the Church and freedom of thought. He was a seeker of truth. He wanted to understand and discern the shades of truth that were revealed in and through Jesus. Uttangi's faith perspectives were always inclusive. His deep Christo-centric faith did not stop him from being open to the other religions and culture. Rather they appear to have enriched him in his own Christian spirituality.

Stanley J. Samartha (1920-2000) - Between two Cultures

Samartha grew up in Basel mission tradition and piety. He was a person who strove to cross the frontiers all his life, without alienating himself from his roots. He found himself at the intersection of cultures and religions. His self-understanding was that of being unmistakably an Indian and distinctively a Christian. Stanley Samartha was the first Indian Principal of BEM Seminary Mangalore who later went on to become the first Director of the Department of Interreligious Dialogue at WCC.

He was deeply concerned about the quality of theological education for the continuation of the mission of God as disciples of Jesus Christ, especially in the Indian and Asian context. A relevant and effective theological education should be committed to, and rooted in, the faith in Jesus Christ and be open to the insights, resources and challenges coming from our religio-cultural heritage. He says and I quote

> "*The critical function of Christian theologians in India and elsewhere is to speak and write courageously against uncritical conformity to tradition, emphasizing that devotion to Christ and discipleship of Jesus in the face of the striking changes taking place in contemporary history demand changed attitudes on the part of Christians to their neighbours in the country and in the world. They need to raise new questions, suggest new answers and broaden the theological space for critical discussion in the freedom of the Spirit within the koinonia of the Church.*"

Stanley Samartha patiently persisted in exploring the theological issues involved, listening to questions and doubts, taking seriously the reservations expressed, but never wavering in his conviction that the churches had to move beyond their traditional exclusivist understandings of truth and of God's presence in a world of cultural and religious plurality.

He was very much concerned that the Indian Church should surmount its ghetto mentality and become outgoing, if it were to take deep roots theologically in the Indian soil and if it were to remain faithful to the mission to which it had been called. Inter-religious dialogue for him was an integral part of Christian mission itself - mission of bearing witness to, and being the channels of God's love as it was manifested especially in the life, death and the resurrection of Jesus Christ. Dialogue to him, meant a silent revolution in terms of attitudinal change, a willingness to listen to one another and to allow the other person to be his/her own spokesperson. It is the willingness to see God at work everywhere, without giving up the integrity of the Christian faith and witness. It has to enable Christians to interact with others in mutual trust and respect, so that mission can be carried out not only for others, but also together with others.

He saw the uniqueness of Jesus' unique ability to evoke wide-ranging positive responses from people of other faiths and ideologies. In this he observed that Jesus was advitiya, the unique one. Hence, he felt that as Indian Christians, we need to listen to others and take their perception of Jesus Christ seriously. The questions of dialogue with Hinduism have everything to do with the relationship between Hindus and Christians in daily life in India and with the position of small church communities in the midst of the dominant Hindu culture. At the time, two theological treatises making waves in the Indian Christian horizon were Unknown Christ of Hinduism and Acknowledged Christ in Indian Renaissance, to which Samartha added a third: The Hindu Response to the Unbound Christ,

He begins his book by stating his conviction that "Christ has already made, and continues to make, an impact on the heart and mind of India." The Church must explore that point, in which case Christianity will not be in competition with Hinduism but in a position to cooperate. For the Church does not possess Christ - that was Samartha's constant argument. Christ is "unbound" and thus universally accessible. In the modern period there are also Hindus who attach great value to this universality and accessibility of Christ. They have responded to the unbound Christ in their own way.

Samartha starts with this theme in his own Christology. He deliberately chooses the monistic tradition as the starting point for Indian theologizing. Though he knew the pitfalls and limitations of Sanskrit tradition fully, he claims that "The all-inclusiveness of the advaita approach has a certain generosity and magnanimity which is reflected in the approach of neo advaitins to other religions". This attitude breaks through the hostility between groups in the population. Though the translator of his book, The Hindu Response to the Unbound Christ into German was Friso Melzer, a former Basel missionary, he obviously felt little affinity for Samartha's work: in his foreword he writes that he did not agree with the book's argument, but that the translation could in any case show that advaita did not offer any promise of a Christology. Samartha held that the Christian faith could teach something to India precisely on this point. After all, if God's love is visible in the life of Jesus Christ and in his death and resurrection, then not only his life story, but history in general receives a new meaning. For Samartha, it was always the earthly history of Jesus of Nazareth, with the cross and resurrection, that continues to determine the image. His Christology is thus called a "cosmic Christology from below." His theological thinking is characterized by his attempt to hold together commitment and openness, knowing that God is always more than our limited and finite perceptions of God. Samartha claimed that one could see that Christ is already present in Hindu religion and thought. Perhaps Samartha was ahead of his time in claiming that Christians should not be in competition with the Hindus or replace Hindu deficiency with Christian uniqueness, but should rather look out for the possibilities of working with Hindus in seeking together the fullness of Christ and His work.

Samartha continued the explorations of a revised Christology and of the relationship of the Holy Spirit to people of other faith traditions, both issues which had been identified in ecumenical consultations as needing further reflection. Some of his writings "One Christ - Many Religions. Toward a Revised Christology claims courageously that the Spirit of God is not the monopolistic possession of the Judeo-Christian tradition. Samartha argued that one could easily identify the works of the Holy Spirit outside the walls of the Christian Church. He also asked his fellow Christians to think of the possibilities of the work of the Holy Spirit in the struggles of liberation, renewal, restoration and reformation.

Samartha argued that while carrying out the mission of God, one must recognize the presence of the Holy Spirit in the renewal movements of other religions without losing his or her commitment to Jesus Christ. Samartha said that God's mission could not be limited by temporal factors, and while the mysterious action of the Holy Spirit could not be bound by visible communal walls, Christian mission had a beginning in the incarnation of God in Jesus Christ, in his life, death, resurrection and the coming of the

Holy Spirit. It is in developing his understanding of mission, that Samartha calls for replacing the word mission with witness. It is Samartha's conviction that witness would help Christians not only claim the Lordship of Jesus Christ in their diaconal ministry, but also help them bring the message of hope to people struggling with various issues and situations.

He claimed that the politicization of religions had a tendency to tear the fabric of society and that dialogue would help to bring harmony and peace among religions and also enable people to establish harmony with one another in addressing human needs. Such dialogue should be carried out without any fear of converting one another to each other's faith. In order to do this effectively, Samartha saw the need for a new definition of evangelism; retelling of the story of Jesus of Nazareth, sharing with people the good tidings about him with joy and humility.

Calling for a better understanding of evangelism and also claiming that mission is wider than evangelism, Samartha said that in countries such as India, churches should see that Christians make an attempt to transform the society by using images of light, salt, leaven, and of the seed growing by itself in secret. Samartha calls us to hold together Christian commitment and openness, knowing that God is always more than our limited and finite perceptions of God.

In the quest of a Borderless Church

Today we live in a neo-colonial, capitalistic world where exclusive communities, club memberships and 'gated' communities are emerging. In such a scenario, how can the Church become a borderless community, discovering and acknowledging Christ among people of living faiths and religions. In the quest of a borderless church, is it possible to do a theology of 'hospitality' as a hermeneutical key? The theological understanding of a borderless community begins with faith in one God, the Creator. God's glory penetrates all creation. It is in the act of creation that 'relationships' are designed and expressed. Everything created is 'related' to each other, and God relates Himself to creation. The theological themes of the call, the election reflect God's readiness to relate and extend relationship to all.

Jesus extended hospitality to those at the margins of society, and those who experienced rejection and marginalization, the small and the least, the poor, the women, the children. The evangelists' theological reflections affirm that hospitality to strangers and acceptance of others is communion with the risen Christ. The biblical understanding of hospitality is not just charity and generosity, but a radical openness based on the affirmation of dignity and justice for all.

Willingness to accept others in their otherness is the hallmark of hospitality. 'Hospitality' is both the fulfilment of the command to love our neighbours as ourselves, and also an opportunity to encounter and discover God anew, to stand where Jesus stood, to recognize the need and to demonstrate and experience empathy. Hospitality creates space for mutual understanding, transformation and even reconciliation. It is an opportunity and a risk.

The Old Testament Prophet of social justice, Micah, encourages us with his beautiful metaphoric exhortation: "but they shall all sit under their own vines and under their own fig trees, and no one shall make them afraid." A community enjoying the fruits of its labour, engaged in knowledge sharing, wise reflections, without fear from within and without, in fuller freedom, and in the presence of the Lord truly reflects a secular community.

Our own Nobel Laureate Rabindranath Tagore dreamt of such a secular land, and called it haven of Freedom: *Where the mind is without fear and the head is held high; where knowledge is free; where the world has not been broken up into fragments by narrow domestic walls; where words come from the depths of truth; where tireless striving stretches its arms towards perfection; where the clear stream of reason has not lost its way into the dreary desert sand of dead habit; where the mind is led forward by Thee into ever widening thought and action; into that haven of freedom , my father, let my country awake.*

The secular space should not be corrupted by divisive and exclusive voices, but should promote the secular spirit of inclusiveness, pluralism, peaceful and a just growing together of all people. If we proclaim *Dharma* to convert communities to the transforming vision of *Saddharma*, we will already have a foretaste of the new humanity.

Contributors

1. Bishop Daniel S. Thiagarajah Ph.D.
   Bishop of the CSI in the Jaffna Diocese
2. Bishop Royce M. Victor Ph.D
   Bishop in CSI Malabar Diocese
3. Rev. Dr. John Samuel Ponnusamy
   Professor, Old Testament
   Principal, Gurukul Lutheran Theological Seminary, Chennai
4. Rev. Dr. Chilkuri Vasantha Rao
   Professor, Old Testament
   Principal, United Theological College, Bangalore
5. Rev. D. Sam Christopher,
   Pursuing DTh in New Testament, SATHRI
   Presbyter, CSI Kanyakumari Diocese
6. Rev. I. Franklin
   Pursuing DTh in
   Presbyter, CSI Thoothukudi - Nazareth Diocese
7. Rev. Dr. L. Jayachitra
   DTh, New Testament

Director, Christian Education Department,
CSI Synod

8. Dr. Laila Vijayan
DTh, Old Testament
United Theological College

9. Dr. C. I. David Joy
Professor, New Testament
United Theological College, Bangalore

10. Rev. Joseph Samuel,
Faculty, KUTS, Trivandrum,
Presbyter, Madhya Kerala Diocese

11. Dr. Gregory T Basker
DTh, New Testament,
Faculty, United Theological College, Bangalore

12. Rev. M. John Sunder,
Presbyter, CSI Medak Diocese

13. Rev. Sagar Sundar Raj
Faculty, Karnataka Theological College, Balmatta, Mangalore

14. Rev Jyothi John Sunder
Presbyter, CSI Medak Diocese

15. Rev. P. Victor Paul
Presbyter, CSI Karimnagar Diocese

16. Rev. Christy Gnanadason
Presbyter, CSI Karnataka Central Diocese

17. Rev. Dr. Mervin Shinoj Boas
Presbyter, CSI Cochin Diocese

18. Rev. Dr. Allan Samuel Palanna
    Faculty, United Theological College, Bangalore
19. Rev. V. Paul Robert Kennedy
    Presbyter, CSI Vellore Diocese
20. Rev. S. Philip Richard
    Presbyter, Diocese of Madras
21. Rev. Dr. Rohan Gideon
    Faculty, United Theological College, Bangalore
22. Rev. Dr. Praveen P.S. Perumalla
    Auxiliary Secretary, Telengana Division
    Bible Society of India
23. Rev. Dr. Vincent Rajkumar
    Director, CSIRS, Bangalore
24. Rev. Dr. D. Rathnakara Sadananda,
    General Secretary, CSI

www.ingramcontent.com/pod-product-compliance
Ingram Content Group UK Ltd.
Pitfield, Milton Keynes, MK11 3LW, UK
UKHW041842190726
13854UKWH00002B/682

9 789390 569144